Homeschool
Field Trips

Th... v

Pa...e

Edu...al

Fi...s

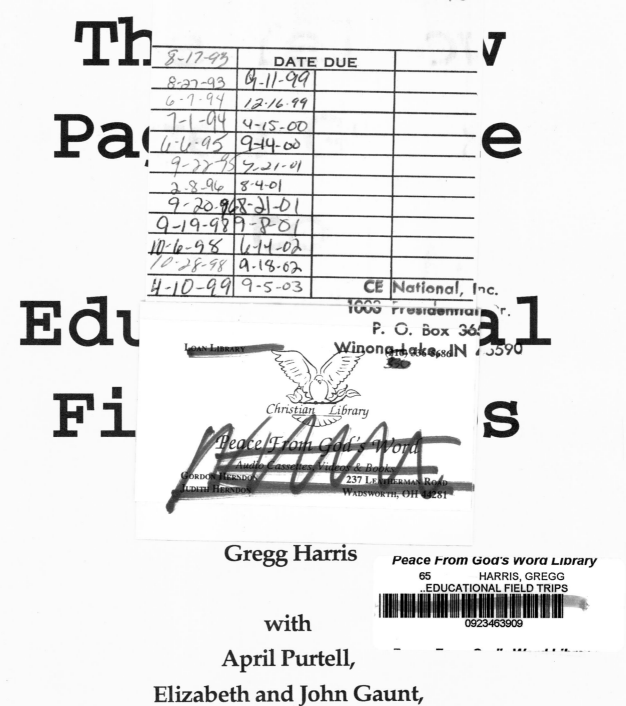

Gregg Harris

with

April Purtell,

Elizabeth and John Gaunt,

and Ross Tunnell

NOBLE PUBLISHING ASSOCIATES
GRESHAM, OREGON

Noble Publishing Associates, the publishing arm of Christian Life Workshops, is an association of Christian authors dedicated to serving God and assisting one another in the production, promotion, and distribution of audio, video, and print publications. For instructions on how you may participate in our association, or for information about our complete line of materials, write to:

Noble Publishing Associates
P.O. Box 2250
Gresham, Oregon 97030

or call (503) 667-3942.

ISBN: 0-923463-90-9

Printed in the United States of America.

PREFACE

*T*he *Yellow Pages Guide to Educational Field Trips* is a valuable resource for any-one involved in education. It is a handbook for turning any place in your community into an educational field trip. Sample forms such as a **Field Trip & Travel Planning / Record** (reprinted from **The Christian Family's Complete Household Organizer** by Gregg & Sono Harris) are included in the appendix in order to make *The Yellow Pages Guide to Educational Field Trips* even more useful.

Destination categories are listed in much the same way you might find them in the Yellow Pages of your local phone directory. They are in alphabetical order and each is organized in the same basic way.

• First, each entry is introduced by giving its background and historical develop-ment. Space is provided for you to write the local destination address, phone, and contact person. This makes your copy of the *Yellow Pages Guide* a personal version for your family's use.

• Second, key concepts and principles about each destination or occupation are explained and illustrated.

• Next, there is a list of possible questions you might want to ask when you are actually visiting the location.

• Fourth, various activities are suggested to increase your in-volvement in the subject. This may be final preparation for the field trip or as follow-up after your visit.

• Next, there is a section containing key vocabulary words. These are listed with check-off boxes to be marked as your student learns each term.

• Finally, there is a section entitled **Tips From Barnabas.** Barnabas is always anxious to share with you some Biblical perspec-tive on each subject studied. Whenever you see him, expect to receive some valuable insights from the Word of God.

CONTENTS

NAME OF PLACE TO VISIT _____

NAME OF CONTACT PERSON _____

PHONE #_____

ADDRESS _____

_____

BEST TIME TO VISIT _____

ADVERTISING AGENCY

Background

Advertising is something that you come in contact with every day. There is advertising on television and radio, in magazines and newspapers, and on billboards. There are also advertisements posted on buses and subways. Often the advertisement is for a product like a car or a soft drink. Sometimes it is for a service such as an airline or a bank. Finally, there are advertisements that promote some value in society, such as not littering or preventing forest fires. These three types of advertising are called *product advertising*, *service advertising*, and *public service advertising*, respectively.

Many different types of organizations advertise. Some create their own advertisements, especially small companies with small advertising budgets. Larger businesses hire advertising agencies to help them create and run their *advertising campaigns*.

The business which hires an ad agency becomes that agency's *client*. The client is known to the agency as the *account*. There is usually one *account executive* to handle each account although exceptionally large accounts may be shared by two or more. The account executive must know everything he or she can about the product or service in order to know the best way to advertise it. He or she keeps in contact with the client in order to work with him on the campaign. He or she is also the one who makes the *presentations* to the client of the agency's recommendations and progress. The account executive must convince the client that the agency's ideas will sell his or her product.

In an advertising agency, different departments work together to create a working ad campaign. The *copywriter* is responsible for the words of the ad. If it is a *print advertising* campaign, the copywriter will create an attention-getting headline and then a body of text to further explain the idea. If it's to be a *broadcast advertisement*, he or she may also suggest appropriate music or sound effects. The copywriter often comes up with short catchy *slogans* which become the client's theme.

The *art director* is responsible for the pictorial content of the ad. First, he or she will draw up a *thumbnail sketch* or *rough*. Eventually, a better drawing, including the copywriter's headline and text, will be laid out and presented to the client. This layout is called a *comprehensive*. If it is to be a television ad, the art director creates a *storyboard*. A storyboard contains ten to twenty sketches which help guide the production people in making the different scenes in the commercial.

The *TV producer* is responsible for making the television commercial. He or she selects the actors, directors, and production studio. He or she also works with the set designers and the wardrobe and make-up people.

Obviously, one of the basic decisions in creating an advertising campaign is deciding which advertising *medium* to use. *Media people* are responsible for this decision. They base their choice on the type of product, the kind of people that buy it most regularly, and the kind of media those people watch, read, or listen to most frequently. Some campaigns combine all of these different types of media.

The *merchandising department* may help the client in designing or changing the packaging of his or her product. It will determine what the package is made of, what its shape is, and what the label looks like. Packaging that is both practical and eye-catching can help to increase sales.

The *research department* tries to find out everything it can about *consumers*: what sort of people use which products and services. What do these people watch, listen to, and read? What is their age, sex, educational status, and level of income? The research department gathers answers to all these questions and counts these answers to create accurate statistics. These statistics help the ad agency to know what type of ad campaign to develop for each client. As you can see, many different departments of an advertising agency must work together to create a successful ad campaign.

Questions You Might Ask At An Advertising Agency

What different kinds of media are used for advertising?

What is the most expensive media to use?

What is the most cost effective?

What is the least expensive?

What is the most unusual?

What are some typical costs of running an ad on television? On radio? In a magazine? In a newspaper? On a billboard?

What are the factors in each of the above media that cause the costs to vary?

Why is it important for the advertiser to know which kinds of people are buying the product?

How is the research done?

What are some of the most common techniques that advertisers use to make a product or service attractive to the public?

What qualities and educational background do advertisers need?

What kinds of accounts do you work on most frequently?

Does your agency specialize?

How many ideas do you usually have to develop before you find one that is acceptable to a client?

How long does it take to complete an ad campaign?

Activities

• Either on television or from different magazines, find an example of an ad that is geared toward:

    A) Business people

    B) Housewives

    C) Retired persons

    D) Teenagers

    E) Children

Notice what the different ads are for and describe how the presentation of each is different and how it is geared to a particular section of society.

• Create a magazine advertisement for:

    A) Your family's car

    B) Your favorite food

C) One of your family's appliances
Include a drawing or photograph, a headline, and copy (text).

• Do library research and write a paper on "Truth in Advertising."

• At dinner have a family fun time by seeing how many commercials, jingles, and slogans you can remember. Then talk about why they were memorable. Start by asking your parents if they can sing the jingle that has the phrase, "A little dab will do ya" or "Rice-aroni."

Vocabulary

❏ Thumbnail Sketch
❏ Product Advertisement
❏ Mass Medium
❏ Account
❏ Presentation
❏ Print Ad
❏ Consumer

❏ Rough
❏ Service Advertisement
❏ Ad Campaign
❏ Merchandising Department
❏ Copywriter
❏ Broadcast Ad
❏ Storyboard

❏ Comprehensive
❏ Public Service Advertisement
❏ Cost Effective
❏ Account Executive
❏ Research Department
❏ Art Director
❏ Blue Line

Tips From Barnabas

Have you ever thought of yourself as an advertisement? As a Christian, the Bible says you are a living ad for the gospel. There are three New Testament passages that express this idea.

In 2 Corinthians 5:20, Paul compares us to ambassadors as though God "were making His appeal through us." In other words, He [God] is using us to make an **appeal** to unbelievers that they should make peace with Him and be saved.

In Titus 2:9-10, Paul is giving instructions to slaves [also appropriate for today's employees] on how they should behave "so that in every way they will make the teaching about God our Savior **attractive**." That is what a good advertisement does.

And in 2 Corinthians 3:2-3, Paul says that the Corinthians are living letters from Christ, "known and read by everybody." People see us, and they form an opinion about our Lord.

Using what you've learned about advertising, make a list of ways that you can be a better "living ad" for the gospel, one that will make it more attractive and appealing to those who are not yet Christians. Don't forget that this is one "product" that everyone can afford. All it costs is yourself. Everyone can give himself to God, and He will make him a new living ad for His Kingdom.

Name brands stand for companies we have come to know and trust. They have a good reputation. Companies spend millions of dollars to promote their brand names. For further study, look up passages in your Bible that talk about a person's reputation and the value of a good name.

AQUARIUM

Background

NAME OF PLACE TO VISIT _____

NAME OF CONTACT PERSON _____

PHONE # _____

ADDRESS _____

_____

BEST TIME TO VISIT _____

Aquariums are places for fish and other water life to live on display. There are both private and public aquariums. Private aquariums are owned by doctors, dentists, schools, restaurants, families and individuals. Some contain goldfish, others have fresh water or salt water tropical fish. You may even own one yourself.

Public aquariums are, of course, much larger. An aquarium may have thousands of fish representing hundreds of *species*. It may include fresh and salt-water fish, fish from warm and cold climates, and water-dwelling amphibians, reptiles, plants, birds and mammals.

A public aquarium is like a zoo for fish. Like good zoos, good aquariums try to recreate the natural environment of the fish and other creatures that they house. Also like zoos, aquariums are built for entertainment, education, and scientific research.

The largest enclosed aquarium is the John G. Shedd Aquarium in Chicago. But most large and medium-sized cities have aquariums. In more temperate areas, especially Florida and Southern California, there are large open aquariums featuring large sea creatures such as whales and sharks.

Aquariums employ many different people to help keep things running smoothly. The director is in charge of the aquarium. He has to oversee the employees, the exhibits, the budget, and the collecting of new *specimens*. The rest of the staff is divided into different departments.

One department's job is to collect new fish for the aquarium. Although aquariums do get some fish through trade, gifts, or breeding, they also must go out and catch some of them themselves.

Depending on what sort of creatures they need to catch, they will go to various places, such as a river, a lake, a sea, or an ocean, and use different methods, e.g., a net, a hook and line, or a diver.

The crew on one of these *expeditions* often includes the director, some of the *curators*, and deep-sea divers. After the fish are caught, they are separated and kept in different holding tanks. Once the boat reaches land, the fish are transported, often by air, back to the aquarium. Sea life is delicate, so getting them to the aquarium as quickly as possible is very important.

Another department is the maintenance department. These people make sure that the aquarium's water, heating, cooling, and electrical systems are all running well. Aquariums usually have back-up systems for all of these things because a loss of power could kill many fish within a matter of hours.

There are also people responsible for the exhibits and the fish themselves. These people set up the exhibits. They study the natural *habitat* of the fish and then try to recreate it. Sometimes they use natural materials, such as plants and rock. Other times they use plastic casts, cement or other imitation *environments*.

Fish in aquariums are fed many different things. Some are fed common seafood, such as shrimp, sardines, herring, or squid. Others are fed more unusual things, such as a special dry food or trout pellets. Some aquariums feature a diver who, once or twice a day, feeds the fish and explains things about them to the visitors.

Questions You Might Ask At An Aquarium

How are the fish caught and brought to the aquarium?

What does the aquarium do if a fish gets sick or dies?

Which kind of educational degrees do you need to work in an aquarium?

How successful are breeding programs?

What is the cost breakdown in running an aquarium?

What impact do aquariums have in preserving species?

How do you keep the tanks clean?

How do you decide which species can be kept together in a single tank?

How many people visit the aquarium yearly?

Where does the money come from to run the aquarium?

Why do you have so many plants in the aquarium?

Are there any dangerous fish in your aquarium?

How do you feed the fish?

Activities

- Choose a fish and a sea mammal that interest you. Find out the following things about them:

  What do they eat?

  Do they live in fresh water or salt water?

  Do they live in a cold or warm climate?

  Are there different types of this same species?

  Are they endangered or threatened?

  If so, why and what can be done about it?

- The blue whale is the largest known creature to have ever existed on this earth. However, it is now in serious danger of extinction. Write a paper on the blue whale, including facts about it, facts about what is being done to save it, and things that still need to be done to help further.

- Set up your own fresh water or salt-water aquarium.

Vocabulary

❏ Curator   ❏ Species   ❏ Specimen

❏ Environment   ❏ Habitat   ❏ Expedition

❏ Aquarist   ❏ Circulation   ❏ Guppy

                         ❏ Tropical

Tips From Barnabas

In Genesis 1:20-21, God created all the animals of the sea, and He gave Adam and Eve responsibility to tend and care for His creation. The earth has been given to mankind as a stewardship to use wisely and for God's purposes, not as a possession to be ruined. In Psalms God makes it clear that each generation is responsible to hand down good things to the children yet to be born. Aquariums are one way in which scientists learn how to use and protect the many living things that live under water. In Jonah 1:17, the Lord provided a "great fish" to swallow Jonah, where he stayed for three days and nights. This could have been a whale, or it may have been a one-of-a-kind fish, prepared for Jonah alone. Do some research on whales if you haven't already and imagine what it would be like to be inside of one for as long as Jonah was. Check your encyclopedia to see if anyone else has been swallowed by a whale and lived to tell about it.

Read all four chapters of Jonah and look on a map of Biblical times to find Nineveh. If you have a Bible handbook, you may want to look up some of Nineveh's history.

In Job a sea creature is described that sounds like a living dinosaur. Read this passage and think about what kind of aquarium you would need to keep a Leviathan on display.

Fish and fishing are very prominent in the New Testament. Jesus' ministry in Galilee centered in several villages where fishing was the main business. It was from these villages that Jesus called several fishermen to be his disciples. What were their names? Remember? They left their nets and boats to follow Jesus, and they became fishers of men (Luke 5:1-11).

Also, several miracles that Jesus performed had to do with fish. As a further study find the miracles that Jesus did which involved fish. Also find the passage were Jesus used a fish to support his claim that He was not a ghost, but that He was Himself in a resurrected body.

NAME OF PLACE TO VISIT _____

NAME OF CONTACT PERSON_____

PHONE #_____

ADDRESS _____

_____

BEST TIME TO VISIT _____

ARCHAEOLOGIST

Background

Archaeology is a relatively new science. Only in the last century did it begin to be approached in a scientific manner. It was born out of the natural human desire to pick up and collect interesting objects. You may have participated in this primitive kind of archaeology as well if you have a collection of Indian arrowheads. Unfortunately, nothing very definite can be learned from haphazard collecting or treasure hunting. The art of searching, as well as the find or *artifact*, must be approached in a painstaking and scientific manner. Some of the greatest finds of archaeology, like the tomb of the Egyptian King Tutankhamun (King Tut) or the ancient city of Troy, took many years of research and hard work before their great treasures were revealed.

Finding these great treasures may seem very exciting and glamourous, but that is really only a very small part of what takes up an archaeologist's time. Finding a great historic monument is sometimes harder than finding a needle in a haystack. Sometimes, as in the case of King Tut's tomb, it is a matter of believing there is more to be found in a particular place and looking where no one has looked before. Sometimes, as in the case of the great pyramids and temples of South America and Mexico, it is a matter of interpreting historical records and moving through almost impenetrable jungles until one finds something. And sometimes, as in the case of Troy, it is a matter of believing that a supposedly mythical or fictional place is actually real and interpreting works of literature as works of history in order to pinpoint a location. Of course, even with works of history or literature to help, it still takes a lot of careful digging and testing of the ground before the exact spot can be found.

It is through this searching and digging process that the science of archaeology comes in. Archaeology, specifically, is the study of artifacts, or man-made objects. It is based primarily on two principles: first, that artifacts found above other artifacts are younger or newer because they were laid down after the older, deeper artifacts, and second, that artifacts found on the same level are from the same time. With these *premises* archaeologists can study cultures in several different ways. They can examine the *vertical development* within a culture by comparing artifacts from different levels and determining the progress of that culture. Archaeologists can also compare the progress of various cultures by comparing their varying vertical developments. Archaeologists can also study the level of development of a culture by examining the *horizontal development*. By examining the artifacts of a particular *stratum*, they can determine the level of diversification of a society, and from that, determine its level of development. Archaeologists can even compare the levels of development and *diversification* among two or more cultures by comparing the collection of artifacts of any stratum with the same stratum from another culture anywhere in the world.

From all this discussion of levels, you can understand their great importance to the science of archaeology. Where something is found is as important as what is found. That is why digging must be done in such a slow and careful manner. It can take an archaeologist a week, a month, or even longer, just to go through a single *cubic foot* of earth. To keep the contents of any given layer clear, detailed drawings of everything on a particular stratum — including rocks and pebbles — are made every few inches or so. Frequent photographs are also taken of the positions of artifacts from different levels and the order of strata. Without these precautions, the order or position of artifacts may become confused and *analysis* would be useless or impossible. It is only through the practice of the *methodologies* for record-keeping and the theories of the importance of relative placement of artifacts that archaeology became a science instead of a hobby, or treasure hunting, or a business.

It may be difficult to find an archaeologist to talk to. However, you may be able to talk to a professor of archaeology at a local college, university, or seminary. If there is no college or university in your area, you could try writing a letter to a professor of archaeology at your state university.

Questions You Might Ask An Archaeologist

What is your experience in archaeology?
Where have you done archaeological work?
What kind of archaeology do you do?
Where do you study; what training and education do you have?
How did you become interested in archaeology?
How long does a normal *dig* last?
How many people are usually involved?
To whom do the artifacts belong after you find them?
What percentage of workers on the dig are volunteers?
What percentage of a *site* do you actually uncover?
How much of your time is spent mapping out the sight and how much is spent digging?
Do you leave the site in good condition for future archaeologists?
What do you do to protect a site in the off-season when you are not digging?
Do you know any ancient or dead languages?
Can an archaeologist actually reconstruct a past civilization?
What was the greatest "find" you have had?

Activities

- In your encyclopedia, read the story of Heinrich Schliemann and the discovery of Troy or any of the stories of the archaeology of Europe.

- In your encyclopedia, read the story of Howard Carter and the discovery of King Tut's tomb, or the Hittite Empire, or any of the stories of the archaeology of the Middle East.

- Read about the archaeology of South America and Mexico.

- Find out if there is now or ever has been archaeology done near where you live.

- With permission, do some archaeological digging of your own, making sure to keep a record of drawings of everything you find on each level.

- Using **National Geographic** or another archaeological journal from your library, write a report about the archaeology of some place that interests you.

Vocabulary

- ❏ Artifact
- ❏ Horizontal Development
- ❏ Cubic Foot
- ❏ Dig

- ❏ Premise
- ❏ Stratum
- ❏ Analysis
- ❏ Site

- ❏ Vertical Development
- ❏ Diversification
- ❏ Methodology
- ❏ Wadi

Tips From Barnabas

The Dead Sea Scrolls are one of the most important Biblical archaeological finds. They were first discovered west of the Dead Sea in 1947 by a shepherd boy. He was following his sheep down the Wadi Qumran and saw a small cave up on a bluff. He tried to throw some rocks into the cave. When he did, he heard a sound of breaking pottery. When he climbed up to the cave and crawled in, he found that his rocks had hit some clay pots. It was inside these pots that the scrolls from the ancient Qumran community had been stored.

Do some research and find out why these discoveries were so important and prepare a report on the Dead Sea Scrolls to share with your family.

Many times in the past, unbelieving men have mocked the Bible accounts of civilizations in the past. One was the Hittite civilization. God said He would wipe out the Hittites, and they were so completely destroyed that unbelieving archaeologists decided they had never really existed. Then in 1936, M. Parrot unearthed many thousands of cuneiform tablets dating from about 1700 B.C. at the city of Mari, located on the Middle Euphrates. These tablets contained the names of Hittite kings mentioned in Genesis 14. Once again Biblical history has been confirmed.

For further study, go to the library and look up some books on Biblical Archeology. Other good sources of Archaeology information are Bible Study books and Bible Dictionaries. Also, if you have a Christian bookstore in your town, there are some excellent books on the reliability of the Bible. Notice how archaeology doesn't "prove" the Bible, but it does substantiate it. The most dependable proof of the truth of Scripture is the witness of the Holy Spirit in our lives, as He opens the Word of God to our understanding.

ARCHITECT

Background

NAME OF PLACE TO VISIT _____

NAME OF CONTACT PERSON _____

PHONE # _____

ADDRESS _____

_____

BEST TIME TO VISIT _____

Architecture is both an art and a science, so an architect must be both an artist and a skilled *technician*. An architect mixes artistic and practical considerations in varying degrees, depending on the building he or she is *designing*. A monument like the Lincoln Memorial in Washington D.C. clearly has more artistic than practical influences. A warehouse building in an industrial area of town, on the other hand, is likely to be more *functional* than artistic. A library or a private home is in between these extremes. These are buildings which must mix mere function with artistic or ornamental elements of design.

We have a tendency to think of architecture only in terms of large, modern buildings or private homes. This is not completely accurate. Architecture can be applied to any type of building, so any civilization that builds is said to have an architecture. Even primitive peoples, if they build, have distinctive forms of architecture. The early American Indians are a good example. Plains Indians built triangular tepees out of long poles covered with animal skin. Northern Indians built wooden longhouses. Southwestern Indians built stone houses in caves in the sides of cliffs. Eskimos build small huts out of ice. There are many reasons for these different kinds of houses. The reasons for the development of the tepee have to do with the life-style of the Plains Indians. These Indians hunted for a living, so they had to follow the herds of animals. Tepees are easily transported. Other reasons have to do with *climate* and *environment*. Eskimos can't build wooden houses even if they want to, because there are no trees in the far north. They use ice because that is the material which is available to them. In the same way, the design of our own modern buildings is effected by the life-style, the material available, and the climate of the area where they are to be built.

An architect must work within many different kinds of limitations. As we have just seen, he or she may be limited by the type, or quantity, or expense of building materials. He or she may also be limited by the size or condition of the area where the building is going to be placed. Is it a hot climate? Is it to be built in a windy area? Finally, the architect is limited by the physical properties of the material that will be used. Any material is only so strong and must be used and supported accordingly. Certain designs, like the *arch* and the *dome*, increase the strength of the material being used. It is mostly through considerations of *tension*, *force* and *gravity* that science enters architecture. These aspects are also dealt with by the building engineer. To help the architect plan for these elements, as well as to keep track of the plans while construction is in progress, he or she will use a *scale drawing* of the finished building, called a *blueprint* or *floor plan*.

So far, we have only talked about architecture in relation to the building of houses or other large buildings. The theories of architecture are often applied to different kinds of planning or different types of construction. There are many sub-fields to architecture. These include furniture design, *landscape design*, and city or urban planning. Some architects concentrate on *interior design*, making the inside spaces more pleasing or easier to work in, while others concentrate on *exterior design,* making the building more attractive from every perspective. *Aesthetics* is the study of why some designs are pleasing while others are not. It is often used to compare and contrast different architectural designs. Engineering is the study of why some designs are more stable, storm and earthquake resistant, easier to heat and cool, and efficient in the use of floor space.

Questions You Might Ask An Architect

In what kind of architecture do you specialize?
Are you involved with city planning and landscape architecture on the projects that you do?
Are there buildings in town which you have designed? Where are they?
How long does it take from the first plan to a finished building?
What schooling or training did you receive?
Do you have to be licensed?
What's the most important attribute for an architect to have?
How important is the site of the proposed building to your design?
How closely do you work with builders and engineers?
How closely do you work with the people who hire you?
What makes a building attractive?

Activities

• In your encyclopedia, read about Frank Lloyd Wright, Christoper Wren, or some other architect.

• Tour around your town looking for different kinds of architectural design. Keep a sketch book of the different kinds of architecture or particularly interesting buildings.

• Design floor plans and perspective drawings for different kinds of buildings (house, library, office building, hospital, etc.) Keep in mind the different needs of the people who will be using the buildings.

• Think about the designs of furniture in your house or your landscaping. Try to come up with ways to change them.

• There are many different schools of architecture which vary among regions and time periods. Create a chart of these different schools of architecture, listing the name, time period, region, basic design elements, materials used, and famous examples.

Vocabulary

- ❏ Technician
- ❏ Environment
- ❏ Tension
- ❏ Aesthetics
- ❏ Floor Plan
- ❏ Exterior Design

- ❏ Design
- ❏ Arch
- ❏ Force
- ❏ Scale Drawing
- ❏ Landscape Design
- ❏ Functional

- ❏ Climate
- ❏ Dome
- ❏ Gravity
- ❏ Blueprint
- ❏ Interior Design
- ❏ Engineer

Tips From Barnabas

Two great building projects in the Bible are the building of the Tower of Babel and the building of Solomon's Temple. The former was an expression of man's pride and rebellion. The latter was an expression of man's honor of God and obedience to His instruction. Read Genesis 11:1-9 and II Chronicles 3:1-5:14 and consider the different results these two examples of architecture created in history.

Many times in the New Testament the growth of the church is compared to building a temple for God with living stones. Each of us is a small part of the great Architect's plan. Location and foundation are important considerations in building. The greatest design will fall to ruin if it doesn't have a solid foundation. Christ's teaching is the only dependable foundation on which to build your life. Look up the following passages and make a list of what you have learned about God's spiritual architecture.

Hebrews 3:1-6
1 Corinthians 3:9
Matthew 16:18
Ephesians 2:19-20

What kind of material will your life add to what God is building?

NAME OF PLACE TO VISIT _____

NAME OF CONTACT PERSON _____

PHONE # _____

ADDRESS _____

_____

BEST TIME TO VISIT _____

ART MUSEUM

Background

Whether or not you enjoy drawing or painting, visiting an art museum can be very rewarding. Most museums display many different artists and many different schools of art. You may also be able to see different *media* of expression such as oil paintings, watercolors, and sculpture.

Everyone has his own preferences regarding what sort of art he likes. Some people prefer realistic art, others like *impressionism*. Others prefer *modern art*. But whichever you prefer, all forms of art have a lot to offer.

The largest art museum in the world is the Louvre in Paris. But most large and medium-sized cities have art museums. Most museums are free of charge or have a day each week that is free of charge.

How to Look At Paintings

There are certain elements of paintings which are the basic elements that form the picture. These are line, shape, space, light, and color. Each of these things helps set the tone and mood of the painting.

For example, horizontal lines are often used to convey serenity. Vertical lines lend feelings of dignity. Curving and swirling lines are used to show a sense of motion. Different shapes are often repeated throughout a painting, but in various colors and contexts. Some colors appear to "come forward" in the painting, others "fall back."

There is so much to even a basic understanding of art, that it cannot be thoroughly discussed here. So, before going to a museum, look in your encyclopedia or go to the library and find a book about *art appreciation*. There will probably be many at your library.

When you go to the museum, look carefully at a few paintings, rather than just glancing at them all. Even if you don't initially care for one, try to understand what the artist was trying to accomplish. What was he or she trying to say? It's much better to try to thoroughly examine a few paintings in this way than to just look casually at one hundred. You can always go back to see more.

Studying Artists and Their Work

Some art museums will have a large collection of the work of one artist. Other museums specialize only in one period or *school of art*. This can be especially useful if you want to do a more in-depth study. In addition to just studying the composition of the paintings, you could also read about the painter's life and about important concerns during the time period that the art represents. Great art often comes out of periods of social change when human passions and ideas are in transition. Art expresses these passions in ways that words often cannot. Images of serenity, faith, hope and honor contrast with images of fear, disillusionment, despair, and rebellion. Art not only reflects society, but it also influences and sometimes changes it. So it can add a lot to your study of art to know about the time period surrounding it.

In the same way, the artist's life will have a lot to do with understanding his paintings. Was the artist also interested in science? Did he or she have to worry about political issues of his or her time? Was the artist deeply religious?

Art Museum Departments and Employees

Art museums employ many different people. Of course, the larger the museum, the more people it can employ in each field, but most museums will have at least one person in each of the following fields.

The *registrar* is the person who records each new *acquisition* that the museum makes. Often works of art are donated to a museum. Sometimes they are purchased. Then the piece is photographed, a description is recorded, and it is numbered. After the value is determined, the piece is then insured against loss.

Often it is the *art historian* who determines the value of a work of art. He or she examines it carefully to determine whether or not it is a *forgery* and, if it is real, how much it is worth.

The *curator* determines how to display the pieces. He or she determines how exhibits will be set up, if they will be changed, where new acquisitions should go, if the art should be placed in a case, behind glass, or left open. Designers then build these cases.

Preparators prepare the pieces for exhibit. They also add any other extras to the exhibits such as individual plaques describing each painting or a large plaque about the artist.

Often art museums have schools which offer art courses in all mediums for both beginning and advanced children and adults. You might enjoy signing up for a class through your local art museum.

There are usually tour guides in museums who give tours of the museum at certain hours every day. This is a good way to be introduced to the museum if you've never visited it before, especially if you don't know much about art. The guides are trained to know a lot about the paintings, statues, and artists represented in the museum and could answer most questions you might have.

Questions You Might Ask At An Art Museum

From where does the museum get most of its funding?
How is the value of a piece of art determined?
What are some ways you can tell if a piece of art is a forgery?
How do you determine which artist's works you will purchase?
How are the paintings/sculptures cared for?
Is it expensive to insure the pieces?
What is taken into consideration when setting up an exhibit?
What training is required for your position?
How did you acquire most of your paintings?
How do you maintain security?

Activities

- Choose an artist that you like who is represented at your art museum. Study his life and his paintings in the museum.

- If your museum offers art classes for children, take one in the medium that interests you the most.

- Create a chart showing the different schools of art. Include the name, time period, regions, characteristics, major artists, and major pieces.

Vocabulary

❏ Medium
❏ Acquisition
❏ Designers

❏ School of Art
❏ Forgery
❏ Preparators

❏ Registrar
❏ Curator

Tips From Barnabas

Art has been used to express man's feelings from the earliest times. Whether it is a painting, sculpture, song, or poem, a true artist is expressing what he or she sees, feels, hears, or thinks, hoping that you, his or her audience, will recognize and share in his or her creation.

While there are periods and schools of "religious art," i.e. art depicting religious subjects, such as Leonardo DeVinci's "Last Supper," try to broaden your thinking to include all legitimate forms of art as expressing **truth**, part of the nature of God. Remember, art is an expressed **image**. In Hebrews 1:3 we are told that Christ is the visible image or representation of the invisible God. That is why we have no need for any graven images or idols to worship. In Genesis 1:26,27 we are told that men and women were made in the image of God. In Romans 1:19,20 Paul says that man can know and understand His eternal power and Godhead by looking at nature, God's handiwork.

Have you ever seen a picture of an ocean that made you think of how powerful God is, or a picture of a mother and child that made you think of love?

Either in a museum or in an art book, choose a few paintings or sculptures that really "speak" to you, and write a paragraph explaining what each says.

If you wish to do additional reading, try Francis Schaefer's How Shall We Then Live, or Dorothy Sayer's chapter on "Toward a Christian Aesthetic" in her book. The Whimsical Christian.

ATHLETE

Background

NAME OF PLACE TO VISIT _____

NAME OF CONTACT PERSON _____

PHONE # _____

ADDRESS _____

_____

BEST TIME TO VISIT _____

There are as many kinds of athletes as there are kinds of sports. Because each sport is different and requires different abilities from its participants, each kind of athlete must train somewhat differently. An athlete will also gain some advantage by matching his body type to the sport he chooses to *train* for. Clearly, a basketball player has a different kind of body than a football player.

Basic training for any sport falls into two categories: training to achieve and maintain general fitness and training for the specific requirements of a particular sport. Most athletes do a lot of running to strengthen their *cardiovascular system*. They will also do a series of exercises including sit-ups, push-ups, chin-ups, jumping jacks, and stretches to keep all parts of their *muscular system* well-*toned*. There may also be some *weight training* to increase strength in general. All these activities would be part of a basic health program to keep themselves *fit*. In addition to this, athletes must train in the particular skills of their sport. Football players practice running plays, throwing, catching, and blocking in the same way that baseball players practice hitting and catching. Catching a football is much different from catching a baseball, and it is important that an athlete learns the peculiarities of his or her sport. Sports which don't require extra apparatus also need to be practiced to the point that reaction by the athlete is automatic; runners must run and wrestlers must wrestle.

Body type, however, is also very important. There are advantages and handicaps for certain sports which no amount of training can provide or overcome. It is almost a requirement for basketball players that they be well above average in height. This is not so in other sports. Jockeys are disqualified if they are not below a certain height. By the same token, it is an advantage to a wrestler to be squat and broad, while most good swimmers are tall and thin. These factors must be considered from the very beginning. It is highly unlikely that an athlete with the wrong type of body will be able to progress very far professionally in a sport for which he or she is maladjusted. Taking part in the right sport or sports, however, can be very exhilarating.

Questions You Might Ask An Athlete

What made you choose the sport you play?

What do you do to train?

What characteristics are necessary to be good at your sport?

Is there a national or international organization that controls the rules of your sport?

What are the risks involved in your sport?

Is your sport an Olympic event?

What are the dangers of training incorrectly?

How long have you been playing your sport?

Is there an ideal age at which to start and end a career in your sport?

What type of equipment is used in your sport?

Activities

- Make a list of sports.

- Using your list of sports, list the physical types which would be best suited to them.

- Using your list of sports, design training programs which would help athletes in that sport.

- Read further on some sport or on how athletes train and write a report.

- Study the medical problems springing from sports and write a report.

- See if you can join a sports team or take a class in some sport.

Vocabulary

❏ Train
❏ Tone

❏ Cardiovascular System
❏ Weight Training

❏ Muscular System
❏ Fit

Tips From Barnabas

The Old Testament has few references to athletics. However, athletics are used in the New Testament, especially by Paul. Even before Alexander the Great, athletic contests held in public stadiums had become popular throughout the known world.

Paul repeatedly uses athletics as a model to explain how our spiritual life works. There are five athletic principles that he uses repeatedly. These are:

1. The Prize   (the motivation)
2. The Discipline   (the training)
3. The Pain   (the obstacles)
4. The Rules   (the procedure)
5. The Goal   (the finish)

Look up the following references and identify which athletic principle is being used to illustrate the Christian life. If you can think of other comparisons between athletics and your spiritual life, add those to this list.

1 Corinthians 9:24
Galatians 2:2
Galatians 5:7
Philippians 3:14
Hebrews 12:1
2 Timothy 4:7-8

AUTOMOBILE

Background

NAME OF PLACE TO VISIT _____

NAME OF CONTACT PERSON _____

PHONE # _____

ADDRESS _____

_____

BEST TIME TO VISIT _____

One of the most influential inventions of the last hundred years is the automobile. From humble, even humorous, beginnings, there are now many automobile manufacturers in many countries all over the world. Over eight million cars were made in the United States alone in 1986. But no matter what the country of origin, no matter what the make, model, shape, color, or size, most cars operate in the same way.

Before the beginning of this century, inventors were attempting to make horse-drawn carriages into self-propelled vehicles. The *engine* is the propulsion machine that turned the automobile into the "horseless carriage." An engine changes the energy of gasoline into power to turn the wheels. The burning of gasoline inside the engine moves the parts of the engine, and this movement is transferred to the wheels. The amount of gas in the engine is controlled by the *accelerator*, or gas pedal; the more gas in the engine the faster the car will move. The major parts of an engine are *cylinders* and *pistons*. Cylinders are upside-down containers about the size of soup cans, and pistons are plugs which move up and down within the cylinders. Most cars have four, six, or eight cylinders. In general, the more cylinders a car has, the more power the car has.

When the accelerator is pressed, *fuel* is pumped from the gas tank to the *carburetor* where it is mixed with air and becomes a *fuel vapor*. The vapor is allowed through a *valve* into the top of the cylinder. The piston then moves up the cylinder and compresses the vapor. When the *spark plug* ignites the compressed vapor, the vapor explodes, forcing the piston downward with great force. The *exhaust*, the waste gas left over after the vapor explodes, is let out of the cylinder by another valve.

The pistons are connected to the *crank shaft*. The force of the explosions in the cylinders turns the crank shaft. The crank shaft turns the *drive shaft*. The drive shaft turns the axle which turns the wheels and makes the car move. The amount of gas in the cylinders and the speed of the pistons are not the only factors which control the car's speed. *Gears* also change the speed of the car by changing the *ratio* of the turning of the crank shaft with the turning of the drive shaft. Gears are wheels with teeth around the outside. Two gears mesh together, and, as one turns the other one is turned. By changing the relative sizes of the gears, you can change the speed that the drive shaft is turning.

The explosions inside the engine and the *friction* caused by various parts of the engine rubbing together causes a lot of heat. If the engine becomes too hot, it will cease to work, so there are two important ways that the engine is cooled. First, to cut down on the friction caused by the pistons rubbing against the inside of the cylinders, *motor oil* is pumped through the engine to make the parts slide more easily. Second, to cool the outside of the engine, water is pumped around the outside of it. The water takes on the heat of the engine and is then cooled by the fan in the front of the car.

Early cars had to be started manually. The driver would have to turn a crank sticking out of the front of the car which would start the crank shaft turning, the pistons pumping, and the spark plugs firing. Modern cars are not like this. Cars are now equipped with a *battery* and a *starter*. When the *ignition* key is turned, electricity is allowed from the battery to the starter (which is a small motor inside the engine). The starter turns the crank shaft until the engine starts to run on its own.

Of course, it takes more than just an engine to drive a car; a driver has to be able to control it. That is why cars are also equipped with steering controls and brakes. The steering wheel is connected to the *steering column,* which is connected, by a different set of gears, to a rod running between the front wheels. When the wheel is turned, the rod (or steering linkage) moves from side to side, pushing and pulling the wheels and making them turn. There are two kinds of *brakes*: *drum brakes* and *disk brakes.* Most cars have drum brakes. The wheels of cars with drum brakes have a lining called a *brake drum.* When the brake pedal is pressed, *brake pads* are pressed against the inside of the brake drums by *brake shoes.* The friction of the pads rubbing against the brake drums slows the car to a stop. With disk brakes, on the other hand, metal *brake disks* are attached to each wheel. The friction to stop the car is caused by a clamp which pinches brake pads on either side of the disk.

Finally, there are many important safety features on an automobile. The most important thing which can be done to increase the safety of the car is to have it checked regularly to make sure that all the parts, especially the brakes, are working properly. Lights are very important on a car. There are many different kinds of lights, and they each have a specific purpose, but in general, they let other cars and pedestrians know what you are doing. Communication is very important among drivers on the road. There are head lights, tail lights, back-up lights, brake lights, parking lights, emergency or hazard lights, and turn signals. Another method of communication between drivers is the horn. It is also important that the driver is able to see clearly all of the time. The headlights help with night driving and the windshield wipers and *defoggers* help in bad weather to keep the windows clear. The most important safety features are the seat belt and a good conscientious driver.

Questions You Might Ask An Auto Mechanic

What is the most common service that you perform?
What is the most frequent cause of automobile breakdown?
What is the benefit of unleaded gas?
Where is the catalytic converter, and what does it do?
How do you fill the car up with gasoline, oil, transmission fluid, brake fluid, and water?
How do you check the oil and tire pressure on a car?
Where did you learn to work on cars?
What are the important things to look for when buying a car?
What are the differences between diesel or rotary engine?
What determines how much gas mileage a car gets?
What is the difference between an "automatic" car and a "stick-shift"?
What needs to be done periodically to maintain a car in good working order?
What makes some cars run better than others?
Do models of cars differ much from year to year?
What is the most important improvement you have seen in cars in the last ten years?

Activities

- With the help of your parents, study your family car. See if you can pick out the parts mentioned here.
- Study the diagram of an automobile in an encyclopedia. Then, without looking, make your own diagram to be sure you know how an automobile works.

- Pick out all the different kinds of lights by their function.
- Do some research on how much safer seat belts make driving/riding in a car and write a report.
- If you live near a science museum, see if it has various engines on display and exhibits to show how they work.
- Take a class on auto mechanics.
- Go to an automobile dealer's showroom and look at the various models and prices. Get some brochures to take home and look at.

Vocabulary

- ❐ Engine
- ❐ Cylinder
- ❐ Valve
- ❐ Crank Shaft
- ❐ Ratio
- ❐ Fuel
- ❐ Starter
- ❐ Drum Brakes
- ❐ Brake Drum
- ❐ Brake Disc

- ❐ Accelerator
- ❐ Carburetor
- ❐ Spark Plug
- ❐ Drive Shaft
- ❐ Friction
- ❐ Defoggers
- ❐ Ignition
- ❐ Disk Brakes
- ❐ Brake Pads

- ❐ Piston
- ❐ Fuel Vapor
- ❐ Exhaust
- ❐ Gears
- ❐ Motor Oil
- ❐ Battery
- ❐ Steering Column
- ❐ Brakes
- ❐ Brake Shoes

Tips From Barnabas

The closest thing in the Bible to an automobile is the chariot. It was used for transportation, as with the Ethiopian in Acts 8. However, its main usefulness was for military purposes. Often the strength of an army was calculated in the number of chariots it had. Kings displayed their legions of chariots to demonstrate their strength. Because of this, Israel was instructed by God not to trust in their chariots but to put their trust in the Lord (Psa. 20:7, Isaiah 31:1).

Today the automobile has become a status symbol which many people use to gain admiration and acceptance. For a Christian, the automobile is a marvelous tool for the advance of the Gospel. Pretend that you are a missionary getting ready for your first term on the field. Decide which country you are going to and then decide what kind of car it would be best to purchase. You may need to do some checking as to the price and availability of gas in that particular country. Make a list of your reasons for selecting a particular car.

Some people have compared taking care of your car with taking care of your spiritual life. See what you can do with that analogy. Use common maintenance procedures that you know are needed to keep a car running and draw the parallels for keeping your spiritual life in good condition.

Name of Place to Visit_____

Name of Contact Person _____

Phone #_____

Address _____

_____

Best Time to Visit _____

BAKERY

Background

We are all familiar with the products of a bakery. On the one hand, some of the most common foods we eat — *staples* — come from a bakery. These staples include all kinds of breads, rolls, and buns. On the other hand, many of the things we consider special treats and desserts come from a bakery. These things are cakes, pies, cookies, and brownies, of course. The differences between these two kinds of products have to do with *chemistry*. The way different ingredients combine and how they react with heat are aspects of chemistry. We will now examine some of the basics of the chemistry of baking.

Baking is one of the earliest ways of preparing food. The earliest baking was drying seeds on rocks in the sun. After this, seeds were placed in water in the sun. The porridge that was produced was then baked on flat rocks. This kind of bread would come out flat, much like a Mexican tortilla or a pie crust. The Egyptians are believed to be the first people to use *leavening agents*. Bread which is leavened has risen and become taller, thicker, and lighter than unleavened bread. Regular sandwich bread is an example of leavened bread.

Bread rises because it is elastic enough to hold bubbles of gas, which are created in the bread, without letting them pass all the way through the bread and out. Only wheat and rye flour have the ability to be leavened, and wheat flour does it better. Therefore, any baked good that needs to be leavened must contain some quantity of wheat or rye flour. These bubbles of gas are created in different ways. Baker's *yeast* is used in most bread. Yeast is composed of living cells which turn sugar into carbon dioxide, a gas, and ethanol, a kind of alcohol. Another method is the use of *sour dough*. Sour dough contains a kind of *bacteria* which is beneficial to man; it creates an acid which in turn *ferments* the sugar into carbon dioxide and ethanol. Sweeter baked goods use a different method of leavening. *Baking soda* is often used because it releases the carbon dioxide which makes the baked goods rise. To control the rate that this gas is released, baking soda is added to certain acids which slow it down. This new mixture is called *baking powder*. A last method for adding bubbles to baked goods is to simply add them already made. This can be done by adding an ingredient which holds air bubbles, like egg whites. Egg whites are whipped into a froth and then added to the batter. This makes a very light texture and is used in the making of such things as angel food cake. Besides flour, water, and leavening, there are a few other ingredients which are found in most baked goods. *Shortening* (butter, oil, or lard) is used to make the batter easier to work and the end result more tender. Milk is often used for flavoring, and sugar is used not only to make it sweeter but to provide something for the leavening agent to work on.

Since the Industrial Revolution in the late nineteenth century, bakeries have become increasingly automated. Before that, everything had been done by hand. In the large industrial bakeries of today you will find a wide variety of specialized machines: mixers, *kneaders*, ovens, slicers, and wrappers. Each of these machines must be run by a specialist for that machine. In smaller bakeries, however, less machinery is used. Each worker in the smaller bakery must be able to do a wide variety of jobs. In many cases, every worker in a small bakery will be a full-fledged baker, capable of doing any of the many baking jobs.

Questions You Might Ask A Baker

How did you get into this business?
What is your favorite part of the job?
What is your most popular product?
Do you have a specialty product line?
Do you have seasonal products?
Do you cater parties?
Do you do wedding cakes and/or other special occasion-type baking?
What kind of ovens do you have?
Who are your customers?
Who is your closest competitor?
Is there much government regulation over your business?
How often does the Health Department inspect the business, and what are they looking for?
Are you privately owned?
What part does nutrition play in your offered line of products?
Do the people who work here have specialized jobs?
What percentage of your work is done by hand and what percentage is done by machine?
Are your employees able to eat all they want?
Do you find yourself snacking a lot?
What training did you receive to become a baker?
Are all your products made fresh every day?
At what time do you have to start work in the morning?
What happens to products which aren't sold?

Activities

- Visit several different bakeries and make a list of the products they sell (perhaps just the different kinds of breads) and how much they charge for each. Then choose one product, bake it yourself, and figure out how much it cost to make. Is it cheaper to make it from scratch or to buy it from the bakery?
- Make a chart of the ingredients of your favorite baked good and list what each one does.
- With help, do some baking of your own. Choose a wide variety of items, including recipes from other countries.

Vocabulary

☐ Shortening
☐ Chemistry
☐ Sour Dough
☐ Baking Soda

☐ Knead
☐ Leavening Agent
☐ Bacteria
☐ Baking Powder

☐ Staple
☐ Yeast
☐ Ferment

Tips From Barnabas

The first Biblical reference to a baker is in Genesis 40. Joseph was in prison because of the trumped-up charges of Potiphar's wife. Two men offended Pharoah, his butler and his baker. While in prison with Joseph, each of them had a dream. Joseph was able to accurately interpret each of their dreams. After the baker was free, he eventually remembered Joseph to Pharoah as one who could interpret his dream. Joseph was brought from prison and placed before Pharoah, and since he was the only one able to interpret Pharoah's prophetic dream he was judged to be the only man to qualify to run the government as the dream became a reality.

While the story of this baker doesn't speak much of the art of baking, it does illustrate an important lesson for all of us. A significant principle from this story centers around the character of Joseph. His life illustrates the verse, "Whoever can be trusted with very little can also be trusted with much" (Luke 16:10). Joseph was faithful with what little he had, and Pharoah entrusted him with very much. He was faithful in prison and God saw to it that he was elevated, second only to Pharoah.

In the New Testament, leaven, one of the key elements used in baking, is used to teach several significant lessons. Jesus uses the illustration of leaven in his parables (Matthew 13) to explain how the Kingdom of Heaven is going to grow. It will be an internal process (like leaven in the loaf), not an external display (like the Pharisees). Jesus also uses the leavening process as an illustration of corrupt teaching. He says in Matthew 16:6, "Beware of the leaven of the Pharisees and of the Sadducees." He later explains that He is talking about the teachings of the Pharisees and of the Sadducees (Mt.16:12). If some of the traditions and attitudes that the Pharisees and Sadducees taught and modeled were followed, they would corrupt the disciples' lives. It would be an interesting study to list some of these teachings and see, if we were to follow them, what affect they would have on our spiritual lives.

It is this later meaning of leaven that Paul uses to argue for the purity of the church. In I Corinthians 5 there is a sinning brother that needs to be removed from the church. If he is not removed, his presence and the church's attitude towards his sin will have a corrupting influence on the rest of the body. To illustrate this truth Paul says, "Don't you know that a little yeast works through the whole batch of dough? Get rid of the old yeast that you may be a new batch without yeast—as you really are" (1Cor.5:6,7).

BANK

Background

NAME OF PLACE TO VISIT _____

NAME OF CONTACT PERSON _____

PHONE # _____

ADDRESS _____

_____

BEST TIME TO VISIT _____

Banks are a very important part of our society. Most people have a bank account of some kind. Usually it is a checking account or a savings account.

There are basically two different types of banks. The first type is national banks. They always have the word "national" in their name and are governed by federal law. The other type is banks with the word "state" in their name or whose name contains neither "state" nor "national." These banks must obey the laws of the state in which they are located.

A bank is run by the president of the bank and its board of directors. The board of directors is made up of approximately a dozen people who choose a person for the job of president. Each of the people on the board is also a stockholder in the bank. Board members make the decisions as to how the bank conducts its business, but they do not always work at the bank. Often they have their own jobs and careers.

The president of a bank does many things. He or she handles a lot of the bank's public relations. He or she tries to get new business for the bank. He or she must understand every aspect of banking and know everything that his or her bank is doing, in order to report to the board. The president is also in charge of all of the other bank officers.

Bank officers are also chosen by the board. Not all of the employees of a bank are officers. Officers must inform the board of any debts that they have or of any businesses they open in addition to their job at the bank. This is to make sure that the officer does not *misappropriate* the banks funds by borrowing money for himself or his business. An employee who is not an officer does not need to report anything about his or her private life.

One of the most common types of accounts is a checking account. You can usually open a checking account with a minimum of one hundred dollars. When you open the account, you receive checks and a ledger in which to record the checks that you write.

A checking account is very convenient. Writing a check for someone is the same as giving him or her money, but it's safer and easier to carry a checkbook than to carry a lot of cash.

If you lose your checkbook or even a single check, you should notify your bank immediately. It can cancel payment on the check so no one else can use it. Almost always when you pay someone with a check they ask for two pieces of identification, but it is still safest to always report a lost or missing check.

Whenever you write a check or *deposit* money in a checking account, always record the transaction in your checking account ledger. This way you can keep track of how much money there is in your account. It is illegal to *overdraw* a checking account, that is, to write a check for more money than is in it. This is what is called a *bounced* check. Banks charge a fee for each bad check that you write, and if you wrote that check to a store it will almost certainly also charge you extra money.

When you have a checking account, the bank will send you a *statement* each month along with all of your *canceled* checks, unless you agree to let the bank keep a record of your checks on microfiche rather than return the actual checks to you. The statement is a record of all the checks that you wrote in the past month, all of the deposits that you made, and the balance at the end of the day before the statement was printed. Most people compare their check ledger with the statement to see if the figures match up. This is called *balancing* a check book.

The other major type of account is a savings account. Savings accounts can usually be opened with only five dollars. Savings accounts earn *interest*, as do some checking accounts. There are short-term savings accounts and long-term ones. Short-term savings accounts are also called passbook accounts. When you open the account, you receive a passbook in which you or a bank teller will record all of your deposits and *withdrawals*.

The reason that you are promising to leave your money in for a long time is that the bank will be able to use your money. The bank invests it in stocks which make money for it. In turn, it pays you more interest so that both you and the bank are making money off of your money.

A long-term savings account also earns interest. In fact, it earns more than a short-term account. However, unlike a short-term account, you agree to leave your money in the bank for a certain period of time. This time can vary from a few months to several years. It is possible to withdraw your money early from a long-term account, but the bank will penalize you.

Another service that banks offer is giving loans. Banks lend money to people who want to make major purchases like homes and cars, to people who are starting a business, and to people who need financial help to go to college.

In the same way that banks pay interest to a savings account, they also charge interest on a loan. This is one of the ways that they make money. So, if you take out a loan, you will have to actually pay back more than you originally received. How much more, depends on how much you took out, how long you had it out, and the current interest rate.

There are many different reasons that a bank lends money, but there are two things that a bank always does before granting a loan. First, if the money is to buy something, the bank will make sure that the item is worth the amount of money it is lending. Second, it will always examine the person who is applying for the loan very closely to make sure that he or she will be able to pay the money back.

A bank is a business just like a store. However, instead of selling a product for money, they offer a service. They handle people's money in exchange for a percentage of that money.

Questions To Ask A Banker

What is the current interest rate that your bank pays to checking accounts, short-term savings, and long-
    term savings?
What does it charge on loans?
Does your bank have different types of checking accounts?
How are they different?
What happens to a check after it is given to someone?
What additional services does a bank offer?
Why is money valuable?
What does the F.D.I.C. do?
Which jobs in the banks are held by officers?

What are the other positions in a bank?
What training is required to be a bank teller?
Why does a bank close down?
How much of the bank's money is actually kept at the bank?

Activities

- Open a savings account.
- Have your parents show you how to balance a checkbook.
- Find a book about the Great Depression of 1929. Write a report on the chain of events that caused this to happen, how the banks were affected, and consequently how people were affected. Also note what the recovery process was and the changes that occurred in banking because of it.

Vocabulary

- ❏ Misappropriate
- ❏ Withdrawal
- ❏ Canceled Check

- ❏ Compound Interest
- ❏ Statement
- ❏ "Bounced" Check

- ❏ F.D.I.C., Deposit
- ❏ Overdrawn

Tips From Barnabas

Banks are places where "treasures" are stored. Christ talked about a heavenly bank where we could store treasures. Starting at Matthew 6:19-21, look up the following Scriptures and write a paper explaining how we can make 'deposits' in a heavenly bank.

Matthew 19:21, Luke 12:33, Philippians 3:8, and 1 Timothy 6:19

There are also several principles given in the book of Proverbs about 'borrowing' and 'lending.' Using a concordance, look these verses up and then discuss with your parents what a Christian's attitude should be towards handling money.

NAME OF PLACE TO VISIT _____

NAME OF CONTACT PERSON _____

PHONE # _____

ADDRESS _____

_____

BEST TIME TO VISIT _____

BARBER

Background

Most of us have had to go to the barber or hairdresser at one time or another. The barber helps us look our best. What other people think about us is often determined by how we look. The barber does not just cut our hair; he or she must think about styling it. Each person requires a slightly different style to look his or her best. All the parts of a haircut must work together – must match. In addition to cutting hair, the barber or hairdresser may wash, curl, straighten, or color it. He or she can take care of anything having to do with hair.

It was not always the case, however, that the only concern of barbers was hair. In the Middle Ages barbers started doing minor *surgery*. This happened first in *monasteries*. Barbers were common in monasteries because *monks* were required to be clean shaven and to have *tonsures*. When monks were later forbidden to draw blood, the barbers, with their sharp instruments, were the logical choice to take up the minor surgical duties that were required. In those days, surgery was not seen as legitimate work for doctors, as it is now. It was seen as more of a craft, like cabinet making, than a real medical skill. In addition to what we would call surgery, the barbers would often take care of dentistry as well. Throughout the late Middle Ages and until the late 18th century, the guilds or unions for barbers and surgeons were the same. It wasn't until 1800 that the *Royal College of Surgeons* was established in England, and the two fields were really separate.

Because the duties of a barber were so varied and so delicate in the Middle Ages, a man would have to serve as an *apprentice* for many years to become a real barber. Now that barbering and surgery are separate, there are barber colleges with two or three-year courses for becoming a barber. These colleges are often open to customers, and it is possible to get a haircut from a student of one of these schools for less money than going to an established barber. Almost every city has one of these schools.

Questions You Might Ask A Barber

How long have you been a barber or a hairdresser?

What kind of training did you receive? Did you go to school to learn it?

Do you like being a barber?

Why did you choose barbering?

What special skills are required in a barber?

Do you have a specialty?

Do you have a regular clientele?

How do you keep up with the latest styles?
Do you give your clients advice on how to take care of their hair?
How long does the average haircut take?
How many clients do you have a day?
What other services do you perform besides cutting hair?
Do you ever teach mothers how to cut their children's hair?
What is the hardest style of hair for you to cut?

Activities

- Research men's and women's hairstyles. Show the many changes in these styles by drawing pictures of the most common style for men and women, starting in the year 1900. Do the same for each ten-year interval (e.g. 1910, 1920, 1930, etc.), up until the present day.
- Write a report on why you think hair styles change.
- Write a report on the history of barbers and surgeons.

Vocabulary

❑ Surgery
❑ Tonsure

❑ Monastery
❑ Royal College of Surgeons

❑ Monk
❑ Apprentice

Tips From Barnabas

Hair is mentioned in Scripture. Remember that the angel of the Lord had told Samson's mother that his hair was never to be cut (Judges 13). What were the consequences that came from his hair being cut (Judges 16)?

In Matthew 10:30, Christ tells His disciples that God has numbered all the hairs on their heads. Why did Jesus say that?

Again in Luke 21:18 Jesus refers to the hairs on the disciples head saying that not one of the hairs of their heads would perish. What was the context of that statement?

In 1 Corinthians 11:3-10 and 1 Timothy 2:9-10, Paul makes several comments relating to hairstyles for Christians. Do you think a person's hairstyle says anything about what they believe about God? Talk about this with your parents and see if you can come up with some principles concerning your personal appearance. What guidance does the Bible give you about your hairstyle and your physical appearance in general?

NAME OF PLACE TO VISIT _____

NAME OF CONTACT PERSON _____

PHONE # _____

ADDRESS _____

_____

BEST TIME TO VISIT _____

BEEKEEPER

Background

You probably never think about where the honey comes from that you use on your toast or biscuits. Sure, everyone knows that bees make honey, but where did your honey actually come from? It's not just gathered haphazardly by people strolling through the woods. In fact, almost all of our honey comes from bees which are professionally farmed. The United States Department of Agriculture estimates that over 260,000,000 pounds of honey are produced by bee farmers – beekeepers – every year in this country. Honey production, however, is not the most important use bee keepers have for bees. Bees perform 80 to 85 percent of all crop *pollination* in the United States. Without pollination, crops couldn't develop. Because of increased use of *pesticides* in recent years, wild insect populations are dying out, and the role of farmed bees has become much more important. Beekeepers set up their hives near crops and allow the bees to pollinate freely. This is vital for American food production.

It takes a good deal of training and experience to handle bees successfully. Most of us think of bees as angry and always ready to attack. This is not necessarily the case. Professional beekeepers are able to handle bees quite a lot, even taking their *hives* apart to extract the honey, without getting stung. One of their secrets is the use of smoke. Smoke pacifies bees. Beekeepers use small, hand-held burners with a small bellows on top. When smoke is blown into the mouth of the hive, the bees stay calm. The other secret is simply knowing how to deal with bees. If the bees are handled by calm and steady hands, they will not attack. Extra vibration would disturb them. As with most animals, the surest defenses against attack are familiarity with the animal and the absence of fear.

There are many different species of bees. The species which originate in Italy and Eastern Europe are most commonly used because of the amount of honey they produce, as well as their good temperament. No matter what the type, however, all *beehives* work the same. There are three types of bees in every hive, and they each have very specific duties. These types are the *queen bee*, the *drones*, and the *workers*. The queen bee controls the hive. She lays the eggs (as many as 2,000 a day) and directs the work of the hive. The drones are the only males in the hive. Since they are unable to perform the tasks that the workers do, their only duty is to *fertilize* the eggs the queen lays. Finally, the workers, who are actually undeveloped females, do everything required to keep the hive going. It is the worker bees with whom we are familiar. These are the ones that leave the hive to collect pollen with which they create honey. Honey is stored inside the hive to feed the young bees. In fact, different kinds of pollen make different kinds of honey.

Questions You Might Ask A Beekeeper

What kind of bees do you keep?
How many bees do you keep?
How much honey do they produce?
Do you use them for planned pollination?
Why did you choose to be a beekeeper?
How long have you been working with bees?
Is it difficult to handle bees?
Are you often stung?
What training did you receive?
Do different types of bees require different kinds of hives?
What different types of honey are there?

Activities

- Find a book that has pictures of the inside and outside of a beehive. Create your own beehive using whatever materials you think would be the most appropriate.
- Research the differences in bee species.
- Write a report on bees and crop pollination.

Vocabulary

❏ Pollination   ❏ Pesticide   ❏ Hive
❏ Queen Bee   ❏ Drone   ❏ Worker Bee
❏ Fertilize

Tips From Barnabas

In Psalm 19:10 and 119:103, the Word of the Lord is compared to honey. Write a paragraph describing why you think honey was chosen for comparison to the Word of God. What are the characteristics of honey that make it so attractive?

In Proverbs 6:6, the characteristics of the ant are used to teach diligence. From what you've learned about bees, write a proverb using the characteristics of bees as illustrations of good character.

Several times honey plays an important part in Bible stories. For some interesting reading, read Judges 14 where Samson makes a riddle about honey. Also read I Samuel 14, about Jonathan and the trouble honey caused him.

NAME OF PLACE TO VISIT _____

NAME OF CONTACT PERSON _____

PHONE # _____

ADDRESS _____

_____

BEST TIME TO VISIT _____

BOOKKEEPING

Background

Can you believe that the same bookkeeping principles that are used today were developed in the 15th century? If you enjoy solving math problems and working with numbers, bookkeeping and accounting might be a profession you would enjoy.

There are two basic jobs that comprise accounting. One is a *bookkeeper*. This person looks for and gathers all the right numbers and *posts* them in the correct places. Then the *accountant* determines the accounting system to be used, uses the information provided by the bookkeeper to generate reports, and interprets the results for the business or agency. An accountant is often a C.P.A. (Certified Public Accountant), which indicates that the accountant has passed a series of tests and is licensed with the A.I.C.P.A. (The American Institute of C.P.A.'s). You can receive information about this organization by writing to 666 Fifth Ave., New York, New York 10019.

The equation upon which all business accounting is based is:

Assets - Liabilities = Net Worth

Assets consist of the things owned by an individual or a business. Your own assets might include a bike, books, some clothes, and a savings account. Each asset has a value that can be defined in dollars.

Liabilities are debts; anything that is owed someone else. You may owe your brother $2.00.

Finally, *Net worth* means *proprietorship* or *capital* and equals what you would have left if you paid off everything that you owe.

So, if you take an *inventory* of your assets, it might look like this:

Bike	$ 50.00
Clothes	$ 100.00
Savings	$ 25.00
Total Assets	$ 175.00

But remember, you owe your brother $2.00. This is a liability.

Total Assets	$ 175.00
Total Liabilities	- $2.00
Your Net Worth is	$ 173.00

Balance Sheet

This is one of the most important reports an accountant will create. It shows the net worth of a business at any particular point in time. You will see a sample on page 42. Assets and liabilities are both divided into two categories: current and fixed. *Current assets* mean cash and other assets such as inventory that will be sold for cash or be used up within a short time, possibly in less than a year. *Fixed assets* mean the assets will probably not be sold for cash in a short period. Machinery and buildings are fixed assets. Look at the sample balance sheet on page 42 to see how this looks.

Profit & Loss Statement (P/L Statement)

A P/L statement is a report that shows how and why the net worth of a business changed during a period of time. This is done by showing its *income* and *expenses*. It is this form that the Internal Revenue Service (IRS) uses to determine how much of a business' income will be taxed. An example follows the balance sheet.

Types of Accounting

There are many different books and courses offered that teach different types of accounting. Accounting Principles, Intermediate and Advanced Accounting, Municipal Accounting, Tax Accounting, and *Auditing* are all different subjects in accounting.

In most large businesses, you will find several different accounting departments. The *accounts payable* department pays all the bills that the firm owes. If the company does not have a separate department to handle keeping track of the inventory, the accounts payable department may do this also. The *accounts receivable* department keeps track of all the money that is owed to the company by its customers, and the *payroll* department handles the paychecks for the company's employees. In smaller businesses, all of these functions may be done by one person.

There are many terms used in accounting: ledgers, accounts, debits and credits, and journal. You may find an accountant to interview at a company which has its own C.P.A. or at a firm of independent C.P.A.'s. Ask him or her to explain what some of these terms mean.

Questions You Might Ask An Accountant

How did you become interested in accounting?
How did you learn to become an accountant?
What do you do most of the time?
What is the difference between a bookkeeper and an accountant?
What do you need to do to become a C.P.A.?
What are the advantages of being certified?
Ask him or her to show you some of the reports he/she does.
Ask him or her to show you a report of accounts payable, accounts receivable, inventory, and explain what these show about the condition of a business.

Ask him or her to show you the various graphs he or she uses, such as line charts, bar graphs, and pie charts.

What filing systems do you use, and what does the term "paper trail" mean?

Do you use a computer in your work, and, if so, what does it do?

Activities

• Create your own balance sheet and profit & loss statement for a pretend business.

• Start your own small business and keep your own books. Even a lemonade stand or a garage sale needs clear accounting.

• Request a copy of an Individual Income Tax Return and also the Schedule C form for businesses from the post office and fill them out.

Vocabulary

❐ Audit
❐ Liability
❐ Capital
❐ Balance Sheet
❐ Expense
❐ Payroll
❐ Liquidity

❐ Bookkeeper
❐ Proprietorship
❐ Current Assets
❐ Profit & Loss Statement
❐ Accounts Payable
❐ Bankrupt
❐ Inventory

❐ Assets
❐ Net Worth
❐ Fixed Assets
❐ Income
❐ Accounts Receivable
❐ Creditor

Tips From Barnabas

God uses accounting principles to explain important concepts from the Bible. Take Salvation, for instance. Abraham believed God and God accounted it to him for righteousness (Rom.4:3). It is the same for us: if we "believe on Him that justifies the ungodly," our faith is "counted for righteousness" (Rom.4:5). Christ's righteousness is deposited into our account.

Make a chart to follow God's accounting of our sin. "The wages of sin is death" (Romans 6:23). "The soul that sins shall die" (Ezekiel 18:4). All men owe a debt to God for their sin. Because Christ is the only man who lived and did not sin, He owes no debt to God.

When Jesus Christ voluntarily died for the sins of humanity, He placed on God's accounting books an asset for which there was no corresponding debt. That is why His death can be transferred to the account of another. His death can pay our debt of death owed because of our sin. His payment, because He was God, is large enough to pay the debt for all the sins of everyone. When I accept Christ's death for my sin, His death is transferred to my account, my life is transferred to His account. Paul states it this way, "For you are bought with a price; therefore, glorify God in your body and in your spirit, which are God's" (I Corinthians 6:20).

Moses had a balance sheet that helped him decide for God.   Read about it in Hebrews 11:24-26.

Jesus used a profit/loss statement to challenge His disciples to an all out commitment of following Him. He asks, "For what is a man profited, if he shall gain the whole world, and lose his own soul? Or what shall a man give in exchange for his soul?" (Matthew 16:26). How would you answer that question?

In another area, it would be impossible to be good stewards of our possessions without some form of accounting. God required Israel to give (10%) of any increase (income). They had to keep good records to know how much their tithe was. Keeping clear and accurate records is a way of honoring God. It reflects our faithfulness and qualifies us for greater service (see Luke 16:10-12).

Can you find the accounting principles that the Apostle Paul uses when he appeals to Philemon to forgive and receive back his runaway slave Onesimus?

To some degree, the equation assets = liabilities + proprietorship can be applied to our spiritual lives. The assets are our positive character traits: honesty, diligence, obedience, and liabilities are our negative traits: dishonesty, laziness, greed, etc. The proprietorship or our net worth would be our spiritual maturity.

Of course, this is not really accurate, for only God knows the real condition of our heart, but it could help us grow if we take a spiritual inventory occasionally.

Make up your own balance sheet, assigning different numerical value for each trait, such as 10 being the highest and 0 the lowest. Figure up your assets, then your liabilities, and you'll be able to find your "net worth." Review it at the end of each month to see if your proprietorship has grown or diminished.

Bulgy Bear Company
Balance Sheet
December 31, 1992

Current Assets:

Cash	$1,200.00
Merchandise (500 Bulgy Bears)	900.00
Accounts Receivable	300.00
(Money owed to you)	
Office Supplies	100.00
Total Current Assets	$2,500.00

Fixed Assets:

Building	$ 30,000.00
Land	10,000.00
Equipment	1,200.00
Total Fixed Assets	$41,200.00

TOTAL ASSETS $43,700.00

Current Liabilities:

Accounts Payable	$ 500.00
(Money you owe to others)	
Wages Payable	300.00
(Wages you owe to employees)	
Total Current Liabilities	$ 800.00

Fixed Liabilities

Mortgage Payment	$ 35,000.00
(Building & Land)	
Notes Payable	1,000.00
(5 years for equipment)	
Total Fixed Liabilities	$36,000.00

TOTAL LIABILITIES $36,800.00

NET WORTH $ 6,900.00

Bulgy Bear Company
Profit & Loss Statement
December 31, 1992

INCOME:

Bear Sales $1,800.00

Expenses:

Cost of Goods Sold:		
Material	$350.00	
Wages	300.00	
Total Cost of Goods:	$650.00	
General Expenses:		
Office Supplies	50.00	
Office Salaries	200.00	
Telephone	50.00	
Total General Expense:	$300.00	

Total Expenses $ 950.00

Net Profit $ 850.00

NAME OF PLACE TO VISIT _____

NAME OF CONTACT PERSON _____

PHONE # _____

ADDRESS _____

_____

BEST TIME TO VISIT _____

BOOKSTORE

Background

If you like to read, a bookstore can be a fascinating place to explore. There are new and used book-stores, *chain bookstores*, and individually owned ones. Some are quite small, others may have several floors. All of them can prove to be very interesting.

New Bookstores. Stores that deal only in new books are often a part of a chain. That is, there are several stores of the same name, owned by the same company, throughout a state, an area, or the whole nation. Sometimes, however, you will also find new bookstores that are single, privately owned businesses.

Bookstores often divide their books by subjects. Some typical divisions are: popular fiction, classics, mysteries, science fiction, romance, cooking, medicine and health, music and drama, religion, psychology, and history.

Sometimes bookstores specialize in a certain area or areas. There are bookstores that carry little other than science fiction, those that carry only mysteries, and some that carry only cookbooks. There are bookstores that carry only Christian-related items and those that carry only books about eastern religions and philosophies.

Bookstores often carry things besides books. You may find calendars, records, tapes, bookmarks, wrapping paper, greeting cards, and even games. The reason for this is partly that people often buy books as gifts and so need wrapping paper and cards as well, and partly because book publishers often sell other things besides books, such as calendars and "books-on-cassette," that is, a cassette of someone reading a book aloud.

All bookstores have one or more buyers who are responsible for knowing what new books are being published, when stock is down, books that the store carries, and ordering all of the books for the store. All publishers distribute catalogues giving descriptions of all their new books coming out. This includes new authors, new books by established authors, a new printing of a previously out-of-print book, or the introduction of a book in paperback.

The buyer looks through these catalogues to get some idea of what he or she will want to order. Next, he or she has a conference with the representative from that publisher. The representative is a salesman of sorts. He or she must know the stores they deal with, what each store specializes in, and what it doesn't carry, in order to know what books to emphasize. The buyer then places the order with the salesman.

For all other books, ones that the store orders repeatedly, there are two sources from which the buyer may order. One, of course, is the publisher. The publishers send lists of all the books they currently publish, along with the newly published books catalogue, or separately, upon request. There are no descriptions of these books, just lists of the titles and the prices. The buyer then indicates the titles and quantities that he or she wants and sends in the order. Often with paperback books you are required to order a certain number (usually at least 25).

The other way of ordering these books is through a *wholesaler*. Wholesalers order books from publishers in huge numbers, then sell these books to bookstores. The disadvantage in ordering from a wholesaler is that you get a lower discount. The advantage is that you get the books much more quickly. It usually takes four to six weeks to get a book from a publisher, but only one to two weeks to get it from a wholesaler. Also, there is no minimum quantity that you are required to order.

There are other people that work in a bookstore as well. There will be sales people and cashiers to help you with your purchase. When books arrive, someone must take them out of the boxes, make certain that everything that was ordered, arrived, by checking the books against the *invoice*, and then put the books on the shelves.

Sometimes books must be returned to the publisher. It may be because the book was defective or damaged, or the book may not be selling well. The book must be boxed up and returned to the publisher.

There are three basic kinds of books. First, there's the hardback book. Hardback books are more expensive, but they last longer and look nicer. Almost all books come out in hardback when they are first published.

Then, there are *mass-market* paperbacks. After a hardback book (especially if its a work of fiction) has been out for one year, it will usually next be published as a mass-market paperback. These are always the same size, about 7" by 4". Most paperbacks are mass-market paperbacks.

The last type is the *trade paperback*. These are paperbacks of all other sizes. Often books are published initially as trade paperbacks. Sometimes hardcover books (especially nonfiction ones) are eventually published as trade paperbacks.

Look on almost any book cover, and you'll find a number on it that is about ten digits long and begins with a zero. This is the *ISBN* or International Standard Book Number. Every title has its own number. If the same title is published in hardback and then in soft back, it will have a different number in soft back. If it goes out of print and then is republished, it will get yet another number.

Used Bookstores. Used bookstores operate in much the same way as a new bookstore. There are cashiers, and people who stock the shelves, and buyers. The buyers do not purchase books from publishers; they buy them second-hand from other people. Then they must decide what to price them. Some stores have flat rates (such as $.50 for paperbacks and $1.00 for hardbacks), while others price each book individually. Of course, since they do not buy books from publishers, there is no need to have anyone to return books.

Questions You Might Ask A Bookstore Owner

Who are the largest publishers?
What publishers does the bookstore order the most from?
How do you decide how many copies to order of a single title?
What is the process for returning books?
How do hardback sales compare with paperback sales?
How do you decide which books to carry?
Are there publishers that specialize in certain fields? What are they?
Which section (fiction, medicine, mysteries, etc.) is responsible for the highest percentage of the store's
     sales?

If it is a used bookstore, how do you determine which books to buy from someone?

How do you determine the price they pay?

How do you determine the price a book will sell for?

Activities

• If you're looking for a particular book, or books by a particular author, or books on a particular subject, there is a set of books that can be very helpful. It's called <u>Books In Print</u>. and a new set is published each year. Go to the bookstore or the library and have someone show you how to use them.

• Organize your books by subject.

• Visit as many bookstores as you can. Make a chart comparing all the bookstores regarding the subjects that they cover and their specialties.

Vocabulary

❑ Chain   ❑ Wholesaler   ❑ Invoice

❑ Mass-Market Paperback   ❑ Trade Paperback   ❑ ISBN

Tips From Barnabas

Since the development of the printing press in 1456, books have been one of the principal means of communicating ideas. Karl Marx's <u>Das Kapital</u> started a revolution. Harriet Beecher Stow's <u>Uncle Tom's Cabin</u> laid the groundwork for the feelings that led to an end of slavery in this country.

Books, whether real or fictional, can have a powerful effect on their readers. George MacDonald's fictional stories helped lay a foundation for C.S. Lewis' later conversion to Christianity. Think of the lives that the Bible has changed.

Go to a Christian bookstore and spend some time just looking at all the different categories of books that are available, e.g. Biographies, Missions, Fiction, Study Guides, Commentaries, and Practical Living.

With the help of your parents and maybe your Pastor, make up a reading list of books for a person your age and read through them, making a written or oral report on each. I think you'll find that if you select your books carefully, they will have a great impact on your life.

BUTCHER

Background

NAME OF PLACE TO VISIT _____

NAME OF CONTACT PERSON _____

PHONE # _____

ADDRESS _____

_____

BEST TIME TO VISIT _____

The butcher is a familiar sight in our local grocery stores. Most Americans eat meat several times a week. The main work of the butcher is to cut and package meat at the store. There are standard *cuts* of meat which are used, and the butcher must know the way to cut meat in order to best take advantage of these specific cuts. You may have seen a chart of the different cuts in the meat department or *butcher shop*. These cuts are not designated at random. Instead, they reflect differences in the quality and taste of the meat. The majority of our meat comes from cows, pigs, sheep, and fowl, including chicken and turkeys. It takes years of practice before a butcher is proficient at cutting the various portions of meat quickly and well.

Questions You Might Ask A Butcher

What training did you receive to become a butcher?

How long have you been doing this work?

What is the basis for the division of different cuts of meat?

What determines the different grades of meat?

Are the divisions of the cuts of meat which are usually made the only ones possible?

Is there a particular problem that you deal with repeatedly in your job?

Why did you decide to become a butcher?

How many knives and tools do you use in your job?

Do you cut all different kinds of meat?

What is the importance of the USDA?

What are the ingredients that go into hamburger and hot dogs?

In your opinion, what is the best cut of beef?

Activities

• Certain cultures have special rules regarding the butchering of animals. Research the Jewish laws regarding the butchering of animals ("kosher") and write a report on it.

• Make a map of the U.S. showing the amount of each kind of meat which is produced in each state or geographical area.

• Learn to identify different cuts of meat by sight.

Vocabulary

❑ Butcher Shop   ❑ Cuts   ❑ USDA
❑ Kosher   ❑ Prime Grade

Tips From Barnabas

Animal sacrifice was often used in the Old Testament for consecration. In Genesis 15, the Lord had Abraham kill and divide a heifer, a goat, a ram, a dove, and a young pigeon, and God passed through the pieces as a confirmation of His promises to Abraham.

In Exodus 29, the butchering of animals was involved in the consecration of the priests. Also in 1 Kings 8:62-66 we're told of the huge sacrifices made at the dedication of Solomon's Temple.

Part of these sacrifices was the draining of blood from the sacrifice. In Hebrews 9:11-28 and 10:1-22, the author of Hebrews draws a comparison between these sacrifices and Christ's blood which was shed for us. Read these passages and discuss with your parents how it is that Jesus's blood cleanses from all sin.

CARPENTER

Background

NAME OF PLACE TO VISIT _____
NAME OF CONTACT PERSON _____
PHONE # _____
ADDRESS _____
_____
BEST TIME TO VISIT _____

Have you ever watched a house being built? It seems that it almost happens overnight. If you've ever looked at *blueprints*, you know how complicated it all is. Unless the owners are building the house themselves, there is usually a *general contractor* in charge. He or she may do a lot of the actual building themselves, or they may *subcontract* most of the work out.

There are many different kinds of carpentry: *framing, finishing, cabinetry,* for example. In this chapter we will look at all the steps involved in building a *residential* home from start to finish. You may talk to a different kind of carpenter, but any carpenter will be able to talk about the woods, tools, and skills that go into his particular type of trade.

Of course, there are many different kinds of wood which come from different trees or are finished in different ways. *Rough wood* is not *planed* or *sanded* and comes in different sizes, such as 2" x 4", which *finishes* down to 1-1/2" x 3-1/2", or 4" x 6", which finishes as 3-1/2" x 5". Some woods are hard, such as oak; others are soft, such as fir. Some woods are expensive, such as rosewood or cherry, while others are inexpensive, such a pine or hemlock. Most framing work is done with fir, while finishing work, such as baseboard and window sills, are often done with oak or hemlock. There are also different *veneers, solid woods, plywood,* or *particle board.* If you go to a lumber yard, make sure that they show you all of these different types of products.

The first step in building is choosing your *lot* and your house plans. After this, the blueprints are ordered or drawn up by an architect. Then all the needed building permits are obtained. All the way through, at different points, the building will have to *pass code* and be done according to specifications in your particular area. Beside the building itself, the plumbing and electricity will also have to pass *inspection* by a public official before you can move in.

After the plans have been chosen, you'll have many decisions to make before you can get a final *bid* or *contract* on what it will actually cost to build the house you've selected. After you've chosen all of your appliances, cabinets, doors, windows, plumbing fixtures, carpeting, flooring, and lighting, your contractor will be able to give you a bid on the total cost of building your new home. You might decide to be the general contractor yourself and work with the subcontractors. This may save you money, but it will take a lot of "know how" and a lot more of your time. After you've signed your contract, you're ready to *break ground.*

This will be an exciting day. This first step will involve *excavating* to prepare the ground for laying the *foundation.* In pouring the foundation, there will be 6"x12" footings and stem walls 6"-8" wide, reinforced with *rebar,* either 3/8", 1/2", or 3/4", which comes in 20' lengths. *Anchor bolts* will be put in the wet concrete every 6' and extend 2" to 2-1/2" above the stem wall. Pier blocks will be used on which to rest the posts. All of this provides the support for the frame of the house. There is another type of foundation that can be used, where a solid concrete slab is poured. It will take approximately *7 man days* to finish the foundation and the flooring.

The next step will be the *subfloor*, which consists of *beams, posts*, and *joists* (which comes from the Latin word 'to support'). 2"x6"x5/8" *tongue and groove* decking will make up the subfloor. You can see how important it is to get the measurements just right, because the weight and alignment of the entire building will all rest on the subfloor and foundation.

After this, the exterior walls will be *framed* up. These are built flat on the ground and then raised. The interior walls will be added, braced to the ground and floor, and then *plumbed level and squared*. After this frame is made, it will be sheathed with 4' x 8', 1/2" or 5/8" plywood. This firms up the first floor before the second floor is added. After the second floor is sheathed, the roof will be rested on the top plate of the exterior framed-up wall. The roof can either be custom-made with rafters, ceiling joists and supports, or be made with *prefabricated trusses* which will be put on 16" or 24" centers. These trusses which you may have seen going down the highway on long trucks are *engineered* to *free span* long distances without needing interior *load-bearing* walls. The trusses or rafters will have been engineered to bear the *dead load*, which is the pounds per square foot the roof can stand, such as from snow, and also to support the *span* of roofing. 1/2" or 5/8" sheathing will be put on the outside of the roof to provide stability. It will take approximately sixty man days to frame and roof a 2500 square foot two-story house.

Going back down to the first floor, the interior floors will be made of 2' x 6' tongue and groove decking. The walls will then be covered with *building paper*, which is impregnated with an asphalt product to produce a vapor barrier. This paper is a 15# felt and will be either stapled or nailed to the frame. This is then covered with siding of some sort. *Insulation* will have been installed in the exterior walls. This *fiberglass* comes in rolls and in different thicknesses, such as 3-1/2" or 5-1/2". 5-1/2" or R19 Insulation will cost more initially, but as with getting the right heating unit, it will save money by making your house more *energy efficient*.

After the interior walls of the first and second floors are completed, the roofing material will be installed. There are several different kinds of material which can be used to roof a house. There are *cedar shakes* which are either sawn or split and come in light, medium or heavy, and random widths, but are 24" long. Cedar has natural oils and is resistant to decay. Split cedar shakes have deep grain grooves that act as runs or ditches for the water to run off. There are also clay tiles and *fiberglass* or *asphalt shingles*. You want to roof the house quickly in order to keep the rain out and let the framing materials dry out. Wood used in framing is *green wood*, which has not been cured or dried, and has a high moisture content, and will need time to dry before the finish work is done.

The finish walls will be made with either *sheet rock*, 4' by either 8', 12', or 16', and 1/2" or 5/8" thick. This is a *gypsum* product in the center and faced with paper. The other option is *plaster*, which is put on to *lathes* that are nailed to the studs.

The next step will be to install the windows and doors to protect the house from the weather. Following this, all the mechanical systems will be installed, such as heating and duct work (the channel that carries conditioned air—either hot or cooled). There are different types of heating units: gas- or oil-fired, electric furnaces, electric area heaters, heat pumps, or solar. Some units may cost more initially, but will save you money in the long run because they work more efficiently and will keep your utility bills down. Also the electrical wiring will be done by a licensed electrician. The plumbing, security system, and telephone wiring will also need to be completed and inspected. For each type of work, a permit is issued from the local government. The costs of these permits pay for the inspection and are based on either the dollar value of the project or the square footage. Local utility companies will put in the gas, electric, water, and sewer, but, of course, there will be *hook-up* charges which may cost hundreds or thousands of dollars. Once the electrical and plumbing work has passed inspection, the inspector will say "approved to cover."

After all this, there are still all the finishing touches, such as: painting after the seams in the sheet rock have been taped and mud put on to provide a continuous seamless wall; the interior doors hung; windows trimmed and cased; baseboards added; cabinets installed in the kitchen and bathrooms; counter tops and appliances completed; trimming out the closets with rods and shelving; ceramic tile work in the bath and/or kitchen; formica installation; and shower doors. The floor covering will go in last to keep it from being messed up.

Finally, the house is almost ready to be moved into, but there is still work to be done outside. Gutters, down spouts, paint or stain for the siding, pouring the garage floor, driveway and sidewalks, and finally, the landscaping.

There will be a final inspection at some point, and the building will be *cleared for occupancy*.

Wow! I bet you never thought about all the decisions, work, and materials that went into putting that roof over your head. I think you can see how much is involved in building just one home. Think how exciting it would be to watch your own home being built or to build it yourself, if you become a carpenter.

Questions You Might Ask A Carpenter

What type of carpentry do you do?
What training have you had?
What made you decide to go into carpentry?
Do you have a favorite wood to work with?
What kinds of things have you built?
What's the largest project you've ever worked on?
What kind of tools do you own?
Have you ever been injured?
How do you feel when a project is done?
Where do you get your materials?
Are you self-employed?
What kind of license or bond do you have?
Do you get your money up front or not until you've completed a job?

Activities

• Find a house being built, check on the progress every few days, and keep a journal on what you see.
• Go to a lumber yard and see the different types and sizes of wood that are available.
• Go to the library and find a project you can build by yourself or with your parents' help.

Vocabulary

- ❏ Blueprints
- ❏ Framing
- ❏ Residential
- ❏ Pass Code
- ❏ Break Ground
- ❏ Anchor Bolts
- ❏ Tongue and Groove
- ❏ Particle Board
- ❏ Prefabricated
- ❏ Load-Bearing
- ❏ Fiberglass
- ❏ Sheet Rock
- ❏ Lathes

- ❏ General Contractor
- ❏ Finishing
- ❏ Rough Wood
- ❏ Inspection
- ❏ Excavating
- ❏ Man Days
- ❏ Veneer
- ❏ Plumbed Level
- ❏ Engineered
- ❏ Dead Load
- ❏ Cedar Shakes
- ❏ Plaster, Hook-Up
- ❏ Contract

- ❏ Subcontract
- ❏ Cabinetwork
- ❏ Lot
- ❏ Bid
- ❏ Foundation
- ❏ Subfloor
- ❏ Solid Wood
- ❏ Squared
- ❏ Free Span
- ❏ Span
- ❏ Green Wood
- ❏ Cleared For Occupancy

Tips From Barnabas

In Mark chapter six, we are told that Jesus was a carpenter. The Apostle Paul talked about himself as an "expert builder" in 1 Corinthians 3:10-14. No matter what our profession, we are all "builders" in the sense that we build something with our lives. By being co-workers with God, we get the chance to build the kingdom of God into our own lives, and to help others around us build it into theirs.

Read the passage in Corinthians and answer the following questions for yourself:

1. What kind of foundation have I laid in my life?
2. Who else has helped build onto it?
3. How can I be careful how I build on this foundation?
4. Does it make a difference what kind of materials I use in building my life?
5. Give some examples from your own life, of building you have done that would be considered "gold, silver or costly stones," and also some examples that would be "wood, hay or straw."
6. Discuss with your parents how you can 'fix' your house, if you've made mistakes in building.
7. Your 'house' won't be complete until the Lord comes back, or you die and go to be with Him. Do you think you will have built a 'mansion' or just a 'shack?' Set some goals that will show what kind of house you want to build with your life and then discuss them with your parents.

CIRCUS

Background

NAME OF PLACE TO VISIT _____

NAME OF CONTACT PERSON _____

PHONE # _____

ADDRESS _____

_____

BEST TIME TO VISIT _____

A circus can be great fun. It you have ever been lucky enough to have been to one, you know this. Even if you have never seen a circus, you probably know something about the kind of entertainment it provides. However, there are many things about the circus behind the scenes that even people who have been to the circus do not know.

The circus season usually runs from early spring through late fall. Since most circuses are performed in tents, they depend on good weather. In the off season, most circuses spend time in the southern United States practicing old tricks and learning new ones. In general, a circus will travel to cities farther north at the height of summer and then farther south as the weather grows colder. Of course, a circus cannot just wander into a town and expect to put on its show. A site must be chosen and *permits* must be obtained before a circus will be allowed to pitch its tents in any town. A circus must also be advertised. It's no use putting on a real show if no one knows you're there. This is why *advance-men* and *women* move through cities and towns about two weeks before the circus arrives. These people put up signs and arrange for television and radio ads.

When the circus arrives early in the morning, the first thing the workers must do is set up the tent. This is done with the help of the circus elephants. Holes are dug for all the poles, including the very large ones that hold up the center of the tent. The tent is then laid in position on top of the poles and the elephants pull the poles upright. There is much to do in order to get the circus ready for the public. After the *big top* is set up, the smaller tents and displays must be arranged. The *side show* tent is set up near the entrance and filled with natural marvels. There are also games and possibly rides for the people who visit the circus. A circus will often put on a parade on its first day in a new town. In between all this activity, the performers use what time they can for further practice.

Finally, in the late afternoon, the show is ready. *Barkers* advertise the side shows, attendants man the rides and games, and inside the big tent the *ringmaster* introduces the acts. Acrobats balance on the tight rope high above the ground or fly through the air from one trapeze to another. One animal trainer makes lions and tigers jump through rings while another directs the elephants who are marching around the tent and balancing on one or two legs at a time. There are dog handlers and tricks on horseback as well, and there are clowns. So many clowns. Each clown has his or her own face make-up and costume that no other clown in the world copies. Finally, when all the fun is over and all the customers have left, the circus personnel must take the circus apart again and move on to the next town.

Questions You Might Ask A Circus Manager

What is your job in the circus?
How long have you worked for the circus?
Does your family have a background in the circus?
Did you receive any special training for what you do?
What special talents do you think are necessary for people who work in a circus?
Why did you choose to work for the circus?
Do you like your job?
What exhibits appear in your side shows?
What animals does your circus use?
How many cities do you perform in each year?

Activities

- Design your own clown character, complete with make-up, clothing, and a name.
- Write a report on the history of circuses.
- Develop a circus act that you can do.

Vocabulary

❑ Permit   ❑ Advance Man   ❑ Advance Woman
❑ Big Top   ❑ Side Show   ❑ Barker

Tips From Barnabas

In Proverbs 17:22, we are told that a cheerful heart or laughter is a good medicine. Much about a circus is done to make us laugh or to awe us. It can help us to forget ourselves and our own problems. Do you think it is a good thing to be able to make others laugh or smile?

In the summer, try to organize a small circus of your own. Maybe you have a dog that can do tricks, or some other pet. Perhaps you can sell peanuts and popcorn. One or two of your brothers or sisters, or maybe a friend, could dress up as a clown and have a water fight. There are many different things you could do. Then invite your other friends and neighbors, and see if you can make them laugh. I'm sure it will make you laugh, too!

CITY GOVERNMENT

Background

NAME OF PLACE TO VISIT _____

NAME OF CONTACT PERSON _____

PHONE # _____

ADDRESS _____

_____

BEST TIME TO VISIT _____

Approximately three quarters of the population of the United States live in *metropolitan* areas that are either in the city proper or in the surrounding suburban areas. It was not always like this. There are two major factors which caused this change and they were both products of the *Industrial Revolution,* which occurred in America and Western Europe in the middle of the nineteenth century. The major effect of the Industrial Revolution was to change the means of production. Before the middle of the eighteenth century, everything was made by hand by skilled *craftsmen.* Afterwards, with the introduction of *mass production* (things being made by machine) and the *assembly line* (things being put together in many easy stages by predominantly unskilled labor), the mode of production changed. With the Industrial Revolution came factories, which had to be manned by a great many people. This meant that work became easy to find in the cities, and great populations of workers developed around the factories. The new workers in the cities had come, of course, from the farms in the country. The reason the farm workers were free to move to the city was the second effect of the Industrial Revolution. Mass production made machinery cheaper and more efficient to run. There was a great increase in the use of machinery on the farms. This meant productivity went up, and fewer people were needed to work on the farms. As we said above, these people found work in the cities.

Since so many of us live in or near cities, it is important for us to understand how they are governed. The form of any city's government is spelled out in its *charter.* The city charter has much the same function as a national or state constitution. It spells out the shape of government as well as the responsibilities and limitations of those people who make up the government. Before an area can become a city, it must get the permission of the state government, meet certain requirements (most importantly have a minimum population designated by the state), and have a charter. There are three basic types of city government. We will discuss them below.

The most common type of city government is called the *mayor-council* government. In this type, the responsibility for governing the city is split between the *mayor* and the *city council.* This responsibility may vary in proportion, and this accounts for the two kinds of mayor-council government: The *strong mayor* type and the *weak mayor* type. In both the strong and weak mayoral systems, the mayor and city council are elected separately. In the strong mayor type of government, the mayor is in charge of *appointing* all the other members of city government such as police chief, fire chief, parks and recreation commissioner, and mass transit board members. The council in a strong mayor system is only in charge of setting city policy and acting as a check on the mayor's power, especially when it comes to the city *budget.* The mayor must still get the council's approval. In a weak mayor system, many of the most important city posts are *elected* by the people instead of being appointed by the mayor. These include city *auditor*, city *treasurer*, city transit board, and city *assessor*. Those positions which are not elected are chosen by the mayor and councilmen together. Under the weak mayor system, the council takes much more responsibility for the budget. In both of these mayor-council types of government, the council members often represent particular sections of the city, often called *wards*. In most cases, neither of these models fits exactly, and city government falls in between these two extremes.

Another form of city government is called the *commission* type. Under a commission type of city government, there is not necessarily a mayor, though one may be chosen from among the membership of the commission to officiate at formal occasions. The commission is usually made up of five members. Under this type of government, no other members of government are elected, and few are appointed. Instead, each commissioner is in charge of a particular branch of city government. This might mean that one commissioner is in charge of *budget* and finance, another is in charge of *public works,* and another is in charge of police and fire departments. A disadvantage to the city commission type of government is the is fact that there is no one person who is in charge of the whole government, and so there is no one idea to direct that government. Another weakness is the fact that each commissioner is not necessarily an expert in the particular branch of government to which he or she has been assigned. Some cities solve this problem by electing certain commissioners to particular, well-defined duties in the government.

The third, and final, form of city government was designed to deal with the weaknesses of the city commission form. This final type is called the *city manager* form of government. As in the city commission form, only a small body of commissioners is elected. Under the city manager form, however, these commissioners hire a city manager to appoint all the other heads of city governmental departments. This solves not only the problem of expertise in a particular governmental department since specialists are appointed to each one, but it also provides a sense of unity for city government as a whole. Under this system, the commissioners are only in charge of choosing a manager and setting down basic city policy. As this form of city government has grown more popular, academic programs have developed to train people specifically to be city managers. This adds the benefits of having a professionally trained planner and a person who is probably not from the local area and so not influenced by local concerns. This makes cleaner government possible.

No matter what form of government a city has, however, it must still provide the same types of services. We are all familiar with these services because they touch our lives every day. First, there are the police and fire departments for our protection. The duties and responsibilities of these departments have been covered elsewhere in this book. The city provides further for our safety by maintaining traffic control and road quality. Cities also supply us with the necessities of water, electricity, and sewer services. In many cases, the city is also in charge of garbage disposal. City government often provides health care through city-run clinics. Mass transit systems are almost always controlled by either an elected or an appointed city board. Public schools are also under the control of city government in cooperation with state government. Finally, the parks and recreation system is another city-controlled service. There is a problem, however, in providing all these services in metropolitan areas. Each city and suburb in a metropolitan area has its own charter and city government. There can often be confusion about who should provide certain services and how it should be done, when laws can be different on opposite sides of the street. Some metropolitan areas even include sections of different states.

Questions You Might Ask A City Manager

What position do you hold in the government of our city?
What are your specific responsibilities?
Do you control a particular area of the government?

Are you elected or appointed?
Is there a difference in the approach to the job if you are elected instead of appointed?
What training did you have for your job?
If your job before this was non-political, how useful was the experience?
How long have you been involved in city government?
Why did you choose to enter politics?
Do you believe you are making a positive difference in our city? What is it?

Activities

- Research the different departments of your city's government, such as civil defense, finance, procurement, planning and zoning, licenses, public health, recreation, etc. Write a report or make a chart comparing and contrasting them.
- Research the type of government your city has and write a report on it.
- Volunteer for the campaign of a local person running for office in city government.

Vocabulary

- ❑ Ward
- ❑ Public Works
- ❑ Craftsman
- ❑ Industrial Revolution
- ❑ Mayor
- ❑ Weak Mayor
- ❑ Elect
- ❑ Assessor

- ❑ Commission
- ❑ City Manager
- ❑ Mass Production
- ❑ Charter
- ❑ City Council
- ❑ Appoint
- ❑ Auditor

- ❑ Budget
- ❑ Metropolitan
- ❑ Assembly Line
- ❑ Mayor-Council
- ❑ Strong Mayor
- ❑ Budget
- ❑ Treasurer

Tips From Barnabas

City government isn't a term you will find in your concordance. However, styles of government are mentioned. Moses was charged with the responsibility of governing the people of Israel from the time of the Exodus from Egypt until his death in the land of Moab. At first he governed alone, meeting with people from morning to evening, settling disputes, and explaining God's will. When his father-in-law visited him, he saw what was going on and said, "What you are doing is not good. You and these people who come to you will only wear yourselves out. The work is too heavy for you; you cannot handle it alone" (Exodus 18:17-20). Moses' father-in-law gave Moses some good advice on how to govern effectively in this difficult situation. Read about it in Exodus 18:5-27.

Today, we live in a country that has a democratic government. What is our responsibility to that government? Also what is the proper function of government? What should be our response when government goes beyond its legitimate function? Some passages to look at are Romans 13:1-7 and I Timothy 2:13-17.

NAME OF PLACE TO VISIT _____

NAME OF CONTACT PERSON _____

PHONE # _____

ADDRESS _____

_____

BEST TIME TO VISIT _____

COMPUTER PROGRAMMER

Background

Computers have become a very important part of our lives. They are used in the world of medicine to conduct tests and to help doctors with diagnoses; in business and government they keep billions of pieces of information at people's fingertips; they are invaluable in the scientific world for conducting research; and they are increasingly being used in the field of education.

Computer programmers are the people who tell computers what to do. Computers consist of two basic parts, *hardware* and *software*. Hardware is the body of the computer, its keyboard, *modem*, etc. — all the parts you can touch. Software is what the programmer is responsible for, that is, the actual program.

Programmers usually work for companies that sell either hardware and software or just software. They are given assignments with deadlines, either on their own or as part of a group, and must have the program completed by a certain date. Often programmers spend much of their time working at home, rather than in the office, and then send their work from their computer to the office computer via a modem.

Computer programs are not written in regular English. There are many different computer languages. *Basic, Pascal, Fortran* and *Cobol* are some of the most common.

Basically there are four things that a computer does. First, it receives information, or *input*. Next, it processes that information. The information is then stored in the computer's memory. And finally, when you want to see that information, it is presented to you as *output*.

Computers have two kinds of memory for storing information. The first is a temporary memory which is stored in *RAM chips* (Random Access Memory). Things stored here will disappear if you do not save them to permanent memory before leaving the program.

Permanent memory is stored outside the computer on tapes or *floppy disks*. In most cases, permanent memory is stored on a hard drive, which may be either inside or outside the computer housing. When you tell it to, the computer writes the information on one of these items, and you can store it for as long as you choose.

The job of a programmer is to get the computer to do these jobs as quickly and smoothly as possible. The first attempt at a program is almost never successful. After the programmer writes a rough draft, he will run the program, see where it can be improved, and then *de-bug* it. A lot of programs must be tested over and over before they work properly.

One of the problems with computers is that they cannot think for themselves. Every step must be told to them. So when a programmer is writing, he must think of every detail. If he leaves out any step, no matter how small, the program will inevitably *crash*.

Some programmers specialize in just that problem. That is, they are trying to solve the problem of computers not being able to think. This is known as the field of *artificial intelligence*. These programmers are trying to create computers that will be able to recognize things, to draw their own conclusions, to take logical steps, even to have creative thought. There is a special computer language used only for work in artificial intelligence called *LISP*.

If you have a home computer, you have probably used it to play games or write letters. It was a programmer who made those things possible.

Questions You Might Ask A Computer Programmer

How did you get started programming?
What sorts of programs are you working on now?
Are there types of programs that you prefer to work on?
What is a computer language?
Is there any computer language that you prefer to work with?
What special schooling have you had?
What is a flow chart?
Does the size of a computer relate to the work that it does?
What is the most powerful computer?
Can one program work on every type of computer?
How does a computer store memory?
What are the dangers in depending too heavily on computers?

Activities

• Find examples of as many different computer languages as possible.
• Learn how to write a simple program in Basic or Pascal.
• Go to a computer store and watch various demonstrations of the computer's abilities. Do some comparison shopping to see which computer you would choose and why, if you were going to buy one.
• Examine different software packages which are available and learn what the following do: word processing, electronic spreadsheets, data base management, and graphics.

Vocabulary

❏ Hardware
❏ Multi-User
❏ Keyboard
❏ Fortran
❏ Ram
❏ Back-Up
❏ Floppy Disk
❏ Hard Disk

❏ Software
❏ PC
❏ Basic
❏ Cobal
❏ De-bug
❏ A.I.
❏ RAM

❏ User-Friendly
❏ Modem
❏ Pascal
❏ LISP
❏ Microchip
❏ Bug
❏ Data Base

Tips From Barnabas

To be a computer programmer you must be able to work in a logical manner; to be able to understand cause and effect. If you understand the law of gravity, you know that if you drop something that weighs more than air, it will fall. When you write a computer program, you need to understand when you put in a command [cause] what the result [effect] will be.

If you read through Exodus 20-21, you can read several of the laws that God gave Israel. They are frequently given as *conditional statements*. **If** you do this, **then** this will happen. Sometimes the words "if" and "then" are not used but are only implied.

Make a chart choosing 12 Proverbs or other verses that you find which show cause and effect. For example:

Verse	Cause	Effect
Prov. 28:19	He who works his land	will have abundant food,
	the one who chases fantasies	will have his fill of poverty.
Matt. 6:33	Seek first His kingdom and His righteousness	and all these things will be given to you as well.

COOK

Background

NAME OF PLACE TO VISIT _____

NAME OF CONTACT PERSON _____

PHONE # _____

ADDRESS _____

_____

BEST TIME TO VISIT _____

Cooking is part of everyday life. Some people will tell you that it is great fun. Others will tell you they dread it. Everyone needs to learn at least enough about cooking to be able to cook for himself. The more you experiment in the kitchen, the more you may become interested in cooking.

Cooking can be divided into various activities. First, is the planning, where you decide on the *menu*, what items need to be purchased, and how many people will be fed. When cooking for a large amount of people, planning is one of the most important aspects. It is here that you will need to know which foods combine well, which will look attractive on a plate together, and what makes a balanced meal. Did you ever think that you might not want to serve two "green" vegetables together? The next step is buying or purchasing the food or equipment you will need. Then comes preparation time. You may need to chop up vegetables, wash fruit, debone a chicken, or marinate the meat. Your next step is the actual cooking, which could be done by steaming, boiling, frying, or baking. There are many different terms which describe the acts of cooking. What does it mean to *sauté* meat or to *clarify* butter? After the cooking, you need to arrange the food attractively in serving dishes or on individual plates. You also need to be able to keep the food either hot or cold, not only for taste, but to insure that it will be safe to eat.

Along with cooking, comes table arranging. One of the first things you probably learned as a child was to help set or clear the table. There are many ways to make a table attractive or very unattractive. You could throw the plates and the silverware on, or you could take a few minutes more and arrange them properly, maybe folding the napkin in a special design and adding a bowl of fruit or flowers for a centerpiece.

One cooking school student I talked to just had her "black box" test as part of her final, after a year of cooking classes. Each student was given a box of various foods and had only thirty minutes to prepare a dinner using what was in the box. They were then graded on taste, appearance, and originality. You might ask your mom or dad if he or she would like to try a "black box" test.

Cooking can be great fun and very creative if you take a little extra time and thought. You don't have to spend a lot of money to make a meal special. A good cook learns to do the best with what he or she has.

If there is a cooking school in your area, try to get a tour or eat a meal at the school's restaurant. If not, try to interview a chef at a restaurant.

Questions You Might Ask A Chef

What would you have to do to serve dinner to a party of twenty?

How do you decide how much food to buy?

What does a *sous-chef* do? What utensils are needed?

How do you keep everything warm/cold?

How do you plan a nutritious meal?

What can you do to make it attractive?

Do you need to go to school in order to be a chef?

How long will you have to study?

What can a chef expect to earn in an average restaurant or in a very luxurious one?

What is a gourmet chef?

How much does cooking school cost?

How long does it last?

Is there an internship program and a placement program?

What do you feel is the most important part of your job?

How often do you hear what the customers think of your cooking?

Activities

- Plan a dinner for your family. Work out the menu and the grocery list. Figure out what it will cost including your time and how much you would have to charge if you were a professional chef. If you're artistic, you may want to design your own *menu*. Try to plan food that will be healthy and also appealing to look at. Try to plan different courses, such as a soup or salad, an entree, and a dessert. After planning and preparing a meal yourself, you may appreciate how much your mother or father does just by cooking for you, and you should also realize how much work goes into a simple restaurant meal.
- Study the basic food groups and find out how many servings of each you should have in one day.
- Get a book on table setting and food *garnishes*. Learn where to put the silverware, plates, glasses and cups. Try making some special food decorations like radish "roses" or apple "birds." Learn how to fold napkins into various shapes.

Vocabulary

☐ Sous-Chef
☐ Menu
☐ Nutrition
☐ Utensils
☐ Groceries
☐ Banquet

☐ Sauté
☐ Garnish
☐ Appetite
☐ Gourmet
☐ Silverware
☐ Smorgasbord

☐ Clarify
☐ Restaurant
☐ Carbohydrates
☐ Cafeteria
☐ Crystal

Tips From Barnabas

Meal times are very important to God. He used meal times to teach some of His most important lessons. In the Old Testament, God planned a very special meal called the Passover. This meal was designed by God to teach history, tradition, and morality. The very items to be eaten had meaning. The way the food was prepared had meaning. This meal was so significant that God intended it to be kept perpetually. It was so structured that in future generations the children would ask their father what the meaning of every aspect of the meal was. Read an account of this meal in Exodus 12.

In the New Testament, Christ initiated a new meal called the Lord's Supper, or what we call Communion. Like the Passover, this meal has special meaning. The very elements of the meal took on new and significant meaning. Read this account in Luke 22:13-23.

Jesus used meal times to teach truth to His disciples. Some of the most important words of Jesus are records of his meal time conversations. Can you remember some of them? If not, ask your parents for illustrations of Jesus' teaching during meal times.

In Revelation 19:9, the wedding supper of the Lamb is mentioned. If you were having to plan this dinner, what would you prepare?

NAME OF PLACE TO VISIT _____

NAME OF CONTACT PERSON _____

PHONE # _____

ADDRESS _____

_____

BEST TIME TO VISIT _____

COUNSELOR

Background

We cannot always feel our best. Sometimes we have problems—either with ourselves or with others—which make us feel angry or sad. Not only can these feelings be uncomfortable, they can also be bad for us physically. Doctors are only now discovering that many physical problems, even disease, can be caused by these bad feelings. They call it *stress*. The best way to alleviate these *emotions* is to talk out the problem and to either clear it up or learn to deal with it. This means not only talking to others, but being able to communicate with yourself—to understand why you have the feelings you do. Many of us either do not know how to communicate our feelings effectively to others or ourselves, or we are made uncomfortable by it. This is what counselors are for. The main task of a counselor is to teach us how to communicate our feelings and feel better.

There are also other kinds of counselors called guidance counselors or advisors. These counselors help us make decisions as to our further education or our career goals. This often means providing information about the entrance requirements of a particular college or university. It also means providing a basic description of the school, including local ones, and any special features it may have. In the case of choosing a career, the counselor would inform us on what the job is like, what the work would entail, what the *salary* is, and any requirements to be met before applying. Whether helping us with a decision about the future or with an emotional problem, counselors are there to make things a little easier. It makes good sense to take advantage of this great resource.

Questions You Might Ask A Counselor

What is the most common problem you deal with?

How are you able to help people?

What training have you received for your job?

How long have you been doing this job?

Why did you choose counseling?

Is your job rewarding?

What are most of your clients like?

Do you ever get clients that you cannot help?

Do you use tests in your counseling?

Do you work with individuals, families, or groups?

Activities

- Research psychological counseling and write a report on it (either the history of it or the various methods).
- Research career and educational counseling and write a report on it.
- Read a book on Christian counseling.

Vocabulary

☐ Stress   ☐ Advisor   ☐ Salary
☐ Intervention   ☐ Confrontation   ☐ Addiction
                        ☐ Emotion

Tips From Barnabas

The Bible also speaks about a particular counselor, One who doesn't live in an office, and who doesn't send any bills. In fact, He gives the best possible advice and direction at all times, and for free. Do you know who this counselor is? Look up the following Scriptures, and answer the questions. If you don't know already, I think you'll know by the time that you're done.

John 14:16   How long will the Counselor be with us?

John 14:26   What will He teach us?

John 15:16   What is another name for the Counselor?

John 16:7   What had to happen before the Counselor could come?

Isaiah 9:6   Who was to be called "Wonderful Counselor?"

Can you think of some ways that the Counselor can help you to make the right decisions? Can He help you learn how to treat other people? Can He help you to have the right attitudes? This Counselor is your best friend! He will always be there when you need help. You just need to ask!

DAMS

Background

NAME OF PLACE TO VISIT _____

NAME OF CONTACT PERSON _____

PHONE # _____

ADDRESS _____

_____

BEST TIME TO VISIT _____

A dam is a wall that holds back water. Dams are built across streams or rivers. Bodies of water are created behind dams, and whether that body of water is a pond or a lake depends on the size of the stream or river. Man-made dams not only create these lakes, but they are also used to create energy. But not all dams are man-made. Long before any human first made a dam, beavers were building them. Beavers build their dams at narrow, shallow points of a stream. Most beaver dams are only a few feet long, but they can range up to two or three hundred feet long. Beavers build dams in order to make ponds deep enough to cover the mouths of their homes. This protects beavers from predators.

There are many types of man-made dams. The type of dam which the builders choose is decided by the placement of the dam ,as well as its intended uses. *Concrete* is the strongest material for building dams. One of the major advantages of using concrete is that it is not porous. Concrete dams come in many shapes. *Gravity dams* use their weight to hold back the water. The width of the base of a gravity dam must be at least two-thirds the height. A gravity dam which is 300 feet high must have a base at least 200 feet thick. A *masonry dam* is a gravity dam built out of concrete blocks instead of poured concrete. A type of concrete dam which does not require as much material as the gravity dam is the *single-arch dam*. An arched dam uses the strength of an arch instead of the weight of the dam to hold the water. An arched dam is shaped like an arch on its side which curves into the upstream side. A *buttress dam* is a fairly long, thin dam with a series of strong supports which extend off the downstream side of the dam. Some dams are not made of cement. An *earth dam* is a giant mound of soil. The largest earth dam, Fort Peck Dam in Montana, is four miles long. Earth dams have to be much larger than cement dams because soil is *porous,* and the extreme thickness prevents seepage.

Despite the fact that there are so many different kinds of dams, all dams have many things in common. First is the body of water which builds up behind the dam. This is usually called a *reservoir.* Second are the basic parts of the dam. The sides of the dam are called faces. The *upstream* side is called the *water face*, and the other side is called the *air face.* The top of the dam is the *crest* and is often a road. The *core* runs through the center of the dam and is surrounded by the *shoulders.* Finally, a dam must be well planned. The type of dam must be matched properly to the site where it will be built. Also the area behind the dam must often be evacuated. The reservoir takes up more room than the original river did, and there is often much flooding connected with the construction of a dam.

Earth dams are usually solid, and so their only purpose is to change water flow and create lakes. Concrete dams, on the other hand, usually have another very important purpose, which is to create electricity. Running through the center of most concrete dams are large pipes called *penstocks*. Water coming through the penstock turns the *turbines* of the *generators,* which make electricity. There is a wire screen at the mouth of the penstock called a *trash rack,* which, keeps debris and fish from entering and clogging the works. At the very bottom of the dam there may be other pipes called *scouring galleries,* which create a current at the bottom of the reservoir to prevent the accumulation of *silt*. Dams can also increase the security of those people living along the river. Dams can control flood waters, but if too much water builds up in the reservoir, the dam can be *overtopped*. To prevent this, dams have *spillways* which can be opened or closed to allow a desired amount of water to run over the dam into the river beyond.

As you can understand, a dam is very disruptive to the use of the river it's built on. For one thing, rivers are major transportation routes. Our rivers and waterways carry much interstate commerce. A way has been devised to get boats past dams; this is accomplished with the use of *locks*. A lock is a water elevator. It works in this manner: if a boat is going *downstream*, it enters the lock from the reservoir, and water is then slowly released from the lock until it is level with the river on the other side of the dam. The boat can then simply move out of the lock and down the river. The same thing can be done going the other way, but, in that case, the lock is filled instead of emptied. It is also important that fish be allowed to move up and down the river. *Fish ladders* were developed to allow fish to get past the dam. They are similar to locks, but instead of just one container which is filled and emptied, there are a series of small ponds, each set just a little higher than the one before. Fish jump from one pond to the next to get past the dam. Finally, even with fish ladders, dams often disrupt the natural way of life for fish. In order to correct this, there are often *fish hatcheries* at dams. A fish hatchery is like a fish farm. Baby fish are hatched, fed, and cared for until they are old enough to be set free, often into the very reservoir created by the dam.

In the best cases, disruption caused by dams can be minimized, and the benefits are great.

Questions You Might Ask A Dam Worker

Do you have a lock, fish ladder, or fish hatchery here?
How much power does the dam produce?
What kind of dam is this?
How old is this dam, and how long did it take to build?
How many people does it take to run the dam?
What steps have been taken to preserve the wildlife around the dam?
How much water pressure can the dam withstand?
What steps are taken to avoid flooding?
What are some things that could happen that would be catastrophic?
How many fish are hatched each year?
What needs to be done to maintain the dam?

Activities

- If there is no dam near you, pick a dam and research it. Find the answers to the above questions.
- Do a research activity on beavers and their dams and write a report.
- Build a model of one of the types of dams listed above.

Vocabulary

- ❏ Concrete
- ❏ Masonry Dam
- ❏ Earth Dam
- ❏ Reservoir
- ❏ Crest
- ❏ Penstock
- ❏ Trash Rack
- ❏ Spillway
- ❏ Fish Hatchery

- ❏ Porous
- ❏ Single-arch Dam
- ❏ Upstream
- ❏ Water Face
- ❏ Core
- ❏ Turbine
- ❏ Scouring Gallery
- ❏ Lock
- ❏ Silt

- ❏ Gravity Dam
- ❏ Buttress Dam
- ❏ Downstream
- ❏ Air Face
- ❏ Shoulders
- ❏ Generator
- ❏ Overtop
- ❏ Fish Ladder

Tips From Barnabas

There is nothing in the Bible that compares to our modern hydro-electric dams. However, if we focus on the function of a dam to hold back water, we have several illustrations of that in Scripture. The most notable is the crossing of the Red Sea. We could call it an Air Dam: "The Lord caused the sea to go back by a strong east wind all that night, and made the sea dry land, and the waters were divided. And the children of Israel went into the middle of the sea upon the dry ground; and the waters were a wall unto them on their right hand, and on their left" (Exodus 14:21-22).

God did a similar thing for Joshua when he led the Children of Israel across the Jordan River at flood stage to occupy the promised land. You can read about it in Joshua 3.

DENTIST

Background

NAME OF PLACE TO VISIT _____

NAME OF CONTACT PERSON _____

PHONE # _____

ADDRESS _____

_____

BEST TIME TO VISIT _____

A dentist is a special kind of doctor who deals exclusively with problems of the mouth, teeth, gums, and jaws. A dentist takes many of the same classes that any other type of doctor would take, but he or she specializes by taking extra classes in dentistry. A dentist must know about more than just his or her specialty. A dentist must know how different parts of the body work together. Even within dentistry, there are sub-specialties. An important one is *orthodontics*. Orthodontists repair damage to the structure of the mouth as well as fixing or straightening natural malformations of the mouth or teeth. This is most commonly done with *braces.*

These major corrections, however, are not the main duty of dentists. It is important to get a dental check-up every six to twelve months. A check-up includes a thorough examination of the teeth for *cavities*. X-rays may even be taken. The dentist makes sure that there is no tooth or gum disease. Finally, with the help of a *dental hygienist*, the dentist thoroughly cleans and polishes the teeth. If the dentist does find a cavity, he drills all the decayed material away and fills the tooth with a special, hard filling material or, sometimes, with gold or silver. If the tooth is in bad enough condition, the dentist must pull it. The dentist will often use *anesthesia* if he or she must pull a tooth. The dentist is concerned to do things in the least painful way possible.

Questions You Might Ask A Dentist

How long have you been a dentist?
Do you like your work? Why?
What special training did you receive?
Do you have a specialty?
What do you do for patients to reduce their pain?
Is it harder to work on adults or children?
Are you bothered by the bad image dentists have?
What are good practices to prevent tooth and gum disease?
What problems do you see most often?
Is an electric toothbrush better than a non-electric toothbrush?
How important is fluoride to teeth?

Activities

- Read further about modern dentistry or its history and write a report.
- Make a log of your dental history.
- Find a diagram of teeth and learn how to identify them.
- Make a list of the different types of dentists, and what each does.
- Find out what a dental assistant does, and how much training is involved.

Vocabulary

☐ Orthodontist   ☐ Braces   ☐ Dental Hygienist
☐ Anesthesia   ☐ Cavity

Tips From Barnabas

In 1 Corinthians 6:19, we are taught that we are temples of the Holy Spirit. At different places in the New Testament, Jesus explained how important it is to be a good steward of what we have. Your body is something of which you are a steward. You should treat it well because it is something that God has given you to take care of. Do you think this is important to God? What can you do to help take care of your teeth?

DOCTOR

Background

NAME OF PLACE TO VISIT _____

NAME OF CONTACT PERSON _____

PHONE # _____

ADDRESS _____

_____

BEST TIME TO VISIT _____

Everyone has had to go to the doctor at one time or another, but not everyone has the same problem. Because there are so many kinds of illnesses, there have to be several different kinds of doctors. Almost all doctors have a specialty — an area of medicine in which they have received special training. Some of these specialties are *surgery, optometry, neurology, obstetrics, pediatrics,* and *podiatry.* Some doctors specialize in sports medicine and are able to care for strains, sprains, and broken bones. Other doctors have special training in *cardiology* and treat problems and diseases of the heart. A very common type of doctor is a *general practitioner,* or G.P. Most family doctors are general practitioners. A G.P. has general knowledge of the most common kinds of illnesses and is able to refer a patient to a specialist if there is a particular problem.

Even though there are many different kinds of doctors, there is one very important thing that they all have in common. All doctors are concerned with helping the sick. When people become doctors, they make a promise called the *Hippocratic Oath.* The Hippocratic Oath is named after an ancient Greek physician, Hippocrates. His oath spells out the duties and responsibilities by which every doctor must abide. They include doing all one can to cure sickness, relieve pain and suffering, and help people who are in need of help. Being a doctor is a very important job, and it is vital that everyone who is a doctor genuinely wants to help people.

Another thing that doctors have in common is the training they receive before they begin to specialize. It is hard work to become a doctor, and it takes a lot of schooling. Before a perspective doctor gets to medical school he or she must spend four years to get a bachelor's degree from an undergraduate college or university. Some people who know early on that they want to be doctors take classes in biology and chemistry, related to how the body works, but it is not necessary to have taken classes like these in order to get into medical school. In medical school a student spends another four years learning about *anatomy, biochemistry, pharmacology,* and generally how the body works and how to cure disease. Even after the student receives an M.D. degree from medical school, he or she is not ready to be a doctor. If the student is going to specialize, he or she may take a year or two of special classes in the field he or she has chosen. A student must also work for a year as an *intern* and two years as a *resident* in a hospital helping doctors with real patients. After all this – twelve years or more from when the student entered undergraduate school – he or she can finally become a doctor.

Even if you have never been sick, you may want to see a doctor occasionally for a *check-up,* or physical examination. A check-up is a standard group of simple tests to determine the general health of the patient. The patient's height, weight, and blood pressure are recorded. Then the doctor listens to the heart and lungs through a *stethoscope.* After that the doctor looks in the eyes, ears, and mouth of the patient and tests the patient's reflexes. The doctor makes sure that the patient doesn't hurt anywhere and has not been having any problems. Finally, the doctor takes a small sample of blood in order to do different kinds of tests. A check-up does not take very long, and it will find almost any problem that a patient may be having.

Questions You Might Ask A Doctor

What type of doctor are you?
What kind of special training did you have to become the type of doctor that you are?
What kind of schooling did you have?
How long have you been practicing medicine?
What do you do in an ordinary day at work?
How many patients do you have?
What can you learn from testing blood?
Is *malpractice insurance* very expensive?
Why did you choose to be a doctor, and why did you choose the area of medicine that you are in?
What do you do in order to keep up with the latest developments in medicine?
What is the most common problem you treat?

Activities

• Ask a doctor or nurse to help you with the following:
  Learn how to take a temperature.
  Learn how to take a pulse.
  Learn how to take blood pressure.
  Learn how to use a stethoscope.
• Pick a particular part of anatomy, such as heart, brain, nerves, liver, etc. and do a report on it.
• Write to a medical school and ask for a recommended list of courses to study if you were interested in
  applying to their school.
• Use your Yellow Pages and make a list of the many different specialties that there are. Next to each,
  write a brief description of what type of medicine is involved in that specialty.
• Get the Well Child Coloring Book and work through it, or draw pictures of different anatomical systems, such as digestive, nervous, or cardiovascular.

Vocabulary

❑ Surgery
❑ Podiatry
❑ Cardiology
❑ Anatomy
❑ Intern
❑ Stethoscope

❑ Optometry
❑ Obstetrics
❑ General Practitioner
❑ Biochemistry
❑ Resident
❑ Malpractice Insurance

❑ Neurology
❑ Pediatrics
❑ Hippocratic Oath
❑ Pharmacology
❑ Check-up

Tips From Barnabas

Colossians 4:14 tells us that Luke was a physician. Find out what you can about his background.

One of the most famous doctors of modern times was Albert Schweitzer. Born in Germany, Dr. Schweitzer and his wife moved to West Africa in 1913 to establish a hospital for the natives. Both Dr. & Mrs. Schweitzer remained in Africa until their deaths. Do some research on him or another medical missionary, such as Wilfred Grenfell, Ida Scudder, or Viggo Olsen. What do you think would be the driving force that would inspire a doctor or nurse to leave his or her home and work in remote parts of the world? In what way would their being doctors help them to share the Gospel?

NAME OF PLACE TO VISIT _____

NAME OF CONTACT PERSON _____

PHONE # _____

ADDRESS _____

_____

BEST TIME TO VISIT _____

ELECTRICIAN

Background

Today we depend on *electricity* for many things. It brings us heat and light. It cools us and entertains us. It cooks, cuts, mixes, and tells us the time. In short, there are hundreds of ways that electricity helps us every day. The modern world could not operate without the vast, ready stores of electricity on which our society draws. Electrical engineers have made this all possible. *Electrical engineering* can actually be broken into two distinct fields, corresponding to the two basic steps in powering our houses. The first is *high power electrical engineering*. This has to do with the creation of electrical power and its storage. Electrical power is created in *generators* by spinning *electromagnets* inside coils of wire. The movement of the magnets creates electricity in the wires. The magnets are attached to turbines (wheels with blades), which are most commonly turned by falling water in a dam or by rising steam, created either by burning *fossil fuels* or with *nuclear power*. These methods are called *hydro-electric* and *thermal*, respectively. The great amount of power created by these methods can be stored and delivered to cities and towns when needed.

It is the other branch of electrical engineering, called *low power electrical engineering* or electronics, with which we are more familiar. Electronics is concerned with utilizing the electric power when it reaches our homes. People who work with electronics are usually called electricians, but there are many specialties within this general title. Among electricians, there are two major types. The first is involved in the building of a new house. He or she wires the house with enough conveniently placed sockets and ample light fixtures. He or she must be very careful to make sure the wiring is safe and that there is no danger of an electrical fire starting. The other kind of electrician is interested in gadgets. In the modern world, there is no shortage of gadgets, which can do almost anything for us. We have become very dependent as a society on our gadgets. Without electricians our world might just stop.

Questions You Might Ask An Electrician

Do you have a specialty?

What training did you receive?

How long have you been an electrician?

What is the most important characteristic for an electrician to have?

Why did you choose electronics?

Is your work dangerous? If so, why?

How is electricity measured?

What does it mean to ground something, and how does one do it?
What's the difference between AC and DC? What are the advantages and disadvantages of each?
What's the difference between a transistor and a microprocessor?

Activities

- Make a list of every electrical device in your house. How many could be replaced with manual activity?
- Write a report on a particular appliance and how it works.
- Write a research paper on what electricity is, how it works, how its uses were developed, etc.

Vocabulary

- ☐ Electricity
- ☐ Fossil Fuel
- ☐ Thermal Power
- ☐ Low Power Electrical Engineering
- ☐ High Power Electrical Engineering

- ☐ Electrical Engineer
- ☐ Nuclear Power
- ☐ Generator

- ☐ Electromagnet
- ☐ Hydro-Electric
- ☐ Turbine

Tips From Barnabas

Electricity is a type of power. It takes some form of energy or power to effect change. If you have an electric stove, you can use the heat to change water into steam.

There are frequent references through the Bible to the power of God. It was the power of God that formed the mountains (Ps. 65:6) and raised Christ from the dead (1 Corinthians 6:14).

Using a concordance, look up the word "power" and make a list of some of the things God can do by His power. Especially keep in mind how the **power** of God can **change** our lives.

NAME OF PLACE TO VISIT _____

NAME OF CONTACT PERSON _____

PHONE # _____

ADDRESS _____

_____

BEST TIME TO VISIT _____

911 EMERGENCY SERVICES
Background

911 is an extremely important telephone number to remember. This is the number to call if you are involved in or see an emergency situation. By calling 911, you will be put in touch with a *dispatcher*. The dispatcher is in contact with all emergency service organizations, including the police department, the fire department, and ambulance services. If you call, the dispatcher will ask you what is wrong and what kind of help you need. Being a dispatcher takes a great deal of compassion, as well as patience. He or she often has to deal with people who are hysterical or in mild shock. The dispatcher must carefully extract all the necessary information from the caller and then contact all those agencies which are needed.

I recently went to the 911 center with a friend who works the "graveyard" shift. They had to "run" me through the computer to make sure that I had no police record or any warrants for my arrest. I asked if they would allow minors to come and watch and was told it was fine, as long as they had no police record.

When you pick up your phone to dial '911', you have little idea of all the wheels that your one call sets in motion. When we first walked into the room where all the dispatchers worked, I could hardly believe my eyes. Of course, Portland, Oregon is a rather large city, so the 911 services here are much larger than they would be in a small town. It takes over a year before anyone is fully trained to handle all the different tasks. The desks were divided into different areas. There was one "bank" of desks to handle the incoming calls and deal with the real emergencies, called the "A" lines. Another series of desks called the "B" lines dealt with calls, that were non-emergencies. A third group of desks handled the medical calls which were transferred to them from the "A" people. Then there were the dispatchers for the different sections of town. There were also a couple of supervisors on duty.

As we plugged our headsets into the phones on the "A" bank and the calls started coming in, I was amazed at all the 911 person had to do. First of all, there is a lot of equipment to handle. There is the phone and *headset* so that your hands are free to type. There is the computer screen to watch while you talk and type at the same time. This keyboard was much larger than a normal keyboard with many extra keys.

After the call is answered, and the person determines it is an emergency, there are 168 different codes by which the call could be classified. At this time, each call receives an *incident* number that will be used to refer to it from then on. Then, the priority of the call is indicated on the screen, such as a #1 priority for a burglary in progress. Next the name, address, and phone number is recorded, along with the pertinent information regarding the emergency. This all sounds very simple, but you have to remember that the people calling are sometimes confused, in shock, or children, and the 911 person has to carefully ask the right questions and get the needed information as quickly as possible. After all the information is recorded in the computer, the information is passed on to the dispatchers, who keep track of where each police car is, and assigned to the closest vehicle that is free to respond to the call. It is the dispatcher who determines which calls need to be responded to first and how many police cars should go.

The duties of the police department and the fire department have been addressed in separate entries. We will take a brief look here at Ambulance Services. The men and women who drive ambulances are required to have some medical training – most importantly, first-aid training. They are called *paramedics* because they provide the first medical care to accident victims. Though they are trained in *first aid*, they must radio into the nearest hospital when they arrive at the scene of an accident. They advise the doctor on duty of the victim's condition, and the doctor can direct any serious first aid that needs to be administered to the patient on the way to the hospital. The care of the paramedics often means the difference between life and death for these victims. It is vitally important if you are in an accident where someone is injured, or witness one, to call for emergency help immediately.

911 is a very important service to our community. The number should only be used for very important situations where help is needed quickly, or there is no other way to get in touch with the local police. Often you can reach the police by calling the nearest precinct directly, when it is not an emergency.

Questions You Might Ask A 911 Worker

What is the most common situation that gets called in?
Are there any particular problems that come up repeatedly in this job?
Why did you choose this job?
Is this job rewarding?
Do people often thank you for your help?
What training did you have to have for this job?
How long have you done this job?
What is the most difficult part of your job?
What are important attributes for a person to have to do this job?
Do you get many prank calls?
How can the public make your job easier?

Activities

- Get in touch with the dispatching agency without calling 911 and ask the above questions of a dispatcher.
- Keep a chart of accidents, crimes, and fires in your town for one month, noting the locations. Determine the busy areas for emergency personnel.
- With your friends or family, set-up a mock "911" calling situation and see how you would respond to various emergencies that they "call to report", such as: a burglary, a traffic accident, a street fight, someone breaking into a neighbor's house, a lost child, someone unconscious or seriously ill, etc.
- Make sure that all your family members know how to call 911 and what information to give.

Vocabulary

❒ Dispatcher
❒ Headset

❒ Paramedic
❒ Incident

❒ First Aid
❒ 911

Tips From Barnabas

Emergencies usually bring panic! When someone is hurt, or there is a great danger, such as from a fire or an armed man, it is difficult to remain calm. You've learned about how to get help by calling "911." But there is Someone else you can call on for help, too. God is always able to hear our cries for help. He can give you the strength to keep calm and the wisdom to know how to handle an emergency situation. Sometimes He even steps in miraculously.

Read the story about Jesus calming the sea in Mark 4:35-41. The disciples didn't have any "911" to call, but they did have Someone even better on board.

Ask your parents to tell you a story about some emergency where they called out to God.

FACTORY

Background

NAME OF PLACE TO VISIT _____

NAME OF CONTACT PERSON _____

PHONE # _____

ADDRESS _____

_____

BEST TIME TO VISIT _____

The word "factory" is short for "manufactory" which means "a place where things are made." This is not completely accurate. Things can be made outside of a factory. A factory uses a specific method. This method was only developed during the middle of the nineteenth century; before that there were no factories. It was the development of that method of production, called *mass production*, that brought about the *Industrial Revolution* and the basic shape of the world today.

Prior to the development of mass production, everything people needed was made by hand: shoes, carts, clothes, dishes, guns, etc. It was with the manufacture of guns that we first see mass production. When everything was made by hand, nothing was exactly the same. Each item was slightly different. This meant that if a part broke, either the whole thing had to be discarded or a craftsman had to make a new part especially for that thing. In the case of guns broken on the battlefield, neither of these options were practical. That is why the idea was developed to make each piece of the gun on a machine instead of by hand. In that way, one could be sure that every piece was exactly the same. Therefore, when a piece broke, a special part didn't need to be made. A few extra parts could be carried along by the army and used to replace any part that broke. Manufacture by machine was also much faster. Hundreds of each part could be made a day.

In the early twentieth century, *Henry Ford* combined the idea of mass production of *interchangeable* parts with another very powerful idea. His idea was the *production line*. Each worker on a production line does one small, simple job, like screwing on a nut. Henry Ford produced cars, of course. On his production line the frames of cars were pulled slowly from one station of the production line to the next. At each station, one simple action was performed. By the time the frame got to the end of the line, it was a complete car. The production line did for workers, what mass production did for products. It made them practically as interchangeable as the parts they worked on. Since each job done on the line is so small and simple, anyone can be trained to do it. Where the majority of workers once had to be skilled *craftsmen*, making things by hand, now the majority are relatively *unskilled*, performing very simple tasks. All factories now use this method of production. Skilled craftsmen are rare these days.

Some of the major things to be considered in how a factory works are: (1) How the materials will be moved from one area to another, (2) what types of machines will be needed, (3) the layout of the factory itself, so that work can flow smoothly, and (4) what type of quality control will be needed. All of these points have to be considered, along with providing the type of environment that will encourage workers to do their best. It takes some creative thinking to be a good factory manager.

Questions You Might Ask A Factory Worker

What is manufactured in here?

How long does the process take from raw material to finished product?

What is the major material you use?

How many steps are there in production?

Do you simply make parts or whole products?

How many different machines are used in production?

What is the major problem you face?

Why did you choose to work in a factory?

Is the factory laid out in a particular order to increase efficiency?

Are there any plans or programs to help keep the employees interested in their work?

Activities

- Design a step-by-step plan for manufacturing some household item.
- Write a report on the effects of the Industrial Revolution.
- Write a report tracing the development of manufacturing of a particular item with which you are familiar.
- Invent your own product – something you've never heard of. Then think of the steps that would be needed in order to produce this item.
- Design an assembly line for cooking a hamburger. Think of the different steps needed, as listed in the last paragraph above.
- If you are an older student, read a biography of Andrew Carnegie or the book In Search Of Excellence by Tom Peters.

Vocabulary

❏ Mass Production

❏ Interchangeable

❏ Unskilled Labor

❏ Industrial Revolution

❏ Production Line

❏ Henry Ford

❏ Craftsman

Tips From Barnabas

There are many different types of factories that produce a multitude of different products. There are certain things that all factories have in common: a system for getting a product from raw materials to finished goods, specialized machines used in that process, and quality control. Each worker may only work on one small part of the finished product. This may make it more difficult for him or her to take pride in the job he or she does. There is less personal involvement between the product and the maker. You can imagine that the craftsman who makes a violin from scratch feels differently about the violin than the factory worker who only screws on one bolt of a car.

We are all born with certain talents, abilities, and interests. Your family will help guide you into the type of work for which you are best suited. You may have to work at different jobs until you can pursue the work that you would like best. Scripture does tell us that we must be diligent, faithful, and honest, whatever our job is. Look up the following Scriptures and make a list of the ways you can honor God in your work, whether as a factory worker, writer, artist or banker.

Exodus 35:30-35
Proverbs 6:6, 10:4, 11:1, 12:11, 13:4, 14:23, 18:9, 22:29, 24:30-31
Ecclesiastes 9:10, 10:18
1 Corinthians 4:2
Ephesians 4:28, 6:5
Colossians 3:22
2 Thessalonians 3:12
1 Peter 2:18

NAME OF PLACE TO VISIT _____

NAME OF CONTACT PERSON _____

PHONE # _____

ADDRESS _____

_____

BEST TIME TO VISIT _____

FARMER

Background

Farming is an extremely important and rewarding career. Very few people have such a close relationship with our daily lives. The farmer grows and raises the food we eat. If there were no farmers, there would be no food for us. Everything that we eat, essentially comes from one kind of farm or another. Therefore, farmers have a lot of responsibility. Good farmers have had a lot of training, usually through experience, though some do take classes.

There are many different kinds of farms, each growing a particular crop. Each of these types of farms has individual requirements for what it needs to be successful. The most important factor is the weather, or *climate,* of a particular region. Particular crops require certain kinds of weather conditions, and in most cases it is useless to try to grow a crop in an area in which the weather is unsuitable. The differences in *orchards* in different regions of the country is a good example. An orchard is a farm made up exclusively of fruit trees. Apples and pears require cool weather and so are found most often in the more northern states of the Northwest, New York, and New England. Oranges, grapefruit, and other *citrus* though, require hot weather. That is why they are most commonly found in places like Florida and California. Farmers are not often completely controlled by the weather, however. Many areas of the country are naturally too dry to grow large fields of strong, healthy crops. In these cases, the farmer will use an *irrigation* system. This way he will be able to give his crops all the water they need.

Plant products, however, are not our only source of food. We also depend on some quantity of meat, and so some farms concentrate on raising animals as food. A farm which raises animals is often called a *ranch.* Location is not as important with ranches as it is for farms. Each animal does, however, have its different kinds of food, sleep differently, and require different kinds of care. There are ranches devoted to cattle, pigs, poultry, and sheep. Among the poultry growers, there is also a difference whether the birds are being raised for their eggs or their meat. Cattle ranching is the same. Some cows are raised to be eaten, while others are raised for their milk.

Often certain jobs on the farm or ranch have to be done at the right time of year. Certain plants must be planted as early as possible in the year, without being planted so early there is a danger from frost. Much of this knowledge is gained by the farmer through experience of doing it every year. In most cases, the farmer is part of a farming family and has learned through the experiences of his parents and grandparents as well. Beyond these experiences, the most important aid for a farmer is the *Farmers' Almanac,* which is put out every year and gives the predictions of important dates for the farmer.

Questions You Might Ask A Farmer

What do you grow or raise?

If the farmer raises crops, how does he or she deal with pests?

If the farmer raises animals, what does he or she do when they get sick?

How does the government subsidize you?

What are the important elements about local climate?

What are the important elements about local soil?

Do you use fertilizers or soil enrichers?

To whom do you sell your crops?

Are they sold before they are even raised?

How do you deal with tragedies, such as drought or flood?

Activities

• Research the weather patterns in your area and make a list of local crops and *livestock*.
• Research the information you can learn from the Farmers' Almanac and make a list.
• Grow some food crops in or around your home.
• Research the different types of farming, such as collective farming, dairying, dry farming, hydroponics, or tree farming.
• Using a blank map of the United States, color code the major crops such as barley, beans, corn, cotton, oats, potatoes, rice, soybean, sugar, vegetables, and wheat.
• Do the same as the above with livestock: cattle, chickens, ducks, hogs, horses, poultry, rabbits, sheep, and turkeys.
• Do a report on the different types of machinery used in farming.

Vocabulary

❐ Orchard
❐ Ranch

❐ Irrigation
❐ Livestock

❐ Climate
❐ Farmers' Almanac

Tips From Barnabas

There are many different activities that must be done to produce a good crop. In 1 Corinthians, Chapter 3, Paul uses farming as an example of how the believers in Corinth came to know the Lord. Read 1 Corinthians 3:5-9. Paul ends by saying that we are God's field. Now look up the definitions for the terms Paul uses and answer the following questions: (Some of the answers are given in the Scriptures; others you will have to figure out for yourself or with your parents' help.)

Who planted the seed?
Who watered the seed?
Who made the seed grow?
What was the seed?
How can I plant seed in other people's lives?
How can I water seed that is already planted?
Is there anything I can do to help the seed grow?

FEDERAL GOVERNMENT

Background

NAME OF PLACE TO VISIT _____

NAME OF CONTACT PERSON _____

PHONE # _____

ADDRESS _____

_____

BEST TIME TO VISIT _____

We are affected every day by the federal government. The primary purpose of the federal government is to provide services that private individuals cannot do for themselves. These services include defense, international relations, and *interstate commerce*. The seat of the federal government is Washington D.C., and so it is called the *capitol*. The shape of the federal government and the way it works was decided in 1787. In that year, representatives of the thirteen original states met in Philadelphia, Pennsylvania, in a Constitutional Convention to write a *Constitution*. They put together a very important document with three parts. These parts are the *preamble,* the body, and the *amendments*. The preamble defines the objectives of the writers of the Constitution. The body of this document spells out the shape the government will take, which has three branches: the *executive*, the *legislative*, and the *judicial*. We will talk about each of these later. The body also makes rules about how states will relate to each other and how the Constitution itself can be amended. The last section is the amendments. The Founding Fathers knew that there would be special circumstances with which the government would have to deal. That is why they made it possible to add rules to the body of the Constitution. There are now twenty-five amendments. The first ten were added immediately. This group of amendments is called the *Bill of Rights*. It assures many freedoms which were not put into the body. The American Constitution is so strong and so well constructed that many nations all over the world have used it as a model for their own constitution.

The Constitution divides governmental power into three parts. The FoundingFathers and their new country had just struggled out from under a monarchy in the American Revolution. They wanted to make sure that no one person gained complete power. Each of the three branches of government has certain power over the actions of the others. This is called the *checks and balances system*. Even with this give and take, the *President*, who represents the executive branch, is still clearly the leader of the government. Not just anyone can be President; there are three main requirements established in the Constitution. The President must be at least thirty-five years of age although no President has ever been this young. The President must also have been born in the United States. Finally, the President must have spent at least fourteen years of his life in the United States; this is so the President understands our country and is able to govern intelligently.

The Constitution also states that the President's *term* of office is four years. That is why there is an *election* every four years and has been since 1788. George Washington had been chosen *chairman* of the Constitutional Convention and was so popular that he was elected as the first President. One cannot simply be elected President; there are several steps which must be taken first. The first thing a *candidate* must do is announce his or her desire to *run for office*. There are usually several people from each *political party* who want to be President. Each state has *primary elections* to determine which of the candidates is most popular with the people. Each party then has a *national convention* to name its choice of who will run in the actual Presidential election. This is usually the person voted most popular during the primaries. At the convention, the party also decides on a *platform,* which is a list of the beliefs and goals of the party. After the convention, the candidate *campaigns* for President. This includes speeches, *debates,* television and radio commercials, and many personal appearances all over the country. There is nothing left then but the election itself. The Presidential election is always held on the first Tuesday after the first Monday in November of election year. Elections for other government officials are held on this same day. But unlike these other elections, people do not vote directly for the President. Instead they vote for *electors.* There is the same number of electors for each state as the number of federal *senators* and *representatives.* There are one hundred members of the *Senate* and 435 members of the *House of Representatives,* so there is a total of 535 electors for the entire country. This body of electors is called the *Electoral College.* The electors of each state usually cast all of their votes for whom ever won the most *popular votes* in that state. The electors are the ones who actually elect the President.

When a person becomes President, he takes on a great responsibility. There are many duties which that person must perform. First, the President is the *chief executive.* His primary responsibility as executive is to enforce the law. Second, the President is commander and chief of the armed forces and can order military action where it is needed. Third, the President is the director of *foreign policy* and guides international relations. He must work to develop laws which are in keeping with the party platform. Fifth, the President is the ceremonial head of state. In this capacity, he greets foreign and domestic leaders, gives parties, and performs other symbolic duties as leader of the country. Finally, the President is the head of the political party to which he belongs. The President must support the party, the platform, and other members of the same party. You can see that the President is busy with these duties almost twenty-four hours a day.

The President does not work alone. As we saw above, as the chief of the executive branch of government, the President's primary concern is the *enforcement* of our laws. To accomplish this, there are twelve executive departments and many independent agencies to watch over specific groups of laws. The heads of the twelve departments, as well as the chiefs of the three main military departments, make up the President's *cabinet.* Through the cabinet, the President can get reports on all aspects of federal law, as well as control the steps taken to enforce the law. The twelve departments are listed here in the order in which they were created. The **Department of State** was the first cabinet department created. Its primary concern is with foreign relations. The *Foreign Service* — including *ambassadors* and their staffs — and *passport* control are responsibilities of the State Department. The federal government could not perform all of its important duties without money. The *Internal Revenue Service* **(IRS)** collects *income tax* to support the financial needs of the government. The IRS is one of the concerns of the **Department of the Treasury,** which also controls the *minting* of new money, *import* and *export customs,* and the *Secret Service,* which originally simply guarded the money. The **Defense Department** is made up of the five branches of the military: the Army, the Navy, the Air Force, the Marines, and the Coast Guard. The Coast Guard is only under the control of the Defense Department during war time; otherwise it is in the Department of Transportation. The **Justice Department** is made up of our national police departmen – the *Federal Bureau of Investigation (FBI),* our national attorney – the *Attorney General,* and our national jail system – the *Bureau of Prisons.* The **Post Office,** led by the *Postmaster General,* is also a cabinet department. The **Department of the Interior** is in charge of national environmental preservation. It controls the *National Park System* and the relations between the federal government and the American Indians. The **Department of Agriculture** deals with farming issues and monitors soil conditions and animal health. It also provides financial assistance to our nation's farmers. The **Department of Commerce** attempts to aid and expand American business. The *Patent Bureau,* the *Census Bureau,* the *Weather*

Bureau, and the *National Aeronautics and Space Administration (NASA)* are all under the control of the Commerce Department. The **Department of Labor** regulates labor relations and labor statistics. It is this department that guarantees a *minimum wage.* The **Department of Health, Education and Welfare (HEW)** is concerned with public well-being. The *Surgeon General,* the *Food and Drug Administration,* the *Office of Education,* and *Social Security* are all controlled by it. The **Department of Housing and Urban Development (HUD)** tries to provide adequate shelter for all citizens. It guides the *Federal Housing Administration* and monitors sewage treatment plants. Finally, the **Department of Transportation,** containing not only the Coast Guard but also the *Federal Aviation Administration (FAA)* and the *National Transportation Safety Board,* works for safer, more efficient travel. These twelve departments make up the cabinet, which answers directly to the President. There are also many independent agencies which monitor other governmental responsibilities. These include the *Interstate Commerce Commission (ICC),* the *Veterans Administration (VA),* and the *Federal Deposit Insurance Corporation (FDIC).* All of the agencies and departments working together form the executive branch of government.

The second branch of the federal government is the legislative. This branch is made up of the Senate and the House of Representatives. The United States legislature is called *bicameral* because it is made up of these two parts. There are many differences between the two parts of the *legislature.* The most obvious is the difference in the lengths of the terms. Senators serve six years each term while Representatives only serve two. This is to make the Representatives more responsive to their *constituency.* Another difference is the number of members of each of these two parts of the legislature from each state. The number of Senators is set at two from each state, so there are one hundred Senators in all. The number of Representatives from each state is determined by the population of the state. The more populated a state is, the more Representatives there are. The primary job of the legislature is the making of *law.* We will discuss the steps in making a law in the chapter on State Government. Another difference between the House and the Senate is the kind of laws they deal with. All laws which deal with *taxation* must start in the House of Representatives because they are closer to the people. Another important difference has to do with appointments that the President makes. The Senate must approve of appointments that the President makes; for example, cabinet members or Supreme Court justices. Since the Senate has to approve of any choice, the President cannot pick just anyone. This is one of the checks that the legislature has on the power of the executive branch. On the other hand, the executive also has an important check on the legislature. The President can *veto* any law that the legislature makes. After a Presidential veto, it is very difficult for that law to become enacted.

The last branch of the government is the judicial. This branch is made up of the *Supreme Court.* The Supreme Court is comprised of nine people, usually judges from lower courts. Supreme Court justices are appointed for life, or until they choose to retire. The job of the Supreme Court is to *interpret* the Constitution. As we have seen, the Constitution is a fairly short document. It only addresses the form and duties of the government, and, in very general terms. Most of our laws are not in the Constitution. The Constitution, however, is the final authority on what is *legal* in the United States. Sometimes the Legislature makes a law that is in conflict with the Constitution. When this happens, the Supreme Court is able to declare a law *unconstitutional,* in which case the law is no longer a law. The Supreme Court also has the power to declare an action of the President unconstitutional, which means that the President cannot do what he is doing. This is a demonstration of the checks that the Supreme Court has over the other two branches of government. The appointing and approving power of the other two branches mentioned above are examples of checks against the Supreme Court. When all three branches of our government work together, it is very strong and much good can be done.

Questions You Might Ask An Elected Official

In what part of the legislature do you work?
What is your party?
What does your party stand for?
How do you work towards those goals?
On what committees do you work?
What legislation have you introduced into the legislature?
How long have you held your position?
What training did you receive for your job?
What was your job before you became a politician?
How do you stay in touch with your local constituency?

Activities

- Research and write a report on one of the government agencies listed here.
- Research and write a report on one of the branches of government.
- Research the checks and balances system and write a report on it.
- Research and write a report on the Constitution.
- Do research on becoming a page. Find out if it would be possible for you to become one.
- Write a report comparing our government system, a representational republic, to another type of government.
- Research the various governmental systems, such as democracy, republic, monarchy, dictatorship, communist, socialist, parliamentary, theocracy, etc. Using a blank map of the world, color code countries by their form of government.
- Role play the passage of a bill, with each family member enacting a different branch of the government.
- Learn the cabinet members' names.
- Write a letter to your state senator or representative.

Vocabulary

- ❏ Interstate Commerce
- ❏ System
- ❏ Bill of Rights
- ❏ Term
- ❏ Candidate
- ❏ Primary Election
- ❏ Campaign
- ❏ Senators
- ❏ House of Representatives
- ❏ Chief Executive
- ❏ Cabinet
- ❏ Ambassador
- ❏ Capitol
- ❏ Amendments
- ❏ Checks and Balances
- ❏ Election
- ❏ Run for Office
- ❏ National Convention
- ❏ Debate
- ❏ Senate
- ❏ Electoral College
- ❏ Foreign Policy
- ❏ Department of State
- ❏ Passport
- ❏ Preamble
- ❏ Constitution
- ❏ President
- ❏ Chairman
- ❏ Political Party
- ❏ Platform
- ❏ Electors
- ❏ Representative
- ❏ Popular Vote
- ❏ Enforcement
- ❏ Foreign Service
- ❏ IRS

- ❏ Income Tax
- ❏ Import Customs
- ❏ Defense Department
- ❏ FBI
- ❏ Postmaster General
- ❏ Department of Agriculture
- ❏ Census Bureau
- ❏ Department of Labor
- ❏ Surgeon General
- ❏ Social Security
- ❏ FAA
- ❏ VA
- ❏ Constituency
- ❏ Veto
- ❏ Legal
- ❏ Executive
- ❏ National Transportation Safety Board

- ❏ Department of the Treasury
- ❏ Export Customs
- ❏ DOT
- ❏ Attorney General
- ❏ Department of the Interior
- ❏ Department of Commerce
- ❏ Weather Bureau
- ❏ Minimum Wage
- ❏ Food & Drug Administration
- ❏ HUD
- ❏ Constitutional Convention
- ❏ FDIC
- ❏ Law
- ❏ Supreme Court
- ❏ Unconstitutional
- ❏ Judicial

- ❏ Mint
- ❏ Secret Services
- ❏ Justice Department
- ❏ Bureau of Prisons
- ❏ National Parks System
- ❏ Patent Bureau
- ❏ NASA
- ❏ HEW
- ❏ Office of Education
- ❏ FHA
- ❏ ICC
- ❏ Bicameral
- ❏ Taxation
- ❏ Interpret
- ❏ Legislative

Tips From Barnabas

From early in man's history, there has been interaction between God's people and national forms of government. The Israelites were cruelly ruled by Pharaoh of Egypt. After a period of being ruled by judges, Israel demanded a king (1 Samuel 8), and God allowed them to have Saul. From this point on, there are a series of good and evil kings, until all of Israel fell under the domination of a foreign power. During Christ's time, Rome ruled over Israel.

Today Christians can be found living under every form of national government that exists: republic, socialist, communist, and monarchy. The relationship between a Christian and the government is often a matter of debate among adults. Some, such as the Amish, Mennonites, and Quakers, call for passivism and non-involvement in political matters. Others demand a Christian democracy.

Scripture in both the Old and New Testaments does address the role of government and the individual's relationship to it. Look up the following Scriptures in each category and discuss with your family what your position should be towards the government and how the government should treat the individual.

Civic Duties
Proverbs 24:21-22; Matthew 17:27, 22:21; Romans 13:1; Titus 3:1; 1 Peter 2:13-14

Governmental Responsibilities
Proverbs 14:34, 16:12, 25:5, 20:28, 29:4,14; 2 Samuel 23:3-4; Psalms 2:10

NAME OF PLACE TO VISIT _____

NAME OF CONTACT PERSON_____

PHONE #_____

ADDRESS _____

_____

BEST TIME TO VISIT _____

FIRE DEPARTMENT

Background

The fire department is a very important part of any community. Firemen are dedicated to protecting the community from spreading fires. They are also very concerned with trying to prevent fires from happening. Fires are very dangerous. They destroy much property and many lives each year. That is why it is important to have alert, well-trained people working on both sides (before and after) of this problem.

The members of the fire department that most of us think of first are the ones who deal with emergencies. First among these are the fire fighters. These are the people who go into the building to put out the fire. This is very dangerous work, and fire fighters receive a lot of training before they battle any real fires. Besides fire fighters, there are other firemen at the scene of the fire. Fire truck drivers must also be specially trained to operate the controls. There are different kinds of trucks, some *ladder trucks* and some *hose trucks*. *Fire chiefs* are on the scene to coordinate fire fighters and the position of the trucks. Other emergency personnel include *paramedics* and other first-aid workers. Paramedics give emergency health care and take injured people to a hospital.

A second purpose which is equally important to the fire department is the prevention of fires; stopping fires before they start. Fire prevention is most often accomplished by inspection. There are many *fire inspectors* working all the time in every city. Because certain kinds of buildings have specific dangers, there are fire investigators who specialize in particular dangers. There are special investigators for factories and hospitals. The *fire marshal* coordinates the fire inspectors' results and suggestions for making buildings safer. Some investigators work with architects and builders to make sure that new buildings are as safe as possible. There are also *arson* investigators who study mysterious fires to determine whether they were accidental or intentionally set. No matter what job these members of the fire department have, they are all very concerned with the public and public safety.

Questions You Might Ask A Fireman

How long have you been a fireman?

Why did you become a fireman?

Do you like being a fireman?

Do you have any special fire-fighting skills?

How much training did you receive before being allowed to fight fires?

What kind of training was it?

How is the fire department funded?

How is the dispatching handled for the fire department?

Are false alarms a problem?
What type of medical services does the fire department provide?

Activities

- Read further on fire-fighting techniques and write a report.
- Keep a chronicle from the newspapers of fires in your town.
- Read further about arson detection and write a report.
- Write a report on fire-fighting equipment.
- Write a report on some of the major fires in history, such as Rome in 64 A.D., London in 1666, or Chicago in 1871.
- Do a report on fire safety in the home.

Vocabulary

- ❏ Ladder Truck
- ❏ Paramedic
- ❏ Arson

- ❏ Hose Truck
- ❏ Fire Inspectors

- ❏ Fire Chief
- ❏ Fire Marshal

Tips From Barnabas

The fire department serves a very important role in our community. Fire destroys, and by calling the fire department, individuals and sometimes entire cities can be saved from destruction.

In a way, individuals and churches can act as fire departments. By winning souls, we can "snatch others from the fire and save them" (Jude 23). Read Proverbs 11:30 and Daniel 12:3 once then discuss with your parents how you can be like a fire department in helping to save others by sharing Christ with them. (For example, fire departments are always alert, watchful, and ready to answer a call for help at any time.) Many young people and older people live in a type of hell, even in this lifetime. Some are addicted to drugs, alcohol, sex, etc. By sharing Christ, we can give them the opportunity to get out of their living "hells" to find a new and free lifestyle of living for Christ.

NAME OF PLACE TO VISIT _____

NAME OF CONTACT PERSON _____

PHONE # _____

ADDRESS _____

_____

BEST TIME TO VISIT _____

FLORIST

Background

Have you ever received flowers from someone? Have you ever sent them? Flowers have long been used to express a variety of feelings. Anything, from a declaration of love, to an apology, to a condolence, can be said with the gift of flowers. And beyond the mere gift of flowers, certain particular flowers have special meaning: white roses for friendship, red for love, and so on. Because there are so many things to be said with flowers (and we all cannot have flower gardens), we have *florists'* shops to go to.

Of course, long ago people could grow any flowers they wanted to on their own or else find them wild. However, with the growth of cities, fewer gardens were possible. People then would have to buy their flowers from street vendors. In the seventeenth and eighteenth centuries, commercial *botany* was developed, and the use of *greenhouses* and the making of *hybrids* became widespread. It is through the use of hybrids that many of the flowers that are familiar to us today came into being. One of the most common florist purchases is long-stemmed roses. These are, of course, hybrid, since they do not appear in nature. They were developed for convenience and to appeal to the needs of people. Florists must know a lot about the working of plants. Through their knowledge and skill, they can create and preserve marvelously delicate flowers. But most florists' shops carry more than just flowers. Florists must be knowledgeable about the care and upkeep of all types of plants.

Questions You Might Ask A Florist

What special training is needed to be a florist?

What do you enjoy most about your work?

Why did you choose to be a florist?

How long have you been doing what you do?

Are there any particular problems which arise often in your job?

What special characteristics are important for a florist?

What is the most common order?

What is your favorite flower?

Do you make special flower arrangements for people?

What flowers and plants are particularly fragile?

How do you send flowers from one part of the country to another?

Activities

- Make a chart of different kinds of flowers and their characteristics.
- Write a report on the development of hybrid flowers/plants.
- Make a flower arrangement.
- Write a report on the different techniques used for flower arranging.
- Grow your own flowers.
- Write a report on the uses of flowers in different festivals and customs.
- Write a report on the differences between annuals, biennials, and perennials.

Vocabulary

❏ Flower
❏ Greenhouse

❏ Florist
❏ Hybrid

❏ Botany

Tips From Barnabas

In Psalm 24:1, we are told that the earth is the Lord's, and everything in it. Nature has its own beauty. In Matthew 6:28-30, Jesus says that not even Solomon, the king, was dressed to compare to a lily. Flowers seem to have a special beauty. They do not provide shade or wood for paper, as trees do, nor water to drink like lakes and rivers. They are not majestic like mountains or awesome as canyons. They are delicate and alive with color. Just looking at flowers can cheer a man or woman's heart.

For part of your spiritual activity, look at some real flowers and write a poem about the glory of God, as seen in nature. For the second part, either from your own garden or by using some of your allowance, take a flower to someone you think could use some cheering up. You might want to include a copy of your poem with the flower(s).

NAME OF PLACE TO VISIT _____

NAME OF CONTACT PERSON _____

PHONE # _____

ADDRESS _____

_____

BEST TIME TO VISIT _____

FUNERAL

Background

Funerals occupy a uniformly important place in all cultures. Even though views about death differ, almost everyone finds a need for the funeral ceremony. For most people, funerals have two major purposes: to comfort the living and to honor the dead. They are a symbolic representation of a change in state. In some cultures, however, they are even more important. They are, in fact, essential *rites of passage*, and it is thought that the soul cannot continue its journey without the prescribed funeral. Because funerals hold such similar places in society, there are many elements which are shared. These include: the formal announcement of death, preparation of the body, some form of religious observance, burial or other form of disposal of the body, a public service, a processional, and mourning.

Among the most striking differences from culture to culture are the ways in which the body is prepared. In most societies, the body is cleansed first. In western societies, after the cleaning, the body is *embalmed*. In this process, the bodily fluids are drained and chemicals are injected to preserve the body. In many other countries, the body is only anointed with oil after cleaning. It is then usually covered in a *shroud* or dressed and put in a *coffin* or casket. Certain cultures have a particular kind of ceremony at this time called a *wake*. A wake is usually held in the same room with the coffin. The purpose of a wake can be either to comfort the living and dead or to protect the dead from spirits. In other cultures, coffins or other containers are not used, and, instead, the body is *cremated*. This is particularly common among Buddhist and Hindu cultures.

In this country we have businesses called *funeral homes*, run by *funeral directors*, through which funerals are arranged and performed. There are 20,000 funeral homes across the country employing almost 60,000 people. Requirements for funeral directors are strict. They must usually complete a two-year course of study in a university and then one to three years of apprenticeship. Finally, each state has an exam which must be passed before a license will be issued. The exams are given through the American Board of Funeral Services Education. The funeral director is then able to prepare the body. The director also arranges for the funeral services (which are usually held in the funeral home), the procession to the cemetery, and the cemetery plot.

Once the funeral is over, any marker in the cemetery stands as a monument, not only to the dead, but also to the history of a family. You can learn a lot about a family from a cemetery. Families often have plots in which graves are grouped together. By matching the dates of the graves, you can pick out parents from children. You can also learn who lived a long time, and who died young. The cemetery is a good place to go to learn about your own family history, but there is more. City history can also be learned: which families were there the earliest, which families are the largest, and which families were prominent. A cemetery is a storehouse of local history.

Questions You Might Ask A Funeral Director

Where did you go to school to become a funeral director?

What did you learn?

Do you enjoy being a funeral director? Why?

What is the most difficult part of your job?

Is it required by law that a corpse be embalmed prior to burying?

What laws govern the operation of funeral homes?

What things can a family do in advance to make the time of death easier to handle?

What expenses are involved in a funeral? The least expensive? The most expensive?

Do you ever conduct the funeral ceremony?

What do you say to help people through this difficult time?

Activities

• Research the funeral rites of another culture or people of the past and write a paper on it.

• Visit the local cemetery. Make a list of your observations about your own family history or local history.

• Write a report on a famous funeral.

Vocabulary

❏ Rite

❏ Coffin

❏ Funeral Home

❏ Embalm

❏ Rite of Passage

❏ Wake

❏ Funeral Director

❏ Shroud

❏ Cremate

❏ Funeral

Tips From Barnabas

Very few people get through life without losing a friend, family member, or other loved one. Death is not something to be feared for the believer. Our hope lies in God's promise of eternal life to those who believe. We still grieve when someone we love dies, because we will miss them. But we do not grieve as "those who have no hope."

Using a concordance, search for these words: "death," "comfort," and "mourn." Then make a list of Scriptures that you could share with someone to comfort them when they are grieving for someone they've lost.

NAME OF PLACE TO VISIT _____

NAME OF CONTACT PERSON _____

PHONE # _____

ADDRESS _____

_____

BEST TIME TO VISIT _____

GARBAGE DISPOSAL/ JUNKYARD

Background

Probably all of us who live in a city or town have seen *sanitation engineers* making their rounds collecting our garbage. Maybe we have even been awakened by them, since they usually work early in the morning. Their job probably does not look very fun to you. They work very early, they must move quickly, their trucks are noisy, and most dogs don't seem to like them. Despite all this, there are garbage people. Part of the reason why people choose to put up with all these negative aspects of their job is because they realize how important the job is. If it weren't for sanitation people, we would soon be buried in garbage.

The primary duty of garbage people is to pick up our garbage on a regular schedule and carry it away to be disposed of. Most garbage is non-reusable. This would include plastic, some paper, and food scraps. These items make up most of our household garbage. This type of *refuse* is usually disposed of by burying in a *landfill*. A landfill is a large pit which is dug usually on the outskirts of town. The size is calculated, so as to be useful for several years. The garbage is placed into the land-fill in relatively even layers. When it is full, the landfill is filled in, and the garbage is covered up. The land over the landfill is then often used for building apartments, parking lots, or whatever the city decides it needs. The land over the landfill can be used as any other piece of land.

Not all garbage, however, is non-reusable. Some can be used again and is called *recyclable*. There are many items of household garbage which can be recycled. The most familiar is probably newspaper. Scouting groups often use *newspaper drives* to collect newspaper and sell it to recyclers to raise money. Another common recyclable item to collect and sell is aluminum cans. Glass bottles are also recyclable but must be divided by color. All of the items which can be recycled are broken down and then reused. Newspaper is dissolved, using water and chemicals. The aluminum cans are melted down, and the metal is reshaped into new cans.

It is not only household garbage which can be recycled. Almost anything made out of steel, iron, aluminum, copper, or brass can be melted down and reused. This is what happens at a junkyard. Junk dealers collect certain types of materials made out of those metals which can be reused. In this way they are like garbage people who specialize. They then sell this material to a junkyard, which is equipped with large pieces of machinery designed to break and cut these pieces of metal down into small pieces, which can be easily melted down and used. The *junk* in the junkyard may take surprising form sometimes. If you visit a junkyard, you may see old cars waiting to be broken up, along with parts of torn-down buildings and, maybe, old sinks and tubs.

Questions You Might Ask A Garbage Man

What kind of facility is this? (Landfill, junkyard, etc.)
What do you do with the material you receive?
Do you buy recyclable material?
What kind of recycling, if any, goes on here?
How much material do you get here in a month; a year?
What is your specific job?
How many years can this landfill be used before it is covered over?
Is this a privately-owned company or a government agency?
What do you do to encourage recycling?
What percentage of garbage is recyclable?
Do you allow people to go through the junkyard and take things?

Activities

• Make a chart of similarities and differences between junkyards and landfills.
• Set up a recycling program in your home.
• Write a report on the differences between open dumps and sanitary landfills.
• Write a report on the two main methods of waste disposal.

Vocabulary

❏ Sanitation Engineer   ❏ Refuse   ❏ Landfill
❏ Recycle   ❏ Newspaper Drive

Tips From Barnabas

In the Old Testament, there are many commands dealing with pollution, both ceremonial and physical. In Numbers 35, we are told that bloodshed pollutes land, and we are not to pollute the land in which we live. In Genesis 1:28, God instructs Adam and Eve to fill the earth and subdue it. God has made us stewards over His earth and its resources. With what you have learned about waste disposal, decide with your family some steps that you can take to help you be a good steward of the earth.

NAME OF PLACE TO VISIT _____

NAME OF CONTACT PERSON _____

PHONE # _____

ADDRESS _____

_____

BEST TIME TO VISIT _____

GAS STATION

Background

Since almost every adult in this country owns a car, gas stations are very important. Just look through your Yellow Pages to get an idea of how many are in your city.

Different gas stations offer different services. Some are only *self-service stations.* You have to pump your own gas, and then you pay a cashier. Others have both self-service and *full-service stations* so you can choose whether you will pump your own gas or have someone else do it, although it usually costs less if you do it yourself.

Although gas stations sell many things, the primary thing they do is pump gasoline. Different types of cars take different types of gasoline. There is regular, unleaded, and diesel gas.

Gas pumps are connected to underground storage tanks. A worker at the gas station regularly checks how much gas is in the tank so that the station will know how much gas to order.

Although most people still pay cash, credit cards are becoming more popular as a way of purchasing gas. They're much more convenient if you're on a long road trip, for instance, because it can be dangerous to carry a lot of cash with you. You use a credit card at a gas station the same way that you do when buying clothes at a department store. The service station worker records the sale, and at the end of the month you receive a bill from the credit card company that you must pay.

Years ago when you went to a gas station, they not only filled your tank with gas but also washed your windows and checked the oil level in your car. Very few places do that now, although they do supply the things that you need to do it yourself. Gas stations also have *tire gauges* so you can check the air pressure in your tires. If there isn't enough air, they also have *air hoses* you can use to inflate your tires.

Most minor car needs can be taken care of at any gas station. They usually have various kinds of light bulbs, windshield wipers, oil, and *anti-freeze* to sell. Some have new and used tires, and using a *tire buck*, they will remove your old tire from your wheel and put on the new one. Some gas stations even have drive-through car washes, and often they have an offer of a free car wash if you fill up your gas tank.

There are also gas stations that have tow trucks and mechanics. These places can fix major problems with your car, as well as the minor ones. They have *lifts* for lifting up cars so the mechanic can get underneath it to work on it. Gas stations can usually fulfill any basic car needs.

Questions You Might Ask A Gas Station Attendant

Why is regular gasoline being phased out?
What's the difference between regular, unleaded, and diesel fuel?
What is the difference between lead content and octane?
Why do different cars require different types of gasoline?
What does gasoline consist of?
Is any training required to be a garage mechanic?
How much do your gasoline holding tanks hold?
How often do you fill up your holding tanks?
How many customers do you service each day?
Why is self-service illegal in some states?

Activities

- Ask your mother or father to teach you how to pump gas.
- Ask them to show you how to check the oil level.
- Ask them to show you how to put water in the radiator.
- Write a report on the major gas companies.
- Research how much of the gas used in this country is from foreign markets. How has this affected the United States?

Vocabulary

☐ Anti-Freeze   ☐ Tire Buck   ☐ Lifts
☐ Air Hose   ☐ Self Service Station   ☐ Full Service Station
                       ☐ Tire Gauge

Tips From Barnabas

A gas station used to be a service-orientated business. Some of the most successful companies in the world have taken the Scriptural idea that service to other people is good and used it to make their company successful. They go out of their way to make their clients feel that they are special and important to them. When you make your field trip to a service station, go to a full-service station and observe how people respond to friendly service.

When you get home, write a paper or give an oral report to your family on what you observed.   Do you think that it would be good for a business to do extra things to serve its customers? Why do you think so many stations have become self-serve orientated, rather than the old-fashioned kind of station where the pump man knew many of his regular customers?

Memorize Galatians 6:10: "Therefore, as we have opportunity, let us do good to all people . . .," and then plan a free neighborhood car wash with some of your friends.

NAME OF PLACE TO VISIT _____

NAME OF CONTACT PERSON_____

PHONE #_____

ADDRESS _____

_____

BEST TIME TO VISIT _____

GLASS BLOWER

Background

Glass is one of the oldest substances manufactured by man. This is because its components are naturally occurring, plentiful, and inexpensive. They are sand, *limestone*, and *sodium carbonate*. Glass could be made purely out of sand, but the *melting point* is so high that it is often impractical. To lower the amount of heat needed, sodium carbonate is added, but glass made out of sand and sodium carbonate alone would *dissolve* in water. One can imagine how difficult it would be to eat or drink out of a vessel that is dissolving. The limestone is added to keep the glass from melting away. The best *ratio* of these three ingredients is 75% sand, 10% limestone, and 15% sodium carbonate. This recipe will make the kind of glass that plates are made of. To make glass that is *transparent*, other ingredients must be added. Most often *magnesia* is added to make clear glass. There are, in fact, many kinds of glass, and each type reflects a different recipe. For example, to color glass, metal oxides are added. Different metals produce different colors.

When glass is made, the ingredients are heated until they melt into a liquid. There are several ways to shape glass as it cools. One of the most common is to pour it into molds. One of the oldest methods used to shape glass is through glass blowing. This technique was developed in Syria in the first century B.C. As glass cools, it gradually becomes stiff and will hold a particular shape. The first blown glass was blown into a mold in order to shape the glass. Later, glass blowers (*gaffers*) learned they could create spherical shapes by simply blowing the glass and depending on the cooling glass to hold the shape. The same technique is used today by modern glassblowers. The *molten* glass is collected on the end of a long hollow pipe. It is then inflated by blowing through the pipe, and able to be shaped. It is kept round during this process by being spun or rolled on a flat surface called a *marver*. Some of the most beautiful pieces of *glass wear* are products of blowing.

Questions You Might Ask A Glass Blower

Where did you learn glass blowing?
Is it a skill that takes a long time to master?
What is the reason you chose to become a glass blower?
What is the composition of the glass that you blow?
Do you use different types of glass?
Is there much demand for your products?
Are your customers companies or individuals?
How long does it take to make a piece?
Where do you get your materials?
What is the most important attribute needed by a glass blower?

Activities

• Write a paper on the history of glass.
• Make a chart showing the different ingredients in different types of glass.
• Make a list of the different types of glass in your house.
• Research how stained glass is made and write a report on it.

Vocabulary

❏ Limestone
❏ Dissolve
❏ Magnesia
❏ Marver

❏ Sodium Carbonate
❏ Ratio
❏ Gaffer

❏ Melting Point
❏ Transparent
❏ Molten

Tips From Barnabas

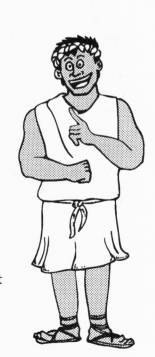

Mirrors are a special type of glass with a reflective backing which makes the glass produce a reflection. There are at least three New Testament references to mirrors or reflections:

1 Corinthians 13:12,   "Now we see a poor reflection; then [in heaven] we
                                    shall see face to face."

2 Corinthians 3:18,   "We . . . all reflect the Lord's glory."

James 1:23-24,   "Anyone who listens to the word but does not do
                                  what it says is like a man who looks at his face in a
                                  mirror and, after looking at himself, goes away, and
                                  immediately forgets what he looks like."

Choose one or all of these verses and write a paragraph or two explaining what the verse means.

NAME OF PLACE TO VISIT _____

NAME OF CONTACT PERSON _____

PHONE # _____

ADDRESS _____

_____

BEST TIME TO VISIT _____

GREENHOUSE

Background

At some time you've probably either given or received a bouquet of flowers or a potted plant. If not, then perhaps you've been in a florist's shop. But, have you ever wondered where these flowers and plants were grown? The answer is, in a greenhouse.

There are both private and commercial greenhouses. Private ones are the greenhouses that people build in or near their own homes. Usually these are *lean-to* greenhouses, which are one slope of glass or plastic built against the side of a building. People have greenhouses because they want to grow their own plants all year long. They may also grow seedlings there during the winter and then *transplant* them outside in the spring or grow their own herbs with which to cook.

Of course, the flowers and plants in florists' shops come from commercial greenhouses. These are usually constructed using an *even-span* design. They have an A-shaped roof, and the roof and walls are constructed out of glass or plastic. Usually they are about fifty feet wide and several hundred feet long. Sometimes there are several standing side by side.

The first greenhouse in America was built by Andrew Fanevile, sometime around 1737. The first greenhouses were used as *orangeries,* where citrus trees were given shelter in the winter.

Today, greenhouses are used for two main purposes. Some commercial greenhouses in the U.S. and Europe produce large quantities of tomatoes, lettuce, and cucumbers. Others are used for plants and flowers.

Plants that are grown in greenhouses can be divided into two types. There are those that need a warm *environment* at night and those that need a cool environment at night. Some greenhouses are devoted solely to one or the other kind. Others have both, and they are divided by a glass or plastic partition.

Some of the plants needing a warm environment at night are: African violets, Banana Plants, Begonias, Caladiums, Ferns, Gardenias, Hibiscus, Oleanders, and many kinds of orchids, palms, roses, and many *tropical foliage* plants.

Some of the plants needing a cool environment at night are: azaleas, cacti, carnations, chrysanthemums, daffodils, figs, fuchsias, geraniums, hyacinths, irises, lilies, marigolds, petunias, poinsettias, primroses, snap dragons, stock, sweet peas, and tulips.

Greenhouses are able to grow tropical and out of season plants all year round because they carefully control conditions, such as heat and *humidity.*

Questions You Might Ask A Greenhouse Worker

Different greenhouses get their heat from different sources. From where does this greenhouse get its heat?

Does it grow plants that need a cool night environment, a warm one, or both?

Does it grow any tropical plants?

If so, where do they naturally grow?

Do plants grow better in a greenhouse than they would if left in their natural environment?

Is only natural light used, or are artificial lights added?

Is the water specially treated, or is it the same that would be used out-of-doors?

How often do you deliver to florists' shops?

What is the ratio of flowers to edible plants in your greenhouse?

What does it mean for something to be organically grown?

What type of fertilizers do you use?

Activities

- Find out what flowers and plants are *indigenous* to your area. Find pictures and/or descriptions of them so that you will be able to recognize them.
- Make a *terrarium*.
- Write a report on *hybridizing*.

Vocabulary

❏ Lean-to
❏ Orangeries
❏ Foliage
❏ Terrarium

❏ Transplant
❏ Environment
❏ Humidity
❏ Hybrids

❏ Even-Span
❏ Tropical
❏ Indigenous

Tips From Barnabas

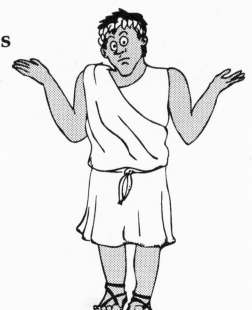

In Genesis 1:11,12, we're told that God commanded the land to produce vegetation. If you get a book on plants, you can learn how photosynthesis transforms the energy the plants get from the sun into growth. You've learned how the greenhouse protects plants from elements too harsh for them to fight against so that they can continue to grow in a protected environment.

Study photosynthesis and use what you know about greenhouses to draw some comparisons about how we grow in Christ, and how His Spirit protects us from the things we could not bear alone. Do you think God puts new Christians into 'greenhouses' until they are strong enough to make it in the world's garden?

NAME OF PLACE TO VISIT _____

NAME OF CONTACT PERSON _____

PHONE # _____

ADDRESS _____

_____

BEST TIME TO VISIT _____

GROCERY STORE

Background

We have all been to a grocery store. It is usually full of busy people hurrying to buy food for their families. Buying food, however, is not the only thing that can be learned at a grocery store. Good *nutrition* is very important for good health, and there is a wealth of knowledge about nutrition in the grocery store. Simply by examining the lay-out of the store, you can learn about the *four food groups*. Breads and grains will be divided into two groups. You will find most of the members of this group in the bakery section of the store, and the rest will be in the pasta section, because pasta is made from grains. The meats and protein will mostly be in the butcher section of the store, though peanut butter, eggs, and beans are also important sources of protein. Most stores group all the dairy products together, including milk, butter and cheese. Fruits and vegetables are also usually all together in the produce section. You will discover, when you locate these sections of the store, that they actually don't take up very much room (usually around the edges) compared with the size of the whole store. The middle part of the store, excluding the sections of inedibles like paper products and beauty aids, is taken up with canned and prepared foods. These products are usually mixtures of foods from various food groups.

Because these food items are not only mixtures of different kinds of food but also have been specially prepared to be packed in cans or boxes, we cannot take their nutritional value for granted. This is where an important element of smart shopping comes in. Since most of the food we buy is not fresh but has been processed in some way, we must learn as much about it as we can. Because of federal law, food manufacturers put nutritional information on the package of food they sell. By reading these messages, we can tell how good some food item is for us. This message will include the percent of the governmentally determined *recommended daily allowance* of certain important vitamins. Other information includes the amount, by weight, of *fat, protein, carbohydrates*, and *sodium*. The number of *calories* per serving is also given. By studying this information, you can learn which foods are better for you and which you should avoid.

Another important skill you can learn by reading labels is becoming a smart shopper. Becoming a smart shopper is a skill that comes only with practice at a store. Part of shopping well is realizing that it is not only the price of an item which is important, but you must also be aware of the size. Here is an example. There are two jars of mayonnaise of different sizes; one is 15 ounces and the other is 36 ounces. The 15 ounce jar costs $1.65, while the larger jar costs $2.88. The smaller jar costs less, but is it the better deal? When we divide 15 into $1.65, we find that each ounce of mayonnaise in the smaller container costs 11 cents. When we do the same to the larger jar by dividing 36 into $2.88, we find that each ounce in the larger jar costs only 8 cents. So the larger jar is the better deal because the price per unit is better. The difference of 3 cents an ounce may not seem significant but when multiplied by 36 ounces, you realize that we have saved over one dollar. When you apply this technique to everything you buy, your savings multiply!

Questions You Might Ask A Grocer

How much business do you do in a week?
How long have you been doing what you do?
Do you think that most people are smart shoppers, or do they not bother to take the time?
What is your job?
Do you have special training to do what you do?
Has working in a grocery store made you a better shopper?
How does the display of products affect how they sell?
What do you do with unsold meat and produce?
Are you part of a chain or an independent store?
Does your store have its own brand of products?
Is it really cheaper to buy generic products?

Activities

- When you go to the store, you will find that there are many different jobs: baker, butcher, produce manager, stocker, bag boys, checkers, and store managers. Ask several different people doing different jobs the above questions.
- Pick several types of food (mayonnaise, sweet pickles, peanut butter, milk, honey, etc.) and make a list, from best bargain to worst, of the brands and sizes.
- Do activity number two again, but list them in order of nutritional value.
- Come up with a few well-balanced and nutritional meal ideas.
- Write a report on one of the largest grocery chains in America.

Vocabulary

❏ Nutrition   ❏ Four Food Groups   ❏ Protein
❏ Carbohydrates   ❏ Fat   ❏ Sodium
❏ Calorie   ❏ Recommended Daily Allowance

Tips From Barnabas

Grocery stores play a very important part in cities. On a farm, much if not all, of the necessary food can be supplied by the farm itself. In a city, most of us depend on the grocery store to provide the food we need. A store run in a godly way will provide good products at honest prices (see Deuteronomy 25:15, and Proverbs 11:1). Make a list of things that a store should and should not do to operate in a Christ-like way.

HANDICAPPED

NAME OF PLACE TO VISIT _____

NAME OF CONTACT PERSON _____

PHONE # _____

ADDRESS _____

_____

BEST TIME TO VISIT _____

Background

At some time in your life, you will almost certainly meet someone who is blind or deaf or has some other handicap. Some people are born with one of these handicaps; others are inflicted with them later in life because of injury or disease.

Blindness

You have probably seen someone blind in a store or walking down the street. You could tell that they were blind because they used a *seeing-eye dog* or a white cane with a red tip. These are two devises that blind people use in order to get around more easily.

Being blind doesn't mean that you must sit at home or have others do everything for you. It simply means that some changes must be made in your lifestyle. Seeing-eye dogs are a good example of specially developed aids for blind people so they may lead independent lives. The dogs are trained to understand things like traffic signals so that blind people can get around easily without the help of another person.

A method of writing for the blind was invented by Louis Braille, who had been blind since childhood. *Braille* is a system that uses raised dots on paper. Each letter and number consists of a different pattern of dots. Blind people read these dots by lightly running their fingers across them.

There is a popular myth that blind people have extraordinary powers of hearing or touch. Although this is not true, it is true that blind people use their other senses better than most sighted people. They will remember how each piece of clothing feels in order to dress themselves. They can often recognize other people merely by the sound of their footsteps or by the way that they smell.

When you are with a blind person, treat him, for the most part, the way you would anyone else. Talk to him in a normal tone of voice; don't talk about him in the third person as if he weren't there, and don't be afraid to use words like "see" if they are appropriate, such as, "Have you seen so-and-so lately?"

Deafness

The deaf are faced with a different set of problems, getting around and taking care of themselves. They may experience great difficulty in the area of communication.

Most deaf people learn *American Sign Language* (ASL) or Signing Exact English (SEE). ASL is not based on the English language; it is a language of its own with its own unique rules and grammar.

Although ASL is good for communication between deaf people, most hearing people do not know it. Some deaf people learn how to speak, although this is difficult because it's hard to reproduce a sound that you have never heard. Some deaf people also learn how to lip read, but again this is easier for some than others.

Note writing can be a time-consuming but effective way of communicating with a deaf person. Unfortunately, some deaf people are also totally or partially *illiterate,* either because educational opportunities for the deaf are still limited or because a person who is only taught ASL, but not taught how to speak, will find the grammar and form of the English language difficult.

If you don't know sign language and you meet a deaf person, look straight at him whenever you talk to him and speak slowly. Feel free to be expressive with your hands and face. If you need to write something out, write it in the same way that you would say it. Don't be surprised if, when he writes something down for you, he switches words around or leaves certain words out altogether. Keep trying, and eventually you will find the easiest method for the two of you to communicate.

Questions You Might Ask A Handicapped Person

For a blind person:
How do you tell the difference between different types of paper money in your wallet?
How do you tell the time?
What sort of sports do you participate in?
What hobbies do you have?
How do you shop for food and clothing?
What work do you do?
Do you have special equipment at your job to help you?

For a deaf person:
Do you have a special kind of telephone?
Do you have a special kind of alarm clock?
Do you have a special kind of door bell?
Are some people easier to lip read than others? If so, why?
Are most of your friends also deaf?
What can hearing people do to make it more comfortable for you?

Activities

- With your parents' permission, spend a day with a blindfold on. See what problems you have and what adjustments you have to make.
- Take a class in ASL. If one isn't offered in your community, find a book on it to teach yourself at least the alphabet (like *The Joy of Signing* by Lottie Riekoff).
- Find a book written in Braille. See how it feels to try to read it.
- Read a biography of a handicapped person, such as Joni Erickson Tada or Hellen Keller, and write a report on it.

Vocabulary

- ❏ Braille
- ❏ ASL
- ❏ Seeing-Eye Dog
- ❏ Illiterate
- ❏ Hearing-Ear Dog

Tips From Barnabas

One of the signs that the kingdom had come was that the blind received sight, the lame walked, and the deaf heard (Matthew 11:4-6). God has often shown His care and provision for those less fortunate. It is a godly principle that the stronger should help the weaker, not ignore or take advantage of them.

People shut off from normal daily activities by their handicaps are often in need of a friend. Take some time to imagine what it would be like to: (1) not be able to hear in a room full of people laughing and talking, (2) never be able to see the sunrise, read a book, or see your parents' faces, and (3) sit in a wheelchair, unable to run and play with other children your age. Now write a paper on what you can do for the handicapped person to help him know that someone cares about him, especially that God cares about him.

NAME OF PLACE TO VISIT _____

NAME OF CONTACT PERSON _____

PHONE # _____

ADDRESS _____

_____

BEST TIME TO VISIT _____

HARDWARE STORE

Background

A hardware store can be a lot of fun. It is full of parts and tools which help people fix or build things. If you are observant, you can learn a lot about how things are made and how they work, simply by examining the parts of things and the tools available in the hardware store. First, you should notice that the store is divided up into parts, and that each department of the store has to do with particular jobs or certain kinds of systems.

There are sections of the hardware store that have to do with building. Many hardware stores have *lumber* departments with boards, *plywood, molding,* and *sheetrock,* for everything from a birdhouse to a family home. Another part of the store will contain the nails and screws needed to hold things together. Nails and screws are often sold by the pound. Another section will hold hinges and handles for doors and cabinets. In fact, you can also buy doors and cabinets and even screen wire for screen doors. Other sections will have paint and wood stain. Hardware stores can often custom mix your paint by adding carefully-measured amounts of dye to white paint and mixing it well on a machine that shakes the can of paint very quickly. Of course, you can't use paint or stain without brushes, rollers, and paint pans, so there is also a section for these. And if you don't want to use paint or stain, there are other wall and floor coverings available. There is probably a section for wallpaper, tile, and panelling.

There are other sections of a hardware store, which are for fixing or installing systems which are inside your house. Most hardware stores have large sections of piping and plumbing supplies, including pipes made out of copper, plastic, and aluminum of all different sizes. There will probably also be a section for plumbing *fixtures.* Sinks, faucets, toilets, and tubs are plumbing fixtures. Hardware stores also have a section devoted to electrical equipment: wire, switches, and plugs. There may also be a section of lamps and other lights. Some stores even have sections of other electrical appliances.

So far, we have seen how diverse departments can work together to make whole systems work. There are many other sections of a hardware store which don't fit so easily with the others. Many stores will have gardening centers with house plants, outdoor plants, and soil. There may also be a section of outdoor tools, like shovels and rakes. There is also a large section of other tools, such as screw drivers, hammers, wrenches, and pliers. There may also be a section of tape, rope, and stationary needs. Hardware stores, then, have almost everything that you might need to make or fix anything around the house. You can learn much from touring a hardware store. Not only can you find out about what parts make up particular home systems, you can also learn something about how each of these parts works.

Questions You Might Ask A Hardware Store Owner

What are the most popular items sold here?

Do you get more professional builders or amateur fixer-uppers in the store?

Have you learned about fixing things around the house by working in a hardware store?

How do you decide what products to carry?

How do you decide which brands to carry?

How are prices determined?

Is there any special training or knowledge needed to work here?

How does the time of year affect your sales?

Do you often give your customers advice?

Do you do your own building and repairs?

What is the difference between a wholesale and a retail hardware store?

Activities

• Make a list of the departments in your local hardware store.

• Make a list of combinations of departments and how they work together.

• Research all the parts of a particular system to see how they work and how they fit together, such as plumbing or electrical systems.

Vocabulary

❒ Lumber   ❒ Plywood   ❒ Molding

❒ Sheet rock   ❒ Fixtures

Tips From Barnabas

In one of George McDonald's books, he gives a glimpse of what a heavenly store would be like, in which nothing would be sold except for the good of the person buying it. Both the seller and the buyer have a responsibility to each other (Proverbs 20:14, and Leviticus 19:35).

A hardware store is full of appliances and gadgets that can make jobs easier. Make a list of questions you should ask yourself before buying. This will help you to be a good steward and avoid impulse buying. You need to know before purchasing it, if you really need the product, and, if so, which particular product has the features you need. Don't be talked into purchasing things you don't need. What do you think of sales people who try to talk you into buying things that you don't really need? Is this what Christ would want them to do?

NAME OF PLACE TO VISIT _____

NAME OF CONTACT PERSON _____

PHONE # _____

ADDRESS _____

_____

BEST TIME TO VISIT _____

HELICOPTER

Background

Most of us have probably flown in a plane at one time or another, but fewer people have ridden in a helicopter. Although both planes and helicopters are airships and even have similarities in methods of flight, they are very different. The major difference between them is the way they take off. If you have been to an airport, you know that an airplane has to be going quite fast to take off. To build up this speed, they need long, straight runways. Helicopters are different; they take off by lifting straight up into the air. This means that they can take off and land in areas which are much smaller than those needed by an airplane. That is why helicopters are much more versatile.

A helicopter is pulled up into the air by the spinning *rotor* on top. The rotor is made up of two, three, or, sometimes, four blades. The upward power, or *lift*, is created by the shape of the blades. This shape is called an *airfoil*. An airfoil is flat on the bottom and rounded on the top. The air must go farther over the top of the airfoil than across the bottom, so the air goes faster. The faster air above the rotor creates a kind of suction which pulls the helicopter up. The power of this suction is controlled by the *pitch*, or angle of the rotor. When the rotor blades are steeply angled, the suction is greater, and the helicopter lifts off. To *hover*, the pilot simply flattens the pitch. The wing of a plane is also an airfoil. An airfoil must be going through the air very fast, for it to work. On a helicopter, it is the rotary motion of the blades which pushes the airfoil through the air fast enough. But since the wings of an airplane are stable, the whole plane must be pushed through the air very fast, for the airfoil to work.

If a helicopter were guided by only one rotor on top, then the motion of that rotor would cause the whole helicopter to spin. That problem is sometimes solved by having two rotors on top spinning in opposite directions, either one on top of another or one at each end of the helicopter. Most helicopters, however, have a small rotor mounted sideways on the tail for stability. A helicopter is maneuvered by tipping the top rotor in the direction the pilot wants to go. Because of this, it can go forward, backward, or sideways. It is easiest, though, for it to go forward, so the pilot will usually turn the helicopter, using the small, sideways rotor on the tail, and fly forward.

The idea for the helicopter has been around for a long time. The first helicopter was designed by the great Italian artist and inventor, Leonardo da Vinci. His design, however, did not work. Many other people have tried since then. In the latter part of the last century and the early part of this one, while many people were experimenting with airplanes, some were working on designs for helicopters. It wasn't until this century that a working design was developed. Helicopters are slower and use fuel less efficiently than airplanes. But because of their maneuverability, ability to hover, and to take off and land in small areas, they are widely used in situations where airplanes are impractical.

Questions You Might Ask A Helicopter Pilot

How are helicopters used in the medical field?
How are helicopters used in the military?
Do you need a special license to fly a helicopter?
How much training is required to fly a helicopter?
Is a helicopter more difficult to fly than an airplane?
How are helicopters used in the police force?
What type of fuel do they use?
How fast can they go?
How high can they go?

Activities

• Lightly hold a spoon sideways under a faucet so that the back of the bowl is in the stream of running water. You might expect the spoon to be pushed away by the water, but, in fact, the opposite is true. This is how an airfoil works; the spoon represents the top of the airfoil, and the water represents the air flowing past.
• Read further on how helicopters work and write a report.
• Make a list of special uses for helicopters.
• There may be helicopter rides available in your area. See if you can ride in one.
• Draw a diagram of a helicopter and label each of the major parts.

Vocabulary

❏ Airfoil   ❏ Rotor   ❏ Lift
❏ Pitch   ❏ Hover

Tips From Barnabas

Technology and team effort are nothing new to mankind. In Genesis 11, we're told the story of the Tower of Babel. They talked together and decided on a plan to accomplish their goal – a tower that reached to the heavens.

"But the Lord came down to see the city, and the tower that the men were building. The Lord said, 'If as one people speaking the same language they have begun to do this, then nothing they plan to do will be impossible for them.'"

You can see this same type of production in the development of the helicopter. Man had dreamed of flying for years; ultimately the airplane was created. Then by using technology and team effort, a new type of craft was designed to be able to take off, land, and hover in a very limited area. Specialized knowledge used for practical purposes (technology) helped achieve the goal, but without the team effort it would have been almost impossible to obtain this type of results.

Read Nehemiah, chapter four. The goal of this people in this chapter was to rebuild the walls of Jerusalem. List some of the ways the people worked together to reach their common goal.

NAME OF PLACE TO VISIT _____

NAME OF CONTACT PERSON _____

PHONE # _____

ADDRESS _____

_____

BEST TIME TO VISIT _____

HISTORY MUSEUM

Background

History museums show us the past. Some are national history museums with exhibits showing significant historical events and objects from all across the country. Some are regional museums depicting, for instance, only the history of New England or the Pacific Northwest. Still others are state or city museums. And some depict only objects and events from one particular subject in history, such as the Civil War or the American Revolution.

There are also historic houses and historic villages. Historic houses are houses that are restored to their original appearance and decorated with either the original furnishings or exact copies. These houses usually belonged to a famous person in history. People are allowed to walk through them and can see what a home was like in that period.

Historic villages are groups of buildings that have been restored to appear as a village of the past. People walk through the different buildings and get a view of what life was like in an ordinary village during that time period. These villages employ people who dress in appropriate costumes and give lectures and demonstrations. Possibly the most popular time period for these houses and villages is the colonial period.

History museums often have a great variety of exhibits. Their *acquisitions* may include clothing, furniture, photographs, newspapers, diaries, various personal possessions, paintings, letters, political memorabilia, ancient artifacts, weapons, and toys. The items may be significant because of their age, their part in history, who owned them, or just as an example of something from a specific time period.

Exhibits may be any combination of objects, photographs, charts, and graphs. The person who decides what the exhibits will be like is the *curator*. The person who does the actual building of any furniture or cases needed is the *designer*, and the person who prepares the backdrop and explanation cards for the exhibit is the *preparator*.

History museums, like other museums, have both permanent and temporary exhibits. Sometimes temporary exhibits are created by museum staff. Other times they are traveling exhibits, often coming from a much larger museum, such as the Smithsonian Institute.

What you will see in a history museum depends partly on its size and emphasis but more on where it is located. For instance, if you are in a state that was one of the original thirteen colonies, you will probably see an exhibit on the American Revolution. If you live in one of the states that took part in the Civil War, you will probably see an exhibit on that. If you live in the West, there will probably be an exhibit on American Indians.

History museums often have educational programs. They frequently sponsor films and lecturers on various historically significant subjects.

Questions You Might Ask A History Museum Employee

From where does the museum get most of its funding?
Which exhibits are permanent?
Which exhibits are temporary?
How does the staff decide what sort of exhibit to display?
Does the museum try to emphasize certain periods in history?
Does the museum try to emphasize certain events?
What kind of education and training have you had?
Where do you get your objects?
Where do you store your objects when not in use?
Do you have a library available for public use?

Activities

• Pick an event, a person, or time period which interests you. Read extensively on it and devise your own exhibit. Since you probably won't be able to obtain actual objects, make do with pictures, charts, and graphs.
• Research and write a report on the founding and growth of the Smithsonian Institute.
• Research and write a report on your local community.

Vocabulary

❑ Acquisitions   ❑ Designers   ❑ Preparators
❑ Curator

Tips From Barnabas

History seems rather awesome, bringing to mind old books and dark hallways, but it is really just a tale or story which attempts to recount the facts as they actually happened. In order to tell a true story, you must remember certain events, including times, people, and places. 1 Chronicles 16:12 tells us to remember the wonders that the Lord has done. The Gospels are histories of Jesus' life. The book of Acts is a history of the early church. A history museum makes history three-dimensional, rather than just words.

Think back over your own spiritual history or your family's together and write a history (story) that would explain your life to someone else. Try also to do at least one exhibit as though it were going to be displayed in a museum in heaven, showing one part of you or your family's spiritual history.

NAME OF PLACE TO VISIT _____

NAME OF CONTACT PERSON _____

PHONE # _____

ADDRESS _____

_____

BEST TIME TO VISIT _____

HOTEL/MOTEL

BED & BREAKFAST

Background

Many of us have visited a hotel or motel at some time or another. Usually they are used when people are traveling. Hotels and motels are, in general, very similar, but there are a couple of important differences. A clue to these differences is the fact that "motel" is short for "motor hotel." Motels are found along highways, usually outside city limits. Motels are usually used by people on longer trips. These travelers often do not want to deal with city traffic and are content to stay near the highway. Hotels are usually used by people who have reached their destination, and who want to be close to the attractions of a city. The other major difference between these two types of establishments is architectural. Most motels are built to be long and flat. This way, each room has a separate door to the outside. In a hotel, however, the doors of the rooms open onto hallways. Hotels usually have only one or two doors from the outside into the *lobby*, while motels have an outside door for every room.

Staying in a hotel or motel can be a real treat. Even though it is usually more comfortable to be at home in surroundings which are familiar, a change can be fun. There are also some special services that go along with staying in one of these places. Hotels often have *room service,* which enables you to order food from the kitchen, and it is brought directly to your room. Motels are much less likely to have this feature because they usually do not serve food at all. Most hotel and motel employees will be able to tell their guests where the city's more interesting sights are located. They might also have suggestions of other places to eat in town. Hotels and motels are often able to wake people up at a certain time in the morning by calling their rooms—a kind of alarm clock. The best part about staying in one of these places when away from home is the *maid* service. Maids bring clean towels and washcloths daily. They also change and make beds. When you are away from home, you don't even have to make your own bed. All in all, hotels and motels are a clean, convenient, comfortable way to live when away from home.

Another even more exciting way to spend a night away from home is to stay in a Bed and Breakfast. Traditionally, Bed and Breakfast is an overnight stay in a private home or small inn where the traveller is treated like a house guest. This has long been a method of lodging when traveling in England and Europe, but only recently has the Bed and Breakfast become increasingly popular in America. Bed and Breakfasts allow you to experience people, as well as, places.

Making *reservations* at a B&B is not like reserving a room at a motel, where you can call twenty-four hours a day and find an open room. B&Bs are more like someone's home. Arrangements should be made during normal hours, well in advance of expected arrival. Also, many of the *amenities* of a large hotel, like *bellhops* and ice machines, will be missing. But this is more than made up by the delightful surroundings and the people you will meet. Expect the unexpected: afternoon tea on the porch, maybe a short walk through the garden, or an explanation of historical significance.

B&B *accommodations* can range from luxurious homes with Old World elegance to unassuming small town homes. You might stay in a lighthouse, on a house boat, or in a restored mansion. All meet basic needs of cleanliness and comfort. All go beyond these basic needs in genteel *hospitality* with warmth and friendliness of the host.

An adventurous spirit, a bit of flexibility, and a sense of humor will help to make your Bed and Breakfast experience a memorable one.

Questions You Might Ask A Hotel/Motel Manager or Bed and Breakfast Owner

What is the average length of stay in your motel?
What special services do you offer?
How long have you been working in this business?
What special training do you have?
Do you own the hotel or just manage it?
Do you ever have to expel guests, and if so, why?
What things should I look for when choosing a hotel/motel/Bed and Breakfast?
What are the different jobs in a hotel?
How do you decide how much to charge?
What are your busy seasons?
How do people make reservations to stay here?
Are you a member of a hotel/motel or B&B association?
Do you require reservations or payment in advance?
Do you have a swimming pool?
Do you have a jacuzzi or hot tub?
Do you provide room service?
What percentage of occupancy do you have to average to make money?
Who do you give discounts to and why?
How old do you have to be to work in a hotel?
Do you offer students summer work?
Who does the repairs when something breaks?
What are your legal liabilities if someone gets hurt on your property?
How many rooms do you have?
What is your capacity?
How often are you booked up?
Do you encourage families with children to stay here?
What special features distinguish your Bed and Breakfast from all the others?

Activities

- Go to several motels and hotels and tell the manager that you are doing a report on motels in the area. Ask if he would assist you in your research project. Then ask the manager if you could see some of the rooms. Ask to see the most expensive and the least expensive. Also ask for a tour of any adjacent facilities, like restaurants, beauty shops, banquet facilities, etc..
- Ask the manager how he attracts customers, and if he has any promotional material you could have. With the material you have collected, make a mini-directory of the hotels you visited, including the range of rates and variety of services offered.
- Pick one of the hotels or motels visited and write a promotional piece. Explain why a couple would want to stay there. Describe the facilities for the children and how they would enjoy staying there.
- Research the number of hotels versus motels in your area. How would you account for the ratio?
- Go to your local library and ask the librarian where you could find books on Bed and Breakfasts. Check out a book that lists Bed and Breakfasts in your area of the country. Have a family conference and pick out a Bed and Breakfast that everyone would like to go to. If able, make reservations to spend a night there. If you aren't able to actually stay there, write to the owners and ask for a brochure and any other information they might have on their establishment.
- Set up a private Bed and Breakfast in your own home. Draw up a set of rules and guidelines for guests. Plan a particularly scrumptious breakfast to wow your guests. And then look for opportunities to have people stay over. Possibly contact your church's missionary committee and ask if the next time a missionary needs a place to stay they might stay at your house. You can also check with organizations that process international students. They often would like to place travelling students in a home overnight.

Vocabulary

- ☐ Lobby
- ☐ Resort
- ☐ Inn
- ☐ Suite
- ☐ Registration
- ☐ Continental Breakfast
- ☐ Hospitality
- ☐ Amenities

- ☐ Room Service
- ☐ Jacuzzi
- ☐ Spa
- ☐ Condominium
- ☐ Reservation
- ☐ Satellite Television
- ☐ Bellhop
- ☐ Accommodations

- ☐ Maid
- ☐ Lodge
- ☐ Lounge
- ☐ Flat
- ☐ Valet
- ☐ Business Discount
- ☐ Elegance

Tips From Barnabas

In Bible times there weren't as many hotels and motels as we have today. In those days there were a few inns, however, a traveler would most often stay in people's houses. It was a sign of hospitality to invite a stranger to spend the night in your home. It was considered a rude insult not to do so. Abraham showed hospitality to three men who came by his tent in Mamre. As it turned out, one of the men was the Lord. During their conversation, the Lord promised that Abraham would have a son by Sarah. See what else they talked about by reading Genesis 19. It was probably Abraham that the verse refers to in Hebrews 13:2, "Do not forget to entertain strangers, for by doing so some people have entertained angels without knowing it."

Some people take the opportunity for hospitality more seriously than others. There was a woman who lived in Shunem who noticed that the traveling prophet Elisha frequently passed by. She encouraged her husband to build an adjacent room so that whenever Elisha visited that area, he had a place to stay. On one such occasion, Elisha called for the woman wanting to show appreciation for her hospitality, and asked her what he could do for her. Elisha was told that this woman had no son. And much to the Shunammite woman's surprise and joy, God granted her a son in response to Elisha's prayer for her.

It is always a blessing to entertain traveling missionaries. It is a rare opportunity to hear firsthand of their ministry. Have you ever considered that when you have your own home you could dedicate one room as a "prophet's chamber" for traveling missionaries? If you do, you will be greatly blessed, like Abraham and the Shunammite woman.

Before we leave the topic of motels and hotels, I want to mention two of the most famous inns in the Bible. Can you think of them? Yes, the inn in Bethlehem and the inn on the Jericho road. The inn in Bethlehem was the place that was too full to house Joseph and Mary, and because there was no room for them in the inn, Jesus was born in a stable.

About halfway to Jericho, on the road out of Jerusalem, there lies an inn in ruins. Tourist guides will point out the parable Jesus taught about the Good Samaritan (Luke 10) and will tell you that this is the inn where the injured man was taken. Whether that is the actual inn referred to, or not, doesn't lessen the importance of "being a neighbor." Read the parable and ask yourself, "If I am to love my neighbor as myself - who is my neighbor?"

NAME OF PLACE TO VISIT _____

NAME OF CONTACT PERSON _____

PHONE # _____

ADDRESS _____

_____

BEST TIME TO VISIT _____

INDIAN RESERVATION

Background

Many states contain *American Indian* reservations. A reservation is a piece of land designated by the Federal government, on which particular Indian tribes can live. The Indians often have nearly complete control of their reservations. These reservations, however, are relatively small areas. This is a major change from the way things were 250 years ago, when the Indians controlled almost all of the land in North America, and people of European descent lived in small areas. This change came about through war, as well as, through *treaty*.

The first thing we must remember is that it is not really accurate to talk about American Indians as only one group. There are many tribes from all over North America who live in different ways, speak different languages, and reacted in different ways to the spread of Europeans. Many Indian *tribes* were friendly to the new arrivals to the Americas. We all know that without the help of North-Eastern Indian groups, the *Pilgrims* would not have survived. Later, in 1805, *Lewis and Clark* were guided by an Indian, *Sacagawea*, when they explored the *Louisiana Purchase*. Unfortunately, friendship was not enough to ensure good relations between the Indians and the Europeans. The major bone of contention was use and control of the land. The Europeans were hungry for land and always pushed for expansion. All of the interactions between Indians and Europeans were ultimately based on the desire of the Europeans for the Indian land.

The official relationship between the Indians and the United States government began in 1787 with the establishment of the *Constitution*. The Constitution gave power to deal with the Indians exclusively to the Federal Government. The government first set up the loosely organized *Indian Department* headed by the *Indian agents*. Later, this organization was formalized as the *Bureau of Indian Affairs*. The attitude of the government towards the Indians becomes clear when we realize that both of these organizations were branches of the *War Department*. It wasn't until much later that official government interaction with the Indians was put under the control of the *Department of the Interior*, where it is to this day.

The goal of most treaties between the United States government and the Indians was to move them from land that the government wanted and put them somewhere else. Usually the land to which they were moved was not as good. A good example is the Cherokee Indians of Georgia. They were forced to walk from their homes to the reservation in Oklahoma. Many died along the way. Soon after this, more oil was found on the reservation land in Oklahoma. Because the government wanted access to the oil, it broke its treaty with the Indians and moved them again. Treaties being broken happened over and over again, and the Indians were moved to smaller and more remote pieces of land. In most of the battles between government forces and Indians, the Indians took the defensive against the army that was trying to move them.

Today, many Indian groups show a lot of pride in themselves and in their heritage. Many tribes are working to preserve their language, culture, dress, and ceremonies. The reservation is the center of this effort. Many tribes have yearly pageants which are open to the public, in which ceremonial dress and dance are displayed. Indian tribes today have not turned in upon themselves, however. There is still an effort to influence local government. Tribes have banded together into governmental bodies called *councils*. The councils work with local governments to preserve, not only fish and wildlife, but also ancient fishing rights claimed by these tribes. All in all, the reservation is a busy center of Indian life and culture.

Questions You Might Ask An Indian

Of what tribe are you?
What are some of your customs that you still practice?
Was your tribe originally located somewhere else? If so, when was it moved?
What are your tribe's traditional religious beliefs?
Do you have yearly festivals?
Does your tribe have a written tradition?
What do you do on the reservation?
What things would you like to see the government do for your tribe?
How is your relationship with the local government?
How big is the reservation, and how many people live there?

Activities

- Investigate the location of Indian reservations in your state or region.
- Read about what kind of Indians inhabit or inhabited your area.
- Research the history of Indians in America and write a paper.
- Using a blank map of the United States, map out the major Indian tribes.
- Write a report on a famous Indian.

Vocabulary

- ❏ American Indian
- ❏ Pilgrim
- ❏ Louisiana Purchase
- ❏ Indian Agent
- ❏ Department of the Interior

- ❏ Treaty
- ❏ Lewis & Clark
- ❏ Constitution
- ❏ Bureau of Indian Affairs

- ❏ Tribe
- ❏ Sacagawea
- ❏ Indian Department
- ❏ War Department

Tips From Barnabas

While the Indians were the original inhabitants of this land, for all practical purposes they have become as aliens. America is also home to many people from many other lands, e.g. the Chinese, the African Americans, the Latins, etc. You might be able to find almost any heritage represented here in the United States.

Scripture speaks plainly as to how we are to treat strangers or aliens that come to our country. Look up the following Scriptures and decide what principles are given for how we are to treat aliens. Discuss these with your parents and decide what your family can practically do to put them into practice.

Exodus 22:21; Leviticus 19:34, 25:35; Deuteronomy 27:19, 31:12; and Matthew 25:35

Also read Exodus 1:6-14, which describes how the Israelites were treated by the Egyptians when they were strangers in Egypt. Are there any people we have mistreated in this way? What should be done to rectify this?

INSURANCE COMPANY

Background

NAME OF PLACE TO VISIT _____

NAME OF CONTACT PERSON _____

PHONE # _____

ADDRESS _____

_____

BEST TIME TO VISIT _____

Insurance is a very important protection against *catastrophic* loss. The idea behind insurance is for a large group of people to pool their money together in order to protect themselves from loss. The idea started in the late Middle Ages when trade by sea became very big business. Sea travel was not as safe then as it is now, and the loss of a boatload of cargo was a frightening prospect. Insurance companies were set up to handle this problem. Each merchant would pay the insurance company a small fraction of the value of his or her cargo, called a *premium,* for an insurance policy. If the boat sank, the insurance company would have enough money to pay the owner the whole value of the cargo. The insurance company could pay off this debt because it had collected money from enough clients.

There are many kinds of insurance available now. By law, in most states, car owners are required to carry accident insurance. This is to protect pedestrians, as well as other drivers. If a driver is involved in an accident, his or her insurance company is required to pay if it is the driver's fault. In this way the accident victim is guaranteed some measure of help. There is also home insurance, which protects people against theft or accident. There is also fire insurance. With these two kinds of insurance, people are able to rebuild their homes or replace stolen or damaged belongings. Two of the most common types of insurance are health and life insurance. These protect a family if the bread winner or winners get sick or die and are unable to support their family or pay the hospital bills. The insurance then acts like the pay check that is not coming in. Nervous fliers can even get flight insurance. It is usually dispensed from machines in the airport. Whatever the type, all insurance protects us against a financial loss that we could not bear.

Questions You Might Ask An Insurance Agent

What kind of insurance do you sell?

What percentage of people in the local area carry the kind of insurance you sell?

What is the average premium ?

What training is required to become an insurance agent?

How long have you been an insurance agent?

Why did you choose to sell insurance?

How is the amount of insurance premiums arrived at?

What are the different types of auto insurance?

What are the different types of life insurance?

What can be done to keep insurance rates as low as possible?

Activities

- Contact several insurance firms in your area and ask the above questions.
- Make a chart of different kinds of insurance and their premiums.
- Make up a budget for a family of five who own their own home, covering all of the different kinds of insurance they will need.
- Find out what types of insurance your family has and the specifics of each policy.

Vocabulary

❏ Insurance   ❏ Policy   ❏ Premium
❏ Agent   ❏ Catastrophe   ❏ Liability

Tips From Barnabas

Y ou buy insurance to help protect yourself from loss. If your house burns down, and you have fire insurance, it will help pay for a new house.

For the believer, God Himself is our insurance that nothing can come to us except what He allows. He does not promise that evil things will never happen to us, but He does insure us that we are secure in His love and care. If our house burns down, our car gets wrecked, or we go to the hospital, we may or may not have fire, auto, or medical insurance, but we can know that God will be there with us.

Read Psalm 112, which describes a man whose heart is secure in the Lord. Discuss with your family how we can feel secure in Christ.

JEWELER

Background

NAME OF PLACE TO VISIT _____

NAME OF CONTACT PERSON _____

PHONE # _____

ADDRESS _____

_____

BEST TIME TO VISIT _____

Jewelry is a very common *wardrobe accessory* today. Almost everyone wears some kind of jewelry at some time. Jewelry includes all kinds of necklaces, bracelets, rings, earrings, broaches, and pins. Watches are even considered to be jewelry, these days. A modern definition of jewelry might be "a bodily decoration which is made of precious or semiprecious materials or is fashioned to look like it is made of one of these materials." It has not, however, always been the case that jewelry was purely ornamental.

The earliest jewelry was made out of animal materials: bone, horn, or teeth. This early jewelry was probably meant to instill the wearer with the characteristics of that animal: wisdom, hunting prowess, or what have you. It was a distinction afforded only to the rich to wear these symbols of power. Until the birth of Christianity, it was common to bury the jewelry which belonged to a person in life with them when they died. This was in the belief that this jewelry would be helpful to the person in the next life. The Egyptians were probably the most ostentatious in this regard. The tombs of Egyptian kings often had several rooms, in order to hold all of the king's treasures.

Since the Middle Ages, the most common metal used in jewelry has been gold. This is not only because of its color and shine. It is also due to the *malleability* of the metal. This makes gold easy to work with. Silver, which is also very malleable, and platinum are also very commonly used in jewelry. *Precious* or *semiprecious* stones are often combined with the precious metals above. By far the most popular precious stones are diamonds. Even though diamond jewelry has become more affordable due to modern techniques of jewelry manufacture, it is still very expensive. This has sparked the creation of artificial diamonds, which are much more affordable. Other popular stones include: rubies, emeralds, sapphires, garnets, opals, jade, and turquoise. Each of these stones has individual characteristics which appeal to different people, and, in some cases, are used for different occasions. Two other materials which aren't actually stones, coral and pearl, are also popular.

Questions You Might Ask A Jeweler

Do you have a specialty or a specific kind of jewelry that you make?
What kind of special training did you receive?
What item makes up the majority of your business?
What is the majority of your clientele like?
Are there any particular problems that you face repeatedly?
What trait is most important in a jeweler?
Why did you choose to be a jeweler?

What is the most popular precious gem?

What determines whether a gem is precious or semiprecious?

What are the different types of gem cuts?

How are stones polished?

What determines the price of a stone?

What's the difference between a carat and a karat?

Activities

- Make a chart of the precious and semiprecious items listed above, including several characteristics.
- Design a piece of jewelry for yourself or a family member.
- Research the different types of gem cuts and make a list of diagrams.

Vocabulary

- ❏ Wardrobe
- ❏ Precious
- ❏ Jewelry

- ❏ Accessory
- ❏ Semiprecious

- ❏ Malleable
- ❏ Carat

Tips From Barnabas

When God created the earth, he also created gems, silver and gold. These precious stones and substances have always been valued by man. They are beautiful in themselves, but they have other properties that make them valuable. God used them in different ways throughout the Bible. In Exodus 28:15-28, the gold and gems of the high priest's breastplate are described; Isaiah 61:10 describes a bride adorning herself with jewels, as an example of how God clothes us with the garments of salvation; and in Revelation 21:19-21 the foundation of different gems of the New Jerusalem is described.

Paul uses precious stones, metals, wood, hay, and straw to represent the building materials of a Christian's life. When judgment comes, it will be by fire, and only gold, silver, and precious stones will survive the test. What remains after the fire will be the basis of the Christian's reward. Read about it in I Corinthians 5:10-15.

Think about what you have learned about jewels and precious metals and consider this question: What materials best represent the kind of building materials you are using to build on the foundation of Jesus Christ?

JOURNALISM

NAME OF PLACE TO VISIT _____

NAME OF CONTACT PERSON _____

PHONE # _____

ADDRESS _____

_____

BEST TIME TO VISIT _____

Background

We all depend on journalism, in some form or other, to stay informed. In fact, people have counted on it to bring them the news for a long time. The first sign of journalism, as we would understand it, was in ancient Rome. Brief *newsletters* were often distributed, telling about the acts of the emperor or the progress of the armies. These newsletters were possible because of the relatively high *literacy* rate among *citizens*. With the fall of the Roman Empire, Europe was plunged into the Dark Ages. Journalism declined with the literacy rate. People depended on wandering *troubadours* to bring them news from other places. This news was completely *oral* and had to be memorized by the troubadours. Literacy and written journalism boomed again with the invention of the *printing press* in the middle of the sixteenth century. *Pamphlets* and newsletters abounded in Europe and, later, in America. These played an important part in stirring up the feelings that led to the American Revolution. The first magazines were started in the early eighteenth century and quickly caught on as another form of passing information.

Photo journalism, which started in the middle of the nineteenth century, foreshadowed the methods of news gathering and conveying we have today. In the twentieth century, we have achieved a new level of communication, and this is reflected in modern journalism. This has been done mostly through the invention of the radio and the television. No longer are we simply told about the news; now we are shown it. We can hear and see the actual events and make judgments for ourselves. This has brought a new freedom of ideas. Today there is so much information available, that we have a wide variety of journalistic forms from which to choose. Newspapers, magazines, radio, and television all have different advantages, disadvantages, and styles. We can choose the way we want the news. The point is, however, not which form we choose, but that we do choose to stay informed.

Questions You Might Ask A Journalist

What form of journalism do you use?

What is its advantage over other forms?

What training did you receive?

How long have you been doing what you are currently doing?

Is there a particular quality which is required of a person working in your media?

Is there a particular problem you face repeatedly?

Why did you choose journalism?

How closely do you work with your editor?

Do you read other journalist's work?

What is the responsibility of journalism in society?

How do you draw the line between protecting individual privacy and publishing news?

Activities

- Make a chart of the characteristics of several of the journalistic media named here. What are their differences?
- Keep a log of news items reported by one of the media listed here.
- Write a paper on "biased journalism," explaining how the different media use their coverage of news events to encourage a particular opinion. In what ways can you "slant" a story, in order to influence your reader/viewer/listener?
- Take an event in your family or neighborhood and write your own news story about it. If you have access to a camera, take photographs to include with your story.
- Do a research paper on the effect of pamphlets and journalism in leading up to the American Revolution.

Vocabulary

- ❏ Newsletter
- ❏ Troubadour
- ❏ Pamphlet

- ❏ Literacy
- ❏ Oral Tradition
- ❏ Photo Journalism

- ❏ Citizen
- ❏ Printing Press

Tips From Barnabas

The gospels and the book of Acts have many of the attributes of journalism. They contain history or news, as seen by eye witnesses or investigators who interviewed eye witnesses (such as Mark who is thought to have obtained much of his information from Peter).

Select one of the following Scriptural events and, using the references given, rewrite it as a newspaper or magazine article.

The Birth of Christ: Luke 2:1-39, Matthew 2:1-23
The Baptism of Jesus: Matthew 3:13-17, Mark 1:9-11, Luke 3:21-22
The Paralytic Healed: Matthew 9:2-8, Mark 2:2-12, Luke 5:18-26
The Crucifixion: Matthew 27, Mark 15, Luke 23, John 19
The Resurrection: Matthew 28, Mark 16, Luke 24, John 20-21

In good journalism, truth is very important, including reporting the facts accurately. Discuss with your family what being a Christian journalist would be like. You may want to subscribe to "**World**" magazine, which covers the news from a Christian perspective, as they say it, "to help lay Christians apply the Bible to their understanding of and response to everyday current events." Write: **World**, Box 2330, Asheville, NC 28802. Subscription rates are $18.00 per year.

LAUNDRY

Background

NAME OF PLACE TO VISIT _____

NAME OF CONTACT PERSON _____

PHONE # _____

ADDRESS _____

_____

BEST TIME TO VISIT _____

Some people never have to think about laundry; they have theirs done for them. Other people take responsibility early for their own clothes, as well as for those of others. Whichever is the case, it is important to have clean clothes. Not only do we feel better about ourselves, but, if we look good, other people will also think better of us and treat us better.

Most homes are equipped with a washing machine and a dryer. This makes the washing of most everyday clothes very convenient. Many apartments, however, do not have individual washers and dryers. If anything, apartment complexes are likely to have communal washers and dryers, which cost a small amount of money to use. People who do not have access to communal machines usually go to coin-operated laundries. These laundry businesses often have ten or so of each machine and usually cost more money than the communal apartment machines. There are also professional laundries and *dry cleaners*. Certain *fabrics* must be washed in special ways, some without the use of water. In the case of these fabrics, the owners have to take the articles of clothing to one of the laundry businesses and have them cleaned by trained professionals with special machines.

Questions You Might Ask A Laundry Employee

What is dry cleaning?
What special machines or techniques do you use?
What kind of special training have you received?
How long have you worked in a laundry?
Why did you choose to work in a laundry?
Are there any special problems you have to deal with in your job?
What special traits are required in a person who works in a laundry?
What ways do you have to remove stains?
What fabrics need to be dry cleaned?
Do you refund someone's money if you can't get his clothes clean?

Activities

• Write a paper on the special techniques used in a laundry.
• Research and write a paper on which fabrics cannot be washed in water and why.
• Research and write a paper on how people did laundry before the invention of washers and dryers, and how people without these conveniences do it now.

- Help do your own laundry with your parents' help. Learn how to sort fabrics by color and type of fabric, and what temperature of water, type of cycle, and load size each group of fabrics needs.
- Get a book on stain removal and make a chart of how to get the major stains out; e.g. grease, heavy dirt, etc.

Vocabulary

❑ Laundry
❑ Press

❑ Dry Clean
❑ Cycle

❑ Fabric
❑ Starch

Tips From Barnabas

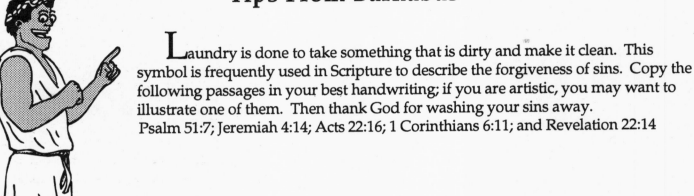

Laundry is done to take something that is dirty and make it clean. This symbol is frequently used in Scripture to describe the forgiveness of sins. Copy the following passages in your best handwriting; if you are artistic, you may want to illustrate one of them. Then thank God for washing your sins away.
Psalm 51:7; Jeremiah 4:14; Acts 22:16; 1 Corinthians 6:11; and Revelation 22:14

LAWYER

Background

NAME OF PLACE TO VISIT _____

NAME OF CONTACT PERSON _____

PHONE # _____

ADDRESS _____

_____

BEST TIME TO VISIT _____

A lawyer's job is very important. A lawyer is part of the system that makes sure laws are obeyed and the guilty punished. After receiving an *undergraduate degree*, which may not specifically prepare a person for a career in *law*, a person wishing to become a lawyer must then go through three or four years of law school. In law school, a person will learn what law is, how it works, and important legal cases which show what is right and what isn't. Our legal system is based on *precedent*. This means that, given the same circumstances, a *court* of law should come to the same conclusion and give the same punishment for two different cases. That is why it is important for a lawyer to know the history of trials in this country. He can then show the court what the court should do in the present case. Another important ability that lawyers learn in school is how to construct and argue a case. It is vital, if you want someone to agree with you, to show him facts in the right order and give good reasons for believing a certain way. This is what lawyers must learn to do. After they are finished with law school, they must pass the *Bar exam*. The *Bar* is the organization of lawyers in any state. By passing the exam, the lawyer proves that he or she is able to do his or her job well. A lawyer must pass the Bar exam in each state he or she will work in.

Because there are so many laws and so many types of laws, lawyers usually must specialize. The type of lawyer we most often think of is the *criminal lawyer*. Criminal lawyers *try* murderers, thieves, and other people who commit major crimes, but they make up only a small portion of the total number of lawyers. Businesses, insurance companies, and banks employ many lawyers to deal with monetary and contract laws. There are other lawyers who deal only with accidents, *wills*, or *divorces*. Some lawyers deal with *civil cases*, which include small thefts (*petty larceny*) or *suits* between two parties who are *suing* each other. Other lawyers don't go to trial at all but simply *advise* their *clients* on what action to take. Lawyers in other countries also specialize and have strictly demarcated duties and responsibilities. Because there are so many laws and so much to know about trying a case, specialization is important because it ensures the best representation of *rights*.

Questions You Might Ask A Lawyer

Where did you attend law school?

What was the most important thing you learned in law school?

What is involved in the Bar exam?

What is your specialty in law?

What did you do to acquire that specialty?

Do you work for a firm?

What are your major duties?

What takes up most of your day?

What kind of win/loss record do you have?

Why did you choose the type of law that you did?

Activities

• Write a report on a particular branch of law.

• Write a report on a particularly important case.

• If you are older and perhaps interested in pursuing law as a career, and your parents agree, you may want to read the book *One L* by Scott Turlow. This is a book about his first year at Harvard Law School. Write a report on the pressures that come with this type of study.

• Do some research and pick a trial case. Then, using your friends and family, "try" the case. You may want to try several different types of cases, sometimes being the judge, the prosecuting attorney, or the defending attorney.

• Research what would be a good pre-law course of study at a college or university.

• If you have a law school in your area, try to attend one of the classes.

• Go to court for a day and write down your observations.

Vocabulary

☐ Undergraduate Degree

☐ Court

☐ Specialize

☐ Advise

☐ Divorce

☐ Sue

☐ Law

☐ Bar Exam

☐ Criminal Lawyer

☐ Trial

☐ Civil Case

☐ Rights

☐ Precedent

☐ State Bar

☐ Client

☐ Will

☐ Suit

☐ Petty Larceny

Tips From Barnabas

A lawyer argues the case of one man or woman before a judge. While not guilty of the crime himself, he sets about to defend one who may or may not be guilty. Christ is described as our advocate with the Father, in 1 John 2:1-2. Even though we are guilty of sin, Christ pleads our case that we may be forgiven because of His sacrifice for us, that the blood He shed paid the price for all of our sins. Even in the Old Testament, Job realized he had an advocate (lawyer) with the Father. Read Job 16:19-21.

Role play a scene with your family, with someone acting as God (the judge), Christ (the lawyer), the sinner (the defendant), and Satan (the prosecuting attorney.)

If your parents agree, you may want to read or watch a video presentation of the story of *The Devil and Daniel Webster*.

LIBRARY

Background

NAME OF PLACE TO VISIT _____

NAME OF CONTACT PERSON _____

PHONE # _____

ADDRESS _____

_____

BEST TIME TO VISIT _____

A library can be a large and confusing place if you are not familiar with it or do not know how to use it efficiently. The first thing to find out about the library you are using is which cataloging system it employs. There are two major systems: The *Dewey Decimal system* and the *Library of Congress* system. The Dewey decimal system assigns three-digit numbers to the major subject groups; sub groups are given further numbers after a decimal. The Library of Congress, on the other hand, uses letters to divide the subject groups and then numbers to designate sub groups. College and university libraries usually use the Library of Congress system, while public libraries are most often on the Dewey decimal system.

Once you know what cataloging system your library uses, you can become familiar with those areas of the library which contain books on the subjects that interest you. Browsing through these areas and finding all kinds of interesting books can be a lot of fun. If you want a specific book, however, the easiest and most efficient way to find it is by using the *card catalog*. The card catalog is a list of all the books a library has. Information about each book is written on a separate card and arranged alphabetically. There are two different groups of cards in the card catalog; two different ways to find the book you want. If you already know the name of the author or the title, or both, you can look in the *"author/ title"* section of the catalog. Here, authors and titles are intermixed alphabetically. Since both the author's name and the book title have separate cards, there will be two cards for every book in this section. If you do not know the author's name or the title of the book, but you do know what the book is about, you can use the "subject" section of the card catalog. Here you will also find the subjects listed in alphabetical order. You can also use the subject section of the catalog if you are not looking for a specific book but want to see all the books a library has on a particular subject.

Since you are going to use the card catalog sometimes, it is a good idea to become familiar with the way information is arranged on the cards. Across the top of the card will be written the author's name (last name first), the title, or the subject, depending on what section you are looking in. Remember that if a title starts with an article ("a," "an," and "the" are articles), then you must look up that title by the second word. Under the author on an author card or the subject on a subject card will be the title of the book. On a title card, the author's name comes second. Third, the publisher's name, the publication date, and maybe a description of the contents will be listed. Even if the contents of the book are not given on the card, a list of subjects will be. The subject listing will help you decide if the book on the card is what you are looking for. (The exception to this rule is works of fiction, which do not have contents or subject listings or any catalog number but are instead filed by the author's last name in its own section.) Finally, in the upper left-hand corner of the card will be the catalog number. You may want to write this number down and take it with you. You now have to find the section of the library that holds the books with numbers similar to the one you want. Books on the shelves of the library will be in numerical order. If you are allowed free access to all the books in a library, then the library is said to have *"open stacks."* If some or all of the bookshelves are closed to the public, then the library has *"closed stacks."* If the library you are using has closed stacks, you must ask a librarian to bring you the books you want to look at.

The last step to a visit to the library is checking out the books you want to take home. There are several different ways that your library might check out books. Some libraries use a computer system to keep track of all the books that are checked out and who has them. Other libraries use cards and write the borrower's name and the date the book is due on the card. Almost all libraries, however, have cards, and you will probably have to get a library card if you want to use the library. You must remember to check out any books you want before leaving the library, and you must remember to bring the books you have borrowed back on time in case someone else wants to use them.

Questions You Might Ask A Librarian

What cataloging system do you use?
Where is the card catalog?
Do you have open or closed stacks?
How long have you been a librarian?
What kind of check-out system do you have?
Do I need a card to use this library?
For how long can books be out?
How many new books do you acquire each year?
What does your acquisition list look like?
How many copies of a book do you usually buy?
Do you repair books yourself?
How much trouble do you have with people not returning books?

Activities

• With a librarian's help, make a chart of the major subject divisions of the cataloging system used by your library.
• Look up your name in the author catalog and see if there is an author with your name.
• Learn the different areas in the library and where different subjects are kept.
• If you need a card to use the library, get one.
• Arrange your books in some type of order similar to the Dewey Decimal system.

Vocabulary

❏ Dewey Decimal System   ❏ Library of Congress System   ❏ Card Catalog
❏ Author/Title Card   ❏ Subject Card   ❏ Open Stacks
❏ Closed Stacks

Tips From Barnabas

One of the most famous Biblical libraries was located in Alexandria, Egypt. It was here that the Septuagent (Greek) version of the Old Testament was translated. Use a Bible handbook or dictionary and write a report on this famous library and the important role the Septuagent played in the development of Scripture.

The books of the Bible are divided into different groups: Pentateuch, Historical, Poetry, Prophets, Gospels, New Testament History, Epistles, and Apocalypse. Make lists showing which books go into which categories.

LOCKSMITH

NAME OF PLACE TO VISIT _____

NAME OF CONTACT PERSON _____

PHONE # _____

ADDRESS _____

_____

BEST TIME TO VISIT _____

Background

There are locks all around us. It seems that everything is locked these days: cars, bicycles, houses, suitcases, briefcases. Anything that we want to keep or which holds things we want to keep must be locked. This is much more common in cities than in small towns. The pressure and difficulty of city life seems to make the possibility of theft or robbery greater. Of course, this isn't only a modern problem; there have always been thieves. This is witnessed by the fact that the oldest known lock was made about four thousand years ago in the Middle East. Locks were widespread by the time of the Egyptian Empire. People have always felt the need to protect their property. Today, to help us do that, we have *locksmiths*.

A locksmith is a person who is well-versed in the workings of all kinds of locks. While there are only two major types (combination and keyed), there is a wide variety of inner workings among locks. He or she must be familiar with the different keys, and which keys go with which locks. One of the most common jobs done by locksmiths is the duplicating of keys; this means grinding in the particular pattern of ridges from one key into a *blank* key. Locksmiths are also often called upon to open locks whose keys have been misplaced. To facilitate this need, mobile locksmiths often have vans with which they can go to the scene with all their equipment. Locksmiths are also needed when building a new house.

Questions You Might Ask A Locksmith

What is the most common problem that you solve?
Do you often go to the scene of a problem?
What training did you receive to become a locksmith?
How long have you been doing what you're doing?
What kind of special equipment do you have?
Could you pick a lock?
Is there such a thing as an unpickable lock?

Activities

• Make a chart of different kinds of locks with their characteristics.
• Write a report on a famous robbery which involved lock picking.
• Research the best types of locks for use in building a new house.

Vocabulary

☐ Locksmith   ☐ Combination   ☐ Blank
☐ Pick

Tips From Barnabas

There are different keys mentioned in Scripture:

Key to Treasure (Isaiah 33:6-NIV)
Keys of the Kingdom of Heaven (Matthew 16:19)
Keys of Death and Hades (Revelation 1:18)
Key to the Abyss (Revelation 20:1)

Keys can be used to open doors. You have to have the right key in order to open a lock. Write a short paragraph on one of the following themes:
1. How does the fear of the Lord open the door to a "rich store of salvation and wisdom and knowledge."
2. How does the Gospel open the door to the kingdom of heaven?
3. How has Christ locked the door of death and hell and given us eternal life?

NAME OF PLACE TO VISIT _____

NAME OF CONTACT PERSON _____

PHONE # _____

ADDRESS _____

_____

BEST TIME TO VISIT _____

MEDICAL CLINIC

Background

There are many different types of medical clinics. Some are general health centers, and others are specialty clinics. Look in the Yellow Pages of your telephone book under "clinics," and you'll see how many different types there are. It would be best if you could go to more than one type and observe the differences between them. If this isn't possible, then try to go to a general medical clinic.

You'll find many different professionals working together in a clinic. Doctors, *nurse practitioners*, registered nurses, pharmacists, secretaries, lab and *x-ray technicians*, and other clerical staff are some of the people you may find in a larger clinic. Correspondingly, there may be many different areas in the clinic. Exam rooms, pharmacy, appointment desk, lab, x-ray room, and medical records room are some of the places you may get to see.

Exam Rooms: Notice what instruments are kept in the room. Is there a blood pressure gauge, *syringes*, tongue depressors, a *thermometer*? What else is in the room? Ask the nurse to explain what the different instruments are used for.

Pharmacy: Ask the pharmacist what his/her different duties are. What sort of education is needed to become a pharmacist? Ask him or her if he or she has a copy of a *Physicians Desk Reference* (PDR) and if he or she will show you how to use it.

Appointment Desk: Is the person who makes appointments a clerical worker or a nurse? Does he or she have other duties, such as collecting patients' fees and billing insurance companies? What questions does he or she ask of patients when making appointments for them?

Lab: What are the duties of the lab technician (tech)? What are the different types of tests that are done in the lab? What equipment is kept there?

X-ray Room: What are all of the duties of the x-ray tech? How many x-rays do they take in a day? What is the most common type of x-ray? What precautions does the x-ray tech take? Why are these precautions necessary?

Medical Records: What information is put into a patient's chart? How is the information ordered? How are the charts filed? How are they labeled? How does a patient go about getting information from his chart? What are the state and federal laws concerning the disclosing of information from a medical chart?

Questions You Might Ask A Medical Practitioner

How do the duties of a registered nurse, a nurse practitioner, and a doctor differ?

How many patients does the clinic see each day?

How many patients does each doctor see?

If you are visiting a general medical clinic, how often do they refer people to specialists?

If you are visiting a specialty clinic, how often are patients referred to them?

What does an RN do to prepare a patient for a doctor or nurse practitioner?

What information is asked of each patient?

What is the difference between *systolic* and *diastolic* pressure?

Is testing done in the clinic, or are the specimens sent to an outside lab?

Why do some patients need to be seen by a doctor instead of a nurse practitioner?

What happens if someone fails to keep an appointment?

Activities

- Have the nurse show you how to take someone's blood pressure and then try it on your own.
- Listen to your heart with a stethoscope.
- Have the nurse or doctor show you how to examine someone's throat, eyes, and ears.
- Have someone show you what a SOAP form is. Fill out this form for yourself and the members of your family.

Vocabulary

☐ Systolic

☐ Syringe

☐ Technician

☐ Diastolic

☐ Physicians Desk Reference

☐ X-ray

☐ Thermometer

☐ Practitioner

Tips From Barnabas

Jesus healed many people during his earthly ministry. Read the account of ten lepers that were healed, Luke 17:11-19. When people help us to get well, we should express our appreciation. Only one of the ten lepers returned to thank Jesus. Why do you think the other nine didn't? Why do you think the Samaritan did?

Do you think the people in the clinic get thanked for their work? If you have a family doctor or naturopath, write him a letter thanking him for taking care of your family. In your prayers, remember to thank God for your health.

If you would like to read a comparison of the church, God's spiritual body, and the way the human body functions, read <u>Fearfully and Wonderfully Made</u> by Philip Yancey and Dr. Bryant.

NAME OF PLACE TO VISIT _____

NAME OF CONTACT PERSON _____

PHONE # _____

ADDRESS _____

_____

BEST TIME TO VISIT _____

MIDWIFE

Background

A midwife is a person who aids a woman in the act of childbirth. Midwifery is one of the oldest professions, as it is mentioned in some of the earliest books in the Old Testament. Midwifery is a highly challenging and complex job, which requires much knowledge and patience. Any number of problems can crop up during childbirth, and the midwife must know exactly what to do and act quickly to protect the health of both the mother and the child. Though the midwife enjoyed a fairly honored place in society in ancient times, the midwife's knowledge was lost during the Middle Ages in the West. This fact was reflected in the sky-rocketing rate of infant mortality, as well as deaths among child-bearing women. A mother in the Middle Ages could not hope for much help if there was a problem in childbirth. It was not until the seventeenth century that wide-spread training of midwives began again and the nineteenth century that training standards were regulated by law. Today there are many training programs for midwives in the United States and Europe. Many more people in the last few decades have turned to midwives and *home births* as alternatives to giving birth in a hospital.

Questions You Might Ask A Midwife

What kind of training did you receive?

Are you a nurse as well?

Why would parents choose to call you instead of going to a hospital?

What is the difference between your help and the help in a hospital?

Why did you choose midwifery?

Are there any problems which you are commonly forced to deal with?

How long have you been a midwife?

What do you do if there is a problem during delivery?

What type of prenatal and postnatal care do you provide?

Are you licensed by the state?

Activities

• Write a report on childbirth.

• Talk to a mother who has given birth at home and used a midwife. Write a report on what the experience was like, both for the mother and the rest of the family.

• Make up a chart listing the advantages and disadvantage of home birth.

Vocabulary

❐ Home Birth   ❐ Midwife   ❐ Childbirth

Tips From Barnabas

Midwives help to bring new life into the world. Birth is a joyous and critical point for every parent. A midwife has studied and become experienced in how to help mothers deliver their children. Read Exodus 1:15-21 and see how the Hebrew midwives served God, and were rewarded by Him. Many spiritual truths are illustrated in the Bible by reference to childbirth. Look up the following verses and explain the truth childbirth is illustrating:

VERSE	TRUTH
John 1:13	
John 3:4	
John 16:21	
Romans 9:11	
Galatians 4:29	
I Peter 1:23	
I John 4:7	

NAME OF PLACE TO VISIT _____

NAME OF CONTACT PERSON _____

PHONE # _____

ADDRESS _____

_____

BEST TIME TO VISIT _____

MONEY

Background

Money is nothing more than whatever people agree to accept in exchange for goods and services. At various times and places, money has been many different things. Shells, beads, metals, stones, and animal hides have all been used as money.

Today most *currency*, including that of the United States, consists of coins and paper money. Different countries have different types of currency. In the United States today, our coins are the penny, nickel, dime, quarter, and half dollar. At one time, one dollar coins were also made. The paper money currently being printed includes the one dollar, five dollar, ten dollar, twenty dollar, fifty dollar, and one hundred dollar bills. At one time two dollar, five hundred dollar, one thousand dollar, five thousand dollar, ten thousand dollar, and one hundred thousand dollar bills were also circulated.

All of our coins are made of *alloys*. Pennies are a zinc and copper mixture. Nickels are a copper and nickel alloy. Dimes, quarters, and half dollars have a copper center surrounded by an alloy of copper and nickel.

All coins in circulation come from *mints* in Denver and Philadelphia. You can tell where a coin was minted by looking at the front of the coin near the date. If there is a small "D" imprinted, it was minted in Denver. If there is no mark, it was minted in Philadelphia.

Paper money is issued by *Federal Reserve Banks*. There are twelve of them in the country, each in a different city. If you look at the front of any bill, you will see a round seal to the left of the central portrait. This seal identifies which federal reserve bank issued the bill. Each bank has its own seal with its own letter in the center of that seal to help identify it.

On the face of each coin and each bill is the portrait of a famous American. Most of them are Presidents, but not all. The portraits are as follows: penny, Abraham Lincoln; nickel, Thomas Jefferson; dime, Franklin D. Roosevelt; quarter, George Washington; half-dollar, John F. Kennedy; (now defunct) dollar, Susan B. Anthony; paper one dollar, George Washington; (now defunct) two dollar, Thomas Jefferson; five dollar, Abraham Lincoln; ten dollar, Alexander Hamilton; twenty dollar, Andrew Jackson; fifty dollar, Ulysses S. Grant; one hundred dollar, Benjamin Franklin.

On the backs of most of the currency, are pictures of various historic buildings such as the Lincoln Memorial or the White House. The exceptions to this are the dime which has a torch and oak branches, the quarter and dollar coins which both have eagles, the half-dollar which has the Presidential seal, the dollar bill which has the Great Seal, and the two-dollar bill which has a picture of the signing of the Declaration of Independence.

Whenever you travel to a different country, you must exchange your U.S. currency for whatever that country's national currency is. How much foreign currency you get for your U.S. dollars depends on the *exchange rate*. If, for instance, you were going to France, and the exchange rate for dollars to francs was 1 to 6.5, then you would get six and one-half francs for every dollar you had.

Money from other countries, especially paper money, is fun to look at if you get a chance. It is often much more colorful than ours, and sometimes different bills are different sizes. There are some similarities though. Many different nations include portraits of famous people from their countries on the front of their bills. Usually the bill's *denomination* is written out both in script and in Arabic numerals.

Money has no *intrinsic value*. It is simply valuable because everyone has decided that it should be. The value of money fluctuates, depending upon the state of the economy. If prices go up, the value of money goes down because you can buy less with it. This is known as inflation.

Questions You Might Ask An Economist

You will probably not be able to go to a mint or talk to an economist. However, if you have the opportunity, I would recommend that you take it. Otherwise, you'll have to find the answers to these questions on your own, or possibly from an officer of a major bank in your area, or a coin collector.

When did paper money first begin to be used in the United States?

Why is paper money more efficient as a means of trade than gold, beads, or just using coins?

What do the economists mean when they say something like, "Today the dollar is worth only 35 cents"?

How does foreign demand for U.S. goods affect how much foreign currency you can get for a U.S. dollar?

Where are the twelve Federal Reserve Banks, and what are their respective "letters"?

Why do you think the bills above $100.00 were pulled out of circulation?

Why is there talk of discontinuing manufacturing the penny?

What happens to old and worn-out bills?

How much money is printed each year in the United States?

Which nation's currency is strongest at the present time?

Activities

- Memorize whose portrait is on each currently circulated U.S. coin and bill.
- Learn the names of the official currency used in the major countries of the world.
- Pretend that you have $75.00 that you want to change to a foreign currency. Find out the current exchange rates and figure out how much you would get for each of the following countries: Great Britain, Canada, Mexico, Germany, France, Italy, India, Russia, Kenya, Egypt, Japan, and Brazil.
- Research and write a paper on the history of money in the world, including the various objects which have been used.

Vocabulary

- ❏ Currency
- ❏ Federal Reserve Bank
- ❏ Intrinsic Value
- ❏ Alloy
- ❏ Exchange Rate
- ❏ Mint
- ❏ Denomination

Tips From Barnabas

Money, money, money . . . Sometimes you would think that it is money that makes the world go around. Scripture has a lot to say about the relationship between man and his use of money. Some people use a lot of time worrying about it, working for it, or even loving it. Money is a medium of exchange. You use it to get something you need or want. There are many books written about Christians and their use of money. With your family you could study Ron Blue's <u>Master Your Money</u> or <u>Money Matters for Parents and Their Kids</u> or attend one of Larry Burkett's workshops.

The following Scriptures talk about the wrong attitude toward money. Look up each one and write a list of things you should or should not do in relation to money.

Ecclesiastes 5:10; Matthew 6:24; 1 Timothy 3:3, 6:10; 2 Timothy 3:2; Hebrews 13:5, and 1 Peter 5:2.

MUSICIAN/ ORCHESTRA

Background

NAME OF PLACE TO VISIT _____

NAME OF CONTACT PERSON _____

PHONE # _____

ADDRESS _____

_____

BEST TIME TO VISIT _____

The world of music is one of the most competitive of career fields. Performers start young and practice hours every day. Composers are often forced to work in other fields as well (often as music teachers), in order to make enough money to live on.

But whether or not you want a career in music, it's important to learn as much as you can about music and to learn to play an instrument if at all possible.

There are five basic classes of instruments: string, woodwind, brass, percussion, and keyboard. Recently some people have added a sixth class: electronic.

Usually the recommended instrument to begin on is the piano. There are various reasons for this. It is extremely versatile. Large amounts of music, from early exercises to concertos, have been written for the piano. In learning to play the piano, the student learns the two most common *clefs* (*treble* and *bass*). It is also the easiest instrument on which to learn about *chords, harmony*, and *accompaniment*.

All of the instruments are important in an orchestra, however. When a composer writes a piece for a specific instrument, a group of different instruments, or a whole orchestra, he or she takes into account the *range* and *timbre* of each instrument. For instance, a trumpet cannot be used to express the same thing that a viola can, and vice versa.

When people say "classical music," they usually are referring to a whole spectrum of music, only part of which is truly classical music. "Classical" music can be divided into four periods: the *Baroque Period*, the *Classical Period*, the *Romantic Period*, and the *Modern Period*. Each period has its own composers and its own particular types of compositions.

Sometimes musicians focus on one period of music or even on one composer and become an expert on it. More often, however, a musician will play all periods of music with relatively equal skill.

Playing in an orchestra is only one of many jobs that a musician might hold. He may play in small groups, like a duet, trio, or chamber group. He may also be mainly a soloist, a commercial player, or a teacher.

Although not all musicians and composers go to college, most do. The most well-known music college in the U.S. is Julliard's in New York City. Classes usually concentrate on composing, performance, theory, or music history.

Questions You Might Ask A Musician

Who influenced you most in your study of music? If it isn't a name that you recognize, ask him or her to tell you about them.

Why did you choose the instrument that you play?

Can you play instruments other than your primary one?

How many hours a day do you practice?

What made you want to become a musician?

Do you have separate instruments for practice and performance?

How did you become interested in music?

What is your favorite composer or piece? Why?

Do you prefer performing solo or with an accompaniment?

Activities

- Go to a performance of your local symphony, orchestra, or chamber group. Notice the distribution of instruments in an orchestra. Why are there so many more strings than brass or woodwinds? Why are the instruments positioned the way they are? Look at the arrangement of the instruments, the audience seating, and the design of the building. Why are these factors significant?

- Find recordings of pieces that belong to each musical period. We recommend: a Bach *Fugue* for Baroque, a Mozart *Concerto* or Beethoven *Symphony* for the Classical Period, and any piece by Liszt for the Romantic Period. The Romantic period has very diverse composers, and it would be better to listen to others as well, if possible. The modern period is so diverse that it is impossible to suggest one composer as being typical of the period. Some of the more famous are DeBussy, Stravinsky, Schoenberg, Bartok, and Copeland. If you can read music, try to obtain the scores to go along with the pieces and follow along as you listen. Just from listening to the recommended pieces, what are some of the differences between musical periods?

- If you have already taken music classes and know some theory, study a Bach chorale. (You'll need both a recording and a score of the music.) Then either take a short Biblical text or write your own *libretto* and write a chorale for it in the same style as Bach.

- Imagine you are a classical musician and write a schedule for what a typical day would be like.

- Write a report on the new field of electronic music.

- Write a report on the life of a famous composer.

Vocabulary

- ❏ Treble Clef
- ❏ Harmony
- ❏ Timbre
- ❏ Romantic
- ❏ Concerto

- ❏ Bass Clef
- ❏ Accompaniment
- ❏ Baroque
- ❏ Modern
- ❏ Symphony

- ❏ Chord
- ❏ Range
- ❏ Classical
- ❏ Fugue
- ❏ Libretto

Tips From Barnabas

Music has often played an important part in worshipping God.

Read Psalm 150 and make a list of all the instruments that are mentioned. Decide which type of instrument each one was: brass, percussion or keyboard.

Talk to you parents about how you think music praises God.

It is interesting to note that music has a definite effect on our spirit. Read how David used music to minister to Saul when an evil spirit troubled him in I Samuel 16:14-23.

NAME OF PLACE TO VISIT _____

NAME OF CONTACT PERSON _____

PHONE # _____

ADDRESS _____

_____

BEST TIME TO VISIT _____

PHOTOGRAPHY

Background

There are several different kinds of photography, and there are different ways to tell them apart. Some pictures are snap shots, and some are still life, but films and video tapes are also photography. Some photography is *photojournalism* and so is concerned with documenting news stories or news worthy people. Photojournalism, then, can have national or international importance; on the other end of the scale would be vacation pictures that would probably only interest the friends and family of the vacationers. Another kind of picture taking could be called art photography. While there are many reasons for calling a particular photograph a work of art, some of them might be that the elements in the photograph are placed in a pleasing arrangement, or that there are elements in the photograph that are usually not seen together, or perhaps the picture was taken at an odd angle in order to show a familiar object in an unfamiliar way. These are only a few of the things that might distinguish a photograph as a work of art. Another aspect which is used to classify photographs is whether they are black and white or color.

The key to differentiating between types of photography is determining the purpose. You can't always tell what type of photo it is by its subject. If the purpose of a photograph is to show that you visited the Grand Canyon this summer, then it is probably a vacation picture. But if the purpose is to show the increasing amount of litter in the Grand Canyon, then it is more likely to be a news photo. On the other hand, if the picture is meant to show the interesting ways clouds gather over the Grand Canyon, then the photograph may be a work of art. That is an example of how three different kinds of photographs can be taken of the same thing. It is the purpose of the photograph that makes the difference.

Have you ever wondered how a camera works? A camera is like a mechanical blinking eye, except the blink works in reverse. The camera's "eye" is almost always closed, and blinks open when a picture is taken. A camera depends on the amount of light there is to take the picture; there can't be too much or too little light, or the picture won't be clear. The amount of light that comes into the camera can be controlled a little by the length of time the "eye" stays open when the picture is taken, and how wide the eye opens when it does. On some cameras the controls are automatic, while on others, the photographer sets the *shutter speed* and *aperture* by hand. Another control that is almost always adjusted by hand is focus. Focus, however, has nothing to do with how much light is let into the camera, but, instead, the distance from the camera to what is being photographed.

There are several kinds of cameras, but they all work on essentially the same shutter-speed/aperture principle. Among the elements which distinguish various types of cameras are the size of film which they take; whether they are movie cameras, video-tape cameras, or still cameras; and whether they have manual or automatic controls for shutter-speed, aperture, and focus. Of all these types of cameras, it is most common that a 35mm still camera will have manual controls. Most other cameras are automatic. And although it may not seem obvious, movie and video-tape cameras work the same way as a still camera. A movie is really just a series of many separate still pictures. Instead of "blinking" only once, like a still camera, a movie camera "blinks" many times a second. When the series of movie shots is shown quickly in close succession, the elements of the pictures seem to move. The more pictures that are taken per second, the more smoothly the elements move.

Of course, a camera by itself cannot take a picture. A camera is a mechanism for efficiently *exposing* a piece of photographic *film* to light. Photographic film is coated with silver nitrate, which reacts with light. The finer, or smaller, the grains of silver nitrate, the clearer the picture will appear. Turning an exposed piece of film into a photographic print is a two-stage process. In the first stage, called *developing*, the exposed film is soaked in a chemical which rinses away the less exposed parts of silver nitrate. This means that the parts of the picture that were lighter retain more silver nitrate than the darker parts. A developed piece of film is called a *negative* because of the way the dark and light parts of the picture get switched. The second stage is called *printing*. In this stage light is shown through the negative onto a piece of photographic paper with the use of an *enlarger*. The picture can be made larger or smaller at this point by moving the negative closer or farther away from the photographic paper. The paper works in the same way as film. The areas which are exposed to greater light will be darker. At this point, the effects of the negative are re-reversed. Silver nitrate was rinsed from the darker areas of the subject of the photograph so now more light gets through these areas. The areas that were light in the subject still have a thick layer of silver nitrate on the negative. No light can get through these areas to the photographic paper, and so those areas will stay light in the print. In black and white printing, the photographic paper only needs to be exposed once, but in color printing, the paper must be exposed three times, each time printing either red, green or blue. The combination of these three colors produces a full color print.

Questions

What type of pictures do you take?
What do you like to photograph the most?
Do you use black and white or color film?
What does the term ASA mean?
Is photography a profession or a hobby for you?
Do you do your own developing? Why or why not?
What type of camera do you use?
What attachments and extra equipment do you use?
Is there a significant difference between different brands of cameras?
Who is your favorite photographer?

Activities

- If you have access to a camera, try taking different kinds of photographs. Try both black and white and color film.
- If you do not have access to a camera, check-out books on different kinds of photography from the library. Study the similarities and differences between the types.

- Read a book on photographic developing and printing and write a report.
- Visit a local photographer or a camera store. Find out how to get started and what to study; make a list of the equipment needed and how much it will cost.
- Choose a famous photographer, examine examples of his or her photography, and write a report about his or her particular photographic style.

Vocabulary

- ❏ Photojournalism
- ❏ Focus
- ❏ Developing
- ❏ Enlarger

- ❏ Shutter Speed
- ❏ Exposure
- ❏ Negative

- ❏ Aperture
- ❏ Film
- ❏ Print

Tips From Barnabas

The camera does operate like the human eye. The eye allows images to be "photographed" on our minds. In Matthew 6:22-23 Jesus says that the eye is the lamp of the body and if the eyes are good the whole body will be full of light. What do you think He was talking about?

In Psalms 119:37, it says to "turn my eyes away from worthless things . . . " and in Proverbs 4:25, it says to "look straight ahead." In a way, our brain records what we see much as a camera makes pictures. With your parents, make a list of things which we should not look at, and a list of positive and enriching things we should look for, for instance Jesus said to "look at the fields' because they are ripe for harvest, that is there are many people ready to be saved.

PLUMBER

Background

NAME OF PLACE TO VISIT _____

NAME OF CONTACT PERSON _____

PHONE # _____

ADDRESS _____

_____

BEST TIME TO VISIT _____

We often do not think of the things around us which make our lives the way they are today. There have been many recent advances that make our lives easier and more comfortable than they have ever been in the past. One of these modern comforts is plumbing. Plumbing brings us clean water, hot or cold, to drink or with which to wash. It also carries away wastes quickly and easily. Many of us do not think of the comforts we have until we do not have them any more. If you have ever been without working plumbing, you have probably met a plumber. A plumber is someone who is knowledgeable in the working of plumbing, and who can get the system working again if it breaks down.

One of the first problems that must be solved by a growing civilization or a city with a large population is plumbing. Not only must sufficient quantities of fresh water be brought into the city, but waste must be carried away. The Romans solved the first part of this problem very well. They constructed many thousands of miles of *aqueducts* (water bridges) to bring fresh drinking water into many of their cities. An efficient *sewage system,* as a way to get rid of waste, was not developed until the late nineteenth century. At first, waste was carried out of cities in carts or buckets. Later, open trenches were dug. The idea was that a stream of water would run through the ditch and carry the waste to a nearby river or lake. This system was very inefficient and unsanitary. Many of the major health problems in the later *Middle Ages* and the *Early Modern Period* (including the many plagues) were caused by the unsanitary nature of sewage removal. These open ditches were breeding grounds for disease.

Finally, in the late 1800's, modern sewage disposal was developed. Public health improved markedly. The materials used in modern plumbing also differ from those used before. Early plumbing had been fashioned out of lead or clay. Lead, however, is bad for the health. Therefore, new materials had to be found. Modern plumbing uses steel, aluminum, copper, and porcelain. These materials are tough and safe.

Questions You Might As A Plumber

How long have you been a plumber?
What kind of training did you receive to become a plumber?
Why did you choose to become a plumber?
Do you enjoy it?
Does plumbing take a lot of study?
What metal makes the best pipes?
What is the most common problem?

Have you ever put in a whole new plumbing system?

Where does the water for the city come from?

How is doing household plumbing different from industrial plumbing?

Activities

- Write a report on the history of plumbing.
- Research the origins of the word "plumbing."
- Write a report on the differences between sewer systems and septic tanks.

Vocabulary

☐ Aqueducts   ☐ Sewage System   ☐ Trench

☐ Middle Ages   ☐ Early Modern Period

Tips From Barnabas

There is nothing very glorious or attractive about plumbing, but it has an important purpose. Without plumbing we would not have water in our homes or sewage disposal from our houses.

Water has always been a key element in civilization. Cities grew up around good water supplies (usually lakes, rivers, springs and wells). One of the ways people insured a good water supply, even during a dry season, was to store it in cisterns. Ancient cities had elaborate plumbing to catch rain water and direct it into huge cisterns. The cisterns became the source of life during a drought.

Jeremiah uses this imagery to illustrate two evils that Israel had committed against God. What were those two evils? (Jeremiah 2:13)

Jesus uses this same imagery to witness to the woman at the well in John 4. Talk to your parents about the ways Jeremiah and Jesus use water supplies to teach truth.

NAME OF PLACE TO VISIT _____

NAME OF CONTACT PERSON _____

PHONE # _____

ADDRESS _____

_____

BEST TIME TO VISIT _____

POLICE DEPARTMENT

Background

The police are a very important part of our community. The main duty of a policeman is to protect us from dangerous people and dangerous situations. Sometimes their protection is *preventative,* and they can stop people who are doing dangerous things before they hurt anyone. Sometimes the police can only go to work after something has happened, in order to keep it from happening again.

The policemen we most often see are *patrolmen*. Their primary responsibility is to patrol traffic in police cars, or *squad cars*. These officers must know all about the traffic laws for the city and state they work for. They are mostly interested in preventative protection. They stop people who are going too fast, or who are breaking some other safety law. If a policeman catches a *law* breaker and stops him, the law breaker is given a *ticket*, which states that he either must go to *court* or pay a *fine*. When there is a more serious problem, the patrolman depends on the *police dispatcher*. The dispatcher takes calls from the public and then sends the nearest patrolmen to the scene of the crime. This way the police can start helping very soon after a problem occurs.

Sometimes *crimes* are committed when a policeman is not around. If it is a serious crime, like *homicide*, a different kind of policeman is assigned to the case. The type of policeman who investigates this type of crime is called a *detective*. The detective will search the scene of the crime for clues. He or she also investigates any weapons found. He interviews anyone who was near the crime scene to find out what they heard or saw. There are several specialists in the police department who can help the detective discover all there is to know about a crime. The fingerprint expert is able to search for fingerprints. When he finds them he dusts them lightly with special powder and takes pictures of them. He can then compare them to the fingerprint file at the police department to see if he can discover whose they are. The *police photographer* not only takes pictures of criminals for the police files, he also takes pictures at the crime scene. These pictures can later be studied over and over again in order to find clues. Finally, a *ballistics* expert studies guns and can tell if a particular bullet has come from a particular gun.

Besides the experts listed above, there are other special police officers who are called in under particular circumstances. The *bomb squad* are specially trained to find and diffuse bombs. Even though members of the bomb squad wear heavy padding, they are still in great danger and must be very careful and brave. Another special branch of the police force is the *canine corps*. In the canine corps, officers are trained to work closely with dogs and to take advantage of the dogs' special abilities to track people, weapons, or drugs. The things that all these various specialists have in common is their concern for people and their strong sense of duty to protect the community.

Questions You Might Ask A Police Officer

How long have you been a police officer?
Why did you become a police officer?
What special training do you have?
Do you like being a police officer?
What is your rank?
What does your particular job entail?
What dangerous situations have you been in?
What are the crime statistics in this area?
What was your most memorable or important arrest?
How large is the police force?

Activities

• Visit your local police station and ask several different officers the above questions.
• Read further on crime-solving techniques.
• Keep a log from your local newspaper on crime in your area.
• Find out the qualifications for becoming a policeman.

Vocabulary

❏ Preventative
❏ Law
❏ Court
❏ Homicide
❏ Police Photographer
❏ Canine Corps

❏ Patrolman
❏ Ticket
❏ Police Dispatcher
❏ Detective
❏ Ballistics

❏ Squad Car
❏ Fine
❏ Crime
❏ Fingerprint
❏ Bomb Squad

Tips From Barnabas

The police are our friends. They should be respected, not feared, unless we break the law. Police men and women are hired by local governments to enforce laws that the governments make.

In the same way, God has always considered it very important to obey the laws that He gives. In the Old Testament, He gave the Ten Commandments (see Deuteronomy 30:15-16). In the New Testament, Jesus commanded us to love God wholeheartedly and our neighbors as ourselves (see Mark 12:30-31), and He gave us the Holy Spirit to enable us to keep His commands. Sometimes, when we disobey His law, our parents or elders in our churches correct us or discipline us, much like a policeman would do. Read the following Scriptures and discuss with your parents how and why they discipline you when you break the rules. (1 Timothy 4:13-16; Deuteronomy 4:9, 31:13; Proverbs 22:6; and Hebrews 12:7-11.)

POST OFFICE

Background

NAME OF PLACE TO VISIT _____

NAME OF CONTACT PERSON _____

PHONE # _____

ADDRESS _____

_____

BEST TIME TO VISIT _____

Have you ever wondered what happens to a letter after you mail it? You can find out from your mailman or your local post office. Be sure that you don't go to the post office during a holiday season, especially Christmas, as the workers will be much too busy to answer all of your questions.

When you write a letter, you put two addresses on it, your own and the address of the person to whom you're sending the letter. Your address is called the return address because it tells the post office where to return the letter to if it cannot be delivered.

There are many different reasons that a letter might not be deliverable. There might not be enough postage on it; or the person to whom the letter was sent may have moved and not left a forwarding address, or you may have just made a small mistake in the address.

Let's examine an address, bit by bit. The first line is the name of the person who will receive the letter. The second line is the street address or post office box number. This tells the postman exactly which house or apartment the letter goes to. The next line has the city and state. This tells the post office where to send the letter after you've mailed it.

The final part of an address is the zip code. This stands for 'Zone Improvement Plan.' The first number stands for one of ten large geographical regions of the United States, the second and third stand for a metropolitan area, and the last two stand for a delivery area within the metropolitan region.

There are different classes of mail. Almost all letters are mailed first class. Magazines and other periodicals are sent second class. Advertisements are sent third class. Books and other packages are usually sent fourth class.

First class mail is more expensive than the other classes, but it gets delivered more quickly as well. Sometimes people will send packages first class because they want them to arrive in time for Christmas or birthdays.

Look at the stamps on a letter you've received, and you'll notice there are marks across them. These marks are a *postmark* or *cancellation*. The stamps have been marked so they cannot be used again. Stamps are cancelled wherever the letter was first processed. This is usually close to where it was mailed from. The postmark will show the city and state where the stamps were cancelled and the date on which they were marked.

The United States Postal Service (USPS) moves millions of pieces of mail every day. To enable them to handle that much, they employ hundreds of thousands of workers and use many different pieces of mechanical and computerized equipment.

If you were to follow a letter that you mailed, you would see something like the following: first, it would be picked up from the mailbox, along with everything else mailed there, by a mail carrier. Next, it is taken to the nearest Section A1 Center. It will be postmarked here and then sorted by zip code.

After being sorted, your letter will be dispatched by truck. Where it goes from here depends on where it is addressed to. If it is going somewhere within about 150 miles of the sectional center, then it will be driven to another sectional center or post office. If it's going further, then it will be taken to an airport. The USPS pays airlines to transport mail. Most domestic commercial flights have mail on board.

Next, your letter will arrive at the sectional center nearest its destination. It is sorted by the last two digits of its zip code and then sent to the appropriate post office. Here it will be sorted again so it can be given to the appropriate mail carrier. Each carrier will then arrange all of his mail, rubber-banding together several pieces of mail that go to the same address, and will order it according to the stops on his route.

Finally, your letter will be delivered. If your letter is undeliverable, the mail carrier will bring it back to the post office after completing his route, along with any money collected for *COD's* (Collect On Delivery), postage due mail, and any letters he has picked up that need to be delivered. There are a lot of steps that a letter must take to get from one place to another, but the post office is able to do it efficiently and quickly.

Questions You Might Ask A Postmaster

What sorts of things cannot be mailed?
What is the proper way to wrap a package that is to be mailed?
Who decides what is pictured on stamps?
Where are stamps printed?
How can someone get a job with the post office?
How many people work at this post office?
How would you describe a typical day?
What determines how long it takes a piece of mail to be delivered?
What is bulk mail?
How large is the average mail route?

Activities

• Do a research paper on Benjamin Franklin and his development of the postal service, along with the government's authority to operate such a service.
• Do a comparison report on the cheapest and fastest ways of communicating.
• Start a stamp collection.
• Write a report on the Pony Express.

Vocabulary

❏ Postmark
❏ Bulk
❏ Postage
❏ Computerized

❏ Cancellation
❏ Rural Route
❏ USPS
❏ Sort

❏ COD
❏ Philatelist
❏ ZIP

Tips From Barnabas

How exciting to get a letter! Did you know that most of the New Testament is letters? Count how many of the books of the New Testament are letters from Paul (ask your parents if you need help.)

If we didn't have the post office, it would be very difficult to communicate in writing across long distances. You would just have to wait for someone going to where you wanted to send your letter, like Paul did (Read Ephesians 6:21-22; also Colossians 4:16).

Now read the "letter" of Philemon and answer the following questions.

1) To whom was the letter written?
2) Who wrote the letter?
3) Who was Onesimus?
4) What did Paul want Philemon to do?

Now, take advantage of your post office and send a letter encouraging someone who lives far away.

NAME OF PLACE TO VISIT _____

NAME OF CONTACT PERSON _____

PHONE # _____

ADDRESS _____

_____

BEST TIME TO VISIT _____

POUND/ PET STORE

Background

A pet is a wonderful thing. Anyone who has been fortunate enough to have a pet knows this. A pet can be a good companion. It is sometimes a playmate and sometimes a friend who will comfort you when you don't feel well. A pet is also a great *responsibility*. It is another life which depends on its owner for a large percentage of the things it needs in order to live. The owner must provide food, shelter, and care when the pet is sick or injured and try to keep the pet as safe as possible. The responsibilities are great with pet ownership, but so are the rewards.

There are several places to get a pet. Some are better than others. The *pound*, or *animal shelter*, is the best place to get a pet. This is because the animals are in some danger at the pound. The danger does not come from the attendants, of course. Animals in the pound are ones which have been lost or *abandoned*. Since there is limited space there, they can only afford to keep the animals for a short amount of time. When their time is up, the animals must be destroyed. Because of this, when you choose a pet from the animal shelter, you are saving it. The most common animals to find in the pound are dogs, although sometimes they also have cats. The next best place to find a pet is in the ads in the newspaper. Often, if these pets don't find new homes, they end up in the pound.

The largest selection of pets can be found in a pet store. You will probably not find birds, and you certainly won't find any fish, at the animal shelter. These are both very popular varieties of pets, and many varieties of each will be found at the pet store. Rabbits and mice are other furry pets which you will only find advertised in the paper or in a pet store. Some people even keep insects, lizards, or snakes. These are also available at the store. Fortunately, animals are not the only things you will find for sale at a store. Anything you might need for your pet is there, too. Food, containers, dishes, toys, and grooming materials are all for sale. The place you choose to go to find your pet depends on what you want. If you are just looking for a companion, you should go to the animal shelter. If you are looking for something specific, however, you will probably need to look in the newspaper or at a pet store.

Questions You Might Ask An Animal Shelter Worker

Pound/Animal Shelter

How long do you keep the animals once they get here?

What kind of animals are most commonly here?

How do animals get here?

What percentage of your animals are selected as pets?

What kinds of animals do you take here?

<u>Pet Store</u>
What are the most popular pets?
What is the most *exotic* pet you have had for sale?
Do most people come to buy or to browse?
What do you do with animals that aren't sold?
What are some of the best pets for young children?
From where do you get your animals?

Activities

• Research a favorite kind of pet.
• Research an exotic pet.
• Research your local animal shelter and write a report on it.

Vocabulary

❏ Animal Shelter   ❏ Exotic   ❏ Pound
❏ Responsibility   ❏ Domesticated   ❏ Abandon

Tips From Barnabas

Man frequently uses stories about animals to tell a deeper truth. Ask your mother and father if you can read some of Aesop's fables or C.S. Lewis', <u>The Lion, The Witch and The Wardrobe</u>.

Then using an animal that you especially like, write your own story about it. Make sure your story has a *moral*.

Read the story in Numbers 22:21-35 about Balaam and his donkey.

NAME OF PLACE TO VISIT _____

NAME OF CONTACT PERSON _____

PHONE # _____

ADDRESS _____

_____

BEST TIME TO VISIT _____

PRISON/JAIL

Background

A prison is an institution for the confinement of people who have been convicted of serious crimes, such as murder, assault or major theft. Prisons are usually run on the state or federal level. Prisons and jails are not exactly the same thing. Jails are usually run on the local or city level. They are also usually for lesser crimes, like minor theft or disturbing the peace. Jails may also be used to hold alleged criminals until their trial. It is only since the last century that confinement in prison has been used as a punishment. Imprisonment replaced *corporal punishment*, *execution*, and *banishment* as the major forms of punishment.

Prisons were used from the twelfth century in England as a place to hold criminals until their cases could be tried. Gradually, this confinement came to be understood as punishment in its own right. Throughout the seventeenth, eighteenth, and nineteenth centuries various theories of imprisonment were tried. These theories ranged from using the prison as strictly a punishment to using the time that the prisoner was interred as a time for *rehabilitation*. Early English prisons did not separate prisoners by sex or seriousness of *crime*. The emphasis was on strict military discipline and hard labor. The desire was to rehabilitate the prisoners, but the conditions were so bad that it was surely a severe punishment. The next method that was tried was *solitary confinement*. It was hoped that solitude would lead to *penitence*, which would lead to rehabilitation. This idea caught on much more strongly in the newly formed United States. Here prisons were constructed so that each prisoner spent time either in his or her cell or in the private yard connected to that cell, and worked on crafts, like weaving or carpentry. This was called the *"separate system."* Not everyone was in favor of the separate system. These opponents came up with a system in which prisoners were not kept strictly separated. In the other system, called the *"silent system,"* prisoners worked together during the day and were only separated at night. Complete silence was enforced at all times, however. A third system was developed in the middle of the nineteenth century called the *"mark system."* Under the mark system, prisoners did not have set *sentences*. Instead, they had to earn a certain number of points for good behavior. Each crime was assigned a certain number of points. These points could be taken away, as well, if the prisoner was involved in mischief. Today, we use elements of all three of these systems in our prisons. Solitary confinement is now used only as a special punishment, and prisoners who behave and follow all the rules of the prison are eligible for early release or *parole*.

Questions You Might Ask A Correctional Officer

What kind of an institution is this?

What kind of crimes have been committed by the criminals here?

How many correctional officers work here?

How many criminals can you house here?
Do you ever have any problems with the prisoners?
What kind of training is required of the correction officers?
How many different positions are there in this correctional institution?
How many repeat offenders are there?
What percentage of inmates will be confined again at some later date?
Are there any statistics on how successful your rehabilitation program is?

Activities

• Write a report on a particular prison in your area.
• Make a chart of crimes and the prison terms prescribed for them in your state.
• Do a research paper on modern-day prison reform.
• Contact someone involved in prison ministries and write a report on your discussion with them.

Vocabulary

❏ Corporal Punishment   ❏ Execution   ❏ Banishment
❏ Rehabilitation   ❏ Criminal   ❏ Solitary Confinement
❏ Penitence   ❏ Separate System   ❏ Silent System
❏ Mark System   ❏ Parole   ❏ Sentence

Tips From Barnabas

A prison is used to confine people—usually those who have broken the law. But sometimes the righteous are put into a prison. Look up each of the following stories and write about why the people were put in prison and how they got out.

Genesis 41   Joseph

John 14   John the Baptist

Acts 5   The Apostles

Acts 12   James

Acts 12   Peter

Acts 16   Paul & Silas

NAME OF PLACE TO VISIT _____

NAME OF CONTACT PERSON _____

PHONE # _____

ADDRESS _____

_____

BEST TIME TO VISIT _____

QUILTING

Background

Quilting is a practical art, or a craft. By definition, quilting is the stitching of two pieces of cloth together, usually with a thick, soft layer of padding in between. On the practical side, thick quilting is useful for padding and for keeping warm. The stitching keeps the padding evenly disbursed. On the other hand, this same stitching provides the opportunity for a wide range of artistic expression.

We are most familiar with the use of quilting for bed covers, but this is not its only use. Quilting has long been used for clothing, especially coats and vests, by the people of Muslim Africa, the Middle East, and the Far East, including China and India. It was also popular in Europe during the Middle Ages. Richer people could use it as padding under their armor, but for poor soldiers it was often all the protection they had. For them, it was very important that the padding was as thick as possible. By the fourteenth century, the quilting of bed covers had become a minor art form in Europe. The high point of its European popularity came between the seventeenth and nineteenth centuries.

Quilting bed covers reached its peak of popularity in the United States in the late eighteenth century. American quilts have a distinctive style. One particularly American style is *"patchwork."* The first patchwork quilts were made from necessity. People who were too poor to afford large pieces of material used scraps left over from the making of dresses or other clothes. These pieces of cloth would be *appliqued* to a large piece of white muslin or simply stitched together in a patchwork pattern. Quilting these colorful top pieces to the other parts of the quilt completed the pattern by following the design of the applique or patchwork. Even though the first patchwork quilts were made of necessity the pattern quickly became popular in the United States. There are now many standard designs of patchwork and appliqued quilts based on the patterns in which the pieces are fit together.

The actual quilting or sewing the top, bottom, and padding together is often done on a frame. The bottom, or lining, is sewn to two cloth-covered poles. The padding is then spread evenly over the bottom, and the colorful top piece is placed over the padding. The pieces are then stitched together following the pattern of the applique or the patchwork.

Questions You Might Ask A Quilter

What kind of quilting do you do most often?

From whom did you learn to quilt?

Do you use a frame to do the quilting?

How long does it take to make a quilt?

How many quilts have you made?

Did your parents or grandparents do quilting?
What are the names of different patterns?
Do you do all your quilting by hand, or do you use a machine?
Do you use all the quilts you make, or do you sell or give some away?
How do you keep your stitches even?
Do you ever use different colors for your quilting thread, or only white?

Activities

• If you can, help make a quilt with someone who knows how.
• On paper, design a pattern for a quilt.
• Come up with your own vocabulary list of quilt patterns.

Vocabulary

☐ Quilt   ☐ Stitch   ☐ Appliqued
☐ Patchwork

Tips From Barnabas

Quilts are made up of smaller pieces or blocks, that make some type of pattern when put together. God is doing the same thing with your life. "Little" events occur, which all fit into God's plan for your life.

Using a piece of graph paper or plain sheets of paper, design six or nine blocks that depict major points in your life. Then put these together with construction paper strips, like a quilt would be made.

NAME OF PLACE TO VISIT _____

NAME OF CONTACT PERSON _____

PHONE # _____

ADDRESS _____

_____

BEST TIME TO VISIT _____

REAL ESTATE BROKER

Background

A house is one of the most important, certainly one of the most expensive, purchases a family can make. A house these days can cost up to $100,000.00 or more. Of course, a family doesn't have to pay that all at once. Usually the first step is to make a *down payment* of at least 10 percent. In the case of a house costing $100,000.00, the down payment would be $10,000.00. That would leave $90,000.00 left to pay. This is usually dealt with through a *mortgage*. A mortgage is a loan from the bank that is for the full amount of the *balance*. The new owners then pay the bank, instead of the person who sold the house. This often works out well for the seller, who then has all of his or her money at once.

There are many considerations when buying a house. First, what size do you need? How many bedrooms or bathrooms? How many cars need to fit in the garage? How many floors do you need? This leads us to the next question. What style do you prefer: colonial, tudor, etc. Do you need a lawn for pets or children? What kind of neighborhood is the house in? Is it safe? Is it convenient to work, markets, or buses? Are there other children of the same age to keep company with? How is the house arranged inside? Do the rooms make sense? Can the right atmosphere be created?

It is the job of the *real estate agent* or *real estate broker* to make sure all the needs and desires of people looking for a house to buy are met. Real estate brokers usually work for firms which are sometimes nation-wide. People who wish to sell their house register the house with a real estate agency. The agency often takes pictures of the house and always learns everything there is to know about the house — focusing on the special features. People who are looking for a home to buy go to these agencies. The brokers working there try to match the descriptions of the house desired by the buyer with the house which has been registered with them. There is some quality, however, which is not contained in any description of a house, but which is essential. A house must become a home to the people who live in it. It must become a place of comfort and warmth, or the house has failed in its purpose. This is a very personal quality, and it must be judged as present or absent by each member of the family living there.

Questions You Might Ask A Realtor

What kind of houses do you have for sale?

How many houses are available?

What are most of your customers like?

Can you provide homes outside of this area?

How do you match house buyers to the right houses?

Do you personally deal with only a small area of town?

Why did you choose real estate as a career?

Do you like what you do?
What training did you have for this job?
How long have you worked in real estate?
Is there a conflict of interest by representing both the buyer and the seller?
Has the market increased?
Is there a building boom?
How are you paid?

Activities

- Make a list of requirements of a house for your family. Compare it to where you live now.
- Design a house you would like to live in.
- Collect several house ads from the local paper for the type of house in which you would be interested and learn to decipher the terminology used (i.e. "quaint" may really mean old, "cozy" may mean small), and also the different abbreviations used in house ads.
- Call a title company and do some research on the paperwork involved in buying a house.
- Contact City Hall and find out the legal requirements for buying a house.

Vocabulary

❏ Down Payment   ❏ Mortgage   ❏ Balance
❏ Broker   ❏ Agent   ❏ Escrow
❏ Earnest Money

Tips From Barnabas

Land is a precious commodity. As we grow in stewardship of all the things God gives us, land is often one of the largest and most expensive possessions we will ever own.

In Numbers 33:54, and 36:7, God distributed the land of Israel to the different clans and established certain laws of inheritance.

Read the parable of the talents (Matthew 25:14-30) and what the godly woman of Proverbs 31:16 did, and make a list of things you could do if you were in charge of a piece of land, in order to be a good steward of it.

RESTAURANT

NAME OF PLACE TO VISIT _____

NAME OF CONTACT PERSON _____

PHONE # _____

ADDRESS _____

_____

BEST TIME TO VISIT _____

Background

Almost all of us have been to some kind of restaurant at some time. It may have been a celebration of someone's birthday or just for fun. It may have been a very fancy restaurant or one that was not so fancy, or anywhere in between. Whatever kind of restaurant it was, it had a lot in common with every other restaurant. If you have been to more than one, you may have noticed some similarities. We will examine those similarities here.

Of course, all restaurants have at least one cook. In fast-food restaurants, these cooks don't usually receive much training though some of them do acquire a lot of experience. In other, fancier restaurants, cooks are required to have more training. In the most impressive restaurants, the cooks often have degrees in cooking and should be called chefs. Often in large restaurants or ones with diverse *menus*, there will be specialty chefs. These cooks will cook specific dishes or use particular ingredients, like beef or pasta.

Most customers, however, never see the cooks who are working in the restaurant. There are other personnel that the public more often deals with. Most restaurants will have a cashier. Fast-food restaurants do not have waiters or waitresses, but almost all others do. In many restaurants, the cashier has double duty and works as a *host* or *hostess* as well. The host or hostess keeps track of *reservations*, sees which tables are in use, and tries to balance the customers among the waiters and waitresses. In other, fancier restaurants, the hosting is done by a separate employee, sometimes called the *maitre d'*.

The last kind of employee needed in a restaurant is the cleaning staff. Dishwashing is one of the most important jobs in the restaurant. It is vital that the dishes and silverware that we use are clean so that disease is not spread. Other cleaning personnel include table cleaners and floor moppers. You can see that the similarities among restaurants are sometimes as important as the differences.

Questions You Might Ask A Restaurant Worker

What kind of work do you do?

What training have you received?

How much experience have you gotten?

What do you like about your job?

Why did you choose to work in a restaurant?

Why did you decide to open a restaurant?

Why did you choose this location?

How do you decide what to serve?

How do you decide how much to charge?

What things must you be careful of in order to satisfy the health department?

Activities

- Research the types of restaurants in your area and make a chart of their similarities and differences.
- Make a chart of employees in different types of restaurants.
- Collect several menus from different restaurants and compare prices.

Vocabulary

☐ Host   ☐ Hostess   ☐ Reservation
☐ Maitre d'   ☐ Menu

Tips From Barnabas

A good restaurant needs more than just good food—it needs good service. If you've ever eaten in several different restaurants, you may have noticed that in some the service was very fast, friendly, and polite. Others may have been very poor—it took a long time to get your food, the waiter or waitress was rude, etc. A good waiter or waitress has learned to be a good servant, which is what a good Christian needs to be. Look up the following qualities of service—both good and bad—and decide how well you would do:

Half-hearted   Humble

Immediate   Indifferent

Joyful   Obedient

Reluctant   Timely

Willing

NAME OF PLACE TO VISIT _____

NAME OF CONTACT PERSON _____

PHONE # _____

ADDRESS _____

_____

BEST TIME TO VISIT _____

SCIENCE MUSEUM

Background

Whether or not you are interested in science, a science museum can be a great place to explore and learn.

There are two basic types of science museums. One is a science and technology museum and the other is natural history museum. Some science museums cover both of these aspects.

A science and technology museum will display exhibits depicting physics, modern technology (such as the space program, modern communication, and transportation), some chemistry, medicine, and the history of science and technology. These museums often have "hands-on" things to do, where you push buttons or pull levers, which start processes that demonstrate scientific properties. The largest museum of this type in the world is the Museum of Science and Industry in Chicago.

Natural history museums usually concentrate on *biology, archaeology, botany, geology,* and *paleontology.* They will often have examples of *taxidermy,* fossils, rocks and minerals, and plants. Usually there will be an exhibit on *ecology* and on the theory of evolution. Sometimes there will also be exhibits on medicine, on primitive or foreign cultures, and on the history of science.

Because of the variety of exhibits in these kinds of museums, they must be set up in many different ways. Some need to be easily accessible because they were designed as "hands-on" exhibits. Others have to be protected by glass because they are valuable or delicate. Others are merely roped-off as an indication that they should not be touched. The person whose job it is to decide all of this is the *curator.* The curator often does research about new *acquisitions* as well.

Many of the exhibits in science and technology museums are sponsored by corporations. The rest are developed by the museum's staff. Sometimes scientific items of historical interest are donated to the museum.

When new acquisitions arrive, the *registrar* records them with a written description, a photograph, and a numbering system. After it is decided how they should be displayed, the *designers* build any necessary cases and furniture. *Preparators* then create the backdrop for the display and any cards or plaques that will be placed by the display to explain it.

Science museums also hire many people with scientific degrees. There will often be *anthropologists,* archaeologists, botanists, *chemists, biologists, physicists,* geologists, *zoologists,* or *engineers* working in the museum, depending on which of the sciences the museum emphasizes.

When going through the museum, try to take your time and read all of the things posted by the exhibits. You'll learn a lot more that way than by just looking at the objects or only trying the hands-on demonstrations. Some museums have staff who give science demonstrations at certain times of the day. Stop and watch one for awhile. Some museums also have complete or partially guided tours.

Most science museums also have an education department. Sometimes they offer classes for both children and adults. Occasionally, they will offer lectures on particular subjects.

Questions You Might Ask A Museum Worker

What are the different ways that the museum acquires its objects?

How does the staff think of new exhibits?

What scientific fields does the museum concentrate on?

Which of the exhibits are permanent, and which are temporary?

How long does a temporary exhibit usually last?

Where does the museum get its funding from?

Does the museum employ volunteers?

What happens to objects that are not on display?

Is the collection insured? How?

Do you have a library which is accessible to the public?

Is there some exhibit or area of study for which the museum is particularly known?

Activities

• Choose a subject in the field of science that particularly interests you. Create an exhibit that demonstrates your subject. The exhibit could be an actual model of something, working or non-working, a chemical experiment, a collection, or a series of charts and graphs. Try to make it both interesting and informative.

• Research and write a report on the history of museums.

• Write a report on a particular science museum.

Vocabulary

❏ Archeology
❏ Curator
❏ Paleontology
❏ Designers
❏ Preparator
❏ Physics

❏ Geology
❏ Registrar
❏ Ecology
❏ Zoology
❏ Biology
❏ Engineer

❏ Taxidermy
❏ Botany
❏ Acquisition
❏ Anthropology
❏ Chemistry

Tips From Barnabas

The largest science museum in the world—is the world! Everywhere you look, you see displays of every type of science imaginable. You can study astronomy, geology, biology, chemistry, any science you can think of, just by walking out your back door. All of these things, life itself, point to the fact that God is. Read Romans 1:20. This teaches us that we can understand the invisible aspects of God's nature by studying the visible aspects of the world He created. The more you learn about science, the more you learn about God. How very full of life He is, how orderly and consistent, and yet how beautiful and majestic. From the tiniest cell to the largest ocean, they can each tell us something about God's character. Choose one of your favorite parts of nature and write a brief paper or poem showing how it reflects God's nature. If you need some help, try reading Psalm 8 or Psalm 36.

SCIENTIST

Background

NAME OF PLACE TO VISIT _____

NAME OF CONTACT PERSON _____

PHONE # _____

ADDRESS _____

_____

BEST TIME TO VISIT _____

Scientific pursuits are widely diverse. Areas of study range from how objects fall, to why plants are green; from how mountains are formed, to how the body uses food; from how chemicals combine, to why planes fly. Despite this great variety in the outcomes of scientific work, scientists in fact do have a lot in common, namely, their methods. Scientific discovery requires painstaking observation and meticulous record keeping. Scientists have developed a many-staged process, called the *scientific method*, for keeping careful track of experimental results. The first step is to state an *hypothesis*. An hypothesis is a possible reason behind the way things work; in a way, it is the scientist's guess. The next step is to do the *experiments*. These experiments must be done very carefully, and all the results must be written down. The experiments are a way to test whether the scientist's guess was accurate. After the experimentation is complete, the results are compared against the hypothesis. The hypothesis can now be modified to be brought closer to the way things actually work. The scientific method is now re-applied to the new hypothesis. The series of experimentation and modification is repeated until the scientist is satisfied that his or her hypothesis accurately reflects the reality of what is being examined.

Physics: Science as a whole can be imagined as a pyramid. The most basic science (a science which deals with the smallest, simplest, most fundamental parts of the physical world) would be the base. Other sciences would be built on this base and would increase in the complexity of the parts of the physical world as they got higher. *Physics* is the base of that pyramid. It is a combination of *math* and *observations* of the actions of objects in the physical world. Math, in fact, is sometimes seen as the most basic science, since the things it studies are not even physical, but only numbers. Physicists observe the most basic occurrences around us. Light, and the way light works, is one of the subjects of physics. Physicists have told us the importance of the speed of light and why we can't go faster than light. *Lasers* are also a product of the study of light. A field related to the study of light is *optics*, or how we see. Everything from a pair of glasses to an observatory telescope is possible because of optics. Physicists also study the reasons for, and the manner in which, things fall. The examination of *gravity* has brought us not only an understanding of why the planets *orbit* the sun, but how we can make objects orbit the earth. With this knowledge of *trajectories*, we have launched orbiting satellites and put men on the moon. There are many more fields based on observation of the world around us, like *meteorology*, *geology*, *astronomy*, and the study of *energy*. Can you think of any more?

The other part of physics is the study of the small objects known to science: *protons*, *neutrons*, and *electrons*, which make up atoms. An *atom* is so small that it cannot be seen even through a powerful *microscope* but through many years of experimentation scientists have gotten an idea of what they must look like. It is believed that an atom is shaped like the *solar system*; the protons and neutrons gather together at the center and the electrons orbit them. There are only about one hundred kinds of atoms, and each of them is made of the same kind of protons, neutrons, and electrons. Because atoms can't be broken down into anything but protons, neutrons, and electrons, they are called *elements*. Physicists have arranged the elements by weight and shape on the *periodic table*. Everything in the physical world is either one of these 103 elements or a combination of elements. The reason there is so much diversity in the world is because combinations of elements are often completely different from the elements themselves. An example is water. Water is a *molecule* of two atoms of hydrogen and one atom of oxygen. Here the liquid water is made from two kinds of gasses. This shows how different a mixture can be from the things that were mixed.

Chemistry: The next step up our pyramid is *chemistry*. Chemistry examines the ways that atoms and molecules combine with each other and the reasons behind these combinations. A chemist is concerned with the various properties of different combinations. Chemistry takes the simple atoms and molecules of physics and creates large, complex *chemicals* which have specific, desirable properties. There is a nearly endless list of everyday contacts we have with the products of chemistry. From the fertilizer in the field making crops larger and more plentiful, to the packaging and preservation of the food in the store, to the very act of cooking, we could not eat the way we do without chemistry. Our personal environment would also be a lot more drab. Dyes for clothes and paints for houses are products of chemistry. Without chemistry, we would have neither the ink in this book or the glue holding it together. Even paper is created through chemistry. Even if it were possible to escape man's use of chemistry, we can never escape nature's use of it. The decay of dead plants into rich *humus* to feed living ones is only one example of this fact.

Biology: The top of our pyramid is *biology* and its related life sciences. Biology studies the ways chemical properties work together in large living systems. Partly because of the wide variety of life forms and partly because of the complexity of the field, there are many subfields and related areas of study with individual emphases. *Botany* is the study of plants, how they grow, how they eat, and what separates them from each other and from animals. *Photosynthesis* is an important part of this study. *Zoology* is not the study of zoos, but of animals. Of course, there are many branches and specialties within zoology. *Entomology*, the study of insects, and *mammalogy*, the study of mammals, are only two examples of subfields of zoology. Finally, there are all the fields related to human biology. *Anatomy*, *physiology*, and *endocrinology* are a few examples of the many fields concerned with the workings of human biology. All this variety is part of the reason for putting biology at the top of the pyramid. The rest of the reason is the complexity of the systems that biologists study. Living organisms are extremely complex. Addressing questions about how chemical interaction produces such great diversities of life or even trying to define life itself, puts biology firmly at the top of the scientific pyramid.

Questions You Might Ask A Scientist

What field of scientific study do you specialize in?

Do you do much research?

What education or training have you had?

How do you use the scientific method?

Why is it important that scientific experiments can be replicated?

How do you keep up with recent scientific theories and discoveries?

What does a scientist do after he feels he or she has made a new scientific discovery?

What kind of equipment do you use in your research?

How long does an experiment take?

Where does most of your funding for research come from?

Activities

- Do further reading on one of the scientific fields mentioned here or one of your own interests and write a report.
- Develop a hypothesis and design an experiment concerning a question you have about the natural world around you.
- Examine the periodic table and learn what the elements are and why they are arranged the way they are.
- Expand the list given here of scientific fields based on observation of the natural world.
- Make a list of everyday objects which are made possible by chemistry.
- Investigate the reasons why certain chemicals can combine and others can't, and write a report.
- Be sure you know the difference between a molecule and a compound.
- Investigate the biological definition of life and write a report.
- Investigate the difference between plant life and animal life and write a report.

Vocabulary

- ❏ Scientific Method
- ❏ Laboratory
- ❏ Math
- ❏ Gravity
- ❏ Meteorology
- ❏ Energy
- ❏ Solar System
- ❏ Electrons
- ❏ Compound
- ❏ Biology
- ❏ Zoology

- ❏ Hypothesis
- ❏ Physics
- ❏ Laser
- ❏ Orbit
- ❏ Astronomy
- ❏ Microscope
- ❏ Protons
- ❏ Periodic Table
- ❏ Chemistry
- ❏ Botany
- ❏ Entomology
- ❏ Anatomy
- ❏ Endocrinology
- ❏ Humus

- ❏ Experiment
- ❏ Observation
- ❏ Optics
- ❏ Trajectory
- ❏ Geology
- ❏ Atom
- ❏ Neutrons
- ❏ Molecule
- ❏ Chemical
- ❏ Photosynthesis
- ❏ Mammalogy
- ❏ Physiology
- ❏ Element

Tips From Barnabas

One of the great debates of this century has been evolution versus creation. In Hebrews 11:3 and in Genesis 1, we are told that the universe was formed at God's command. The scientist tries to explain "how" the universe came about. There are Christian "scientists" who use the scientific method to explain how God created the heavens and the earth. Two of these men are Dr. Henry Morris of Institute of Creation Research (ICR) in California and Dr. Don Chittick.

Try to find a book that explains the thinking of both sides. Truth will always stand up to the light of examination. Pretend you are a scientist on either side and try to answer questions that your parents and family ask you. Be able to give facts to support what you believe.

```
┌─────────────────────────────────────────────┐
│                                             │
│  NAME OF PLACE TO VISIT_____     │
│  NAME OF CONTACT PERSON_____     │
│  PHONE #_____      │
│  ADDRESS _____      │
│  _____      │
│  BEST TIME TO VISIT _____      │
│                                             │
└─────────────────────────────────────────────┘
```

SCUBA DIVER

Background

As the cold water (around 45 degrees) of the Puget Sound floods your suit, you're shocked at how warm you still are. As you snorkel out to 15 feet before descending, you get your first view of the ocean's floor, and you're hooked. A Dungeness crab scuttles away, the barnacled rocks have an unbelievable diversity of color, and the fish seem to accept you as part of their family. You've entered a new world with its own laws and culture, but it took a lot of preparation to get here.

Go to a dive shop, talk to a diver, watch Jacque Cousteau on PBS or a video on diving, and learn what you can about this fascinating sport.

Certification: Skin divers (divers using only snorkels for their air supply) do not require *certification*. A *scuba* (**s**elf-**c**ontained **u**nderwater **b**reathing **a**pparatus) diver must be certified by a qualified instructor before he/she is allowed to purchase or rent equipment or obtain air fills. The two main organizations which certify divers are P.A.D.I., and N.A.U.I.

Classes are offered through colleges or underwater dive shops. Classes can last anywhere from two to three days to six months. After your basic certification, you can advance to different degrees of certification all the way to instructor.

Equipment: Equipment is an important part of diving. If the diver will be in cold water, fresh or salt, he will need more equipment than the diver in *tropical* waters.

The following is a partial list of items most frequently used: Mask, *Snorkel, Fins, Air Tank, Buoyancy Compensator (BC), Regulator, Depth Gauge, Air Pressure Gauge,* Compass, *Weight Belt, Wet Suit, Dry Suit,* Hood, Gloves or Mittens, Boots, and Lights.

If you go to a dive shop or talk to a diver, ask him to show you each of the items listed. When diving in cold water, you may wear/carry between thirty and seventy pounds, so it is critical that you have been properly instructed in the use of each piece of equipment and have practiced the skills needed to keep you safe.

Skills: You will first need to be able to swim and to feel comfortable in the water. You will then learn to use a snorkel and swim with fins. Children can learn these skills, and if you are interested in becoming a diver this would be the best place to start.

You will then learn to use your regulator and air tank. Ask to be shown how to attach the regulator to the air tank and try breathing through it. You would then learn how to *clear* your regulator and also your mask if they get flooded with water. You would also learn how to "buddy breathe." Ask for someone to show you how this is done. You would also learn the different tows for helping another diver in trouble.

Work: If you are interested in diving as a job rather than just sport diving, you might consider underwater welding, nuclear diving, treasure hunting, search and rescue, harvesting roe offshore in Alaska, working for the navy, or research and development. There are many different types of work which require diving skills.

Questions You Might Ask A Scuba Diver

Why do you always need to dive with a "buddy?"
What level of certification do you have?
How many dives have you made?
Where are some of the places you have dived?
Which was the most exciting? The most dangerous?
What are some of the physical laws that affect a diver?
What are some of the hazards of diving?
What is the difference between a wet suit and a dry suit?
Are there any personality traits that are important for a good diver to have?
What got you interested in diving?
What is the most exciting part of diving for you now?

Activities

- Do some research on the physical laws that effect diving, e.g., Charles' Law, Boyle's Law, and Dalton's Law.
- Do a report on diving medicine, covering the different things that can happen to a diver, usually because he is breathing pressurized air.
- Make a list of some of the most famous dive spots and find out why each is considered so ideal (e.g. the Cayman Islands, Hawaii, Washington's San Juan Islands, the Florida Keys, Truk Lagoon, the Blue Hole in Belize, the Great Barrier Reef in Australia, and the Red Sea).

Vocabulary

❏ Certification
❏ Mask
❏ Air Tank
❏ Depth Gauge
❏ Wet Suit

❏ Scuba
❏ Fins
❏ Buoyancy Compensator
❏ Air Pressure Gauge
❏ Dry Suit

❏ Tropical
❏ Snorkel
❏ Regulator
❏ Weight Belt
❏ Clear

Tips From Barnabas

Diving equipment often reminds me of the armor of the Lord listed in Ephesians 6. Using what you've learned, make your own comparisons between spiritual qualities and a diver's equipment; i.e., the mask of God's Word helps us to see clearly.

NAME OF PLACE TO VISIT _____

NAME OF CONTACT PERSON _____

PHONE # _____

ADDRESS _____

_____

BEST TIME TO VISIT _____

SECRETARY

Background

Y ou may think of a secretary as someone who sits behind a desk typing all day. This may be part of a secretary's job, but probably not the most important part. The most important part of this job is taking care of his/her superior. There may be many different things that need to be done. There may be *correspondence* to answer, letters to be typed, *bookkeeping* to be done, papers to file, mail to be opened, reports to be filled out, and *appointments* to keep track of. In fact, a secretary is almost like a second brain for his/her boss.

There are many different levels at which secretaries work: a general typist or clerk typist, a personal secretary, or an executive secretary. Each level requires different skills and levels of *proficiency*. One secretary may be able to type at 40 *wpm*, another at 100 wpm. You may need to take *shorthand* or to be able to *transcribe* tapes. Some secretaries need to have a pleasant phone voice to deal with all the calls that an executive receives.

A good secretary, one that thinks ahead and plans for his/her boss, is worth a fortune, as any boss will tell you.

Some secretaries specialize in different fields such as medicine or law.

Skills
Some of the skills that a secretary may need are, typing, 10-Key, writing, shorthand, filing, spelling, and transcription

Questions You Might Ask A Secretary

What do you do with most of your time?

What characteristics do you think are important for a good secretary to have?

How long have you been a secretary?

Do you enjoy your work?

What is the hardest part of your job?

Did you have any special training to prepare for your job?

What machines do you use in the office?

How many people work in the same room with you?

Is the environment pleasant? If so, what makes it that way?

What would you change?

Activities

• See if you can find a Gregg shorthand book and transcribe the first couple of sentences in Tips From Barnabas.
• Ask your parents for a business letter. Retype the letter, using the same format.
• Have someone read the background section of this Secretary section out loud and type while they talk. This is what transcription would be like.

Vocabulary

❏ Appointment   ❏ Shorthand   ❏ Inventory
❏ Correspondence   ❏ Proficiency   ❏ Transcribe
❏ Bookkeeping   ❏ WPM

Tips From Barnabas

You might think of all the writers of the Scripture as secretaries for God. They took something that God wanted understood and put it down in a form that others could retain and understand.

In the Old Testament, there were many scribes. In some ways, these men were like secretaries; they copied Scripture.

Ezra was an important scribe in the Old Testament. Find a Bible dictionary and see what you can learn about him. There are letters in chapters 1, 4 , 5, and 7 of Ezra and some inventories. Try typing one of these letters.

In chapter 6, there is a memo from the King. Memos are usually used to communicate between people in the same organization and are less formal than a business letter. Try writing or typing a memo to your Mom or Dad.

In chapter 2, there is a census of people. Using an adding machine or calculator, add up the figures given. In chapter 1 there is an inventory of gold and silver dishes. Take an inventory of part of your home: the pots and pans, bedding, canned goods, or other items.

Can you see how God used secretaries to keep things orderly and help record history?

NAME OF PLACE TO VISIT _____

NAME OF CONTACT PERSON _____

PHONE # _____

ADDRESS _____

_____

BEST TIME TO VISIT _____

STATE GOVERNMENT

Background

The government of a state takes on much the same form as the federal government. When a state becomes a state, it must *ratify* a state *constitution* in a *Constitutional Convention*, just as the United States did in 1787. State constitutions are very much like the national one, so state governments are very similar to their national counterpart. All state governments are made up of three parts: the *executive*, the *legislative*, and the *judicial*. Every state but Nebraska has a *bicameral* legislature, meaning they have both a *senate* and a *house of representatives*. There are differences, however, between governing a single state and a group of states. Some of these will become apparent below.

The *governor* of a state, as its *chief executive*, takes on much the same roll as the President who is the chief executive of the entire country. Some of the governor's duties are different than the President's. For instance, the governor does not need to make foreign policy decisions. Many of the other categories of duties, however, though on a smaller scale, can be applied to the governor. As chief executive of the state, the governor's primary duty is to *enforce* the laws of the state. To help him or her do this, the governor is in charge of the state police and the state chapter of the *National Guard*. The governor is empowered to call on either of these groups when trouble arises. Second, it is the responsibility of the governor and his staff to put together the *budget* proposal and present it to the legislature. The governor tries to estimate the amount of money which will be needed to run the state for the next year. Third, the governor is responsible for appointing certain members of the executive staff, as well as the state supreme court. Fourth, the governor has certain legislative duties and ways in which he or she interacts with the legislative branch. Though the legislature itself performs the duty of changing a bill into a law, the governor's signature is required in most cases to finalize the legislature's decision. If the governor sees a need, he or she, too, can introduce a bill as a suggestion for action. Finally, the governor interacts with the judicial branch by having the power to grant *reprieves* or *paroles* to prisoners.

There are other similarities between state and federal government. Because the duties of the governor are so great, he or she must have a fairly large staff of other administrators, much like the President's cabinet. The second in command in state government is the *lieutenant governor*. Much like the Vice President, the lieutenant governor must take over running the state if something ever happens to the governor. Also, like the Vice President, the lieutenant governor is chairman of the senate. The *secretary of state* acts as record keeper for the actions of all three branches of government. The *treasurer* keeps track of all money coming into the state *treasury*. He or she is also in charge of writing the checks to pay the bills of the state. To make sure everything is done correctly, the *auditor* (in some states called the *comptroller* or the *auditor general*) must keep track and okay all the checks written by the treasurer. The *attorney general* is the chief trial lawyer for the state and represents the state in court when necessary. Finally, the *superintendent of public instruction* is in charge of keeping the schools functioning as they should. The major difference between the President's cabinet and the governor's state executives is that the state officials are elected separately and not appointed. This is not a problem when the whole staff is of a particular *political party*, but when more than one political group is represented, getting the work of the state done can be a problem.

The second branch of state government is the legislature. Much like the federal legislature, its primary duty is the passage of laws. We will see here the steps needed for an idea to become a law. Anyone can have a good idea which can be turned into a law. What must be done first is to write the idea in the correct form. An idea in this correct form is now a *bill*. This bill must be introduced to the legislature by a member of that group. When it is introduced, it is numbered and put on the *calendar* for discussion. A *lobbyist* is a person who works for a particular *special interest group* and tries to convince members of the legislature to introduce certain bills. The first step that the full legislature will take is to assign the bill to a committee. Each member of the legislature will belong to twenty or more committees. These committees are specialized groups, each of which deals with bills from a relatively narrow range of topics. The committee will study the bill, perhaps hold hearings on it, and decide on the action they will take. It will either send it back to the *floor* unchanged, change or amend it and send it back, or *pigeon-hole* it, which means not changing it or sending it back. When a bill is pigeon-holed, it is dismissed and will not progress any further on the way to becoming a law. When a bill is sent back to the floor, it is put before either the entire house of representatives or the whole senate depending on where it was introduced. All the members are then able to *debate* the bill. The bill may be agreed on as it is or it may be changed again. It may even be *tabled*, in which case it progresses no further. Once a bill is *passed* in one half of the legislature, it is sent to the other half. There it must go through all of the same steps it went through in the first half: introduction, numbering, assignment to committee, passage back to the floor, and passage by entire membership. If the bill passes through the second half of the legislature without change, then it goes on to the chief executive (the governor on the state level, the President on the national level) to be signed into *law*. If the second half of the legislature passes the bill only after making some change to it, then it must go to a special committee made up of members from both the house and the senate. This is called a conference, or compromise, committee. This committee must draft a bill that both parts of the legislature will approve. After the committee is finished, the bill is put again before the entire membership of the legislature. If it is passed, it can be sent on to the chief executive.

The last branch of the state government is the *supreme court*. Like the national Supreme Court, the state court interprets the Constitution and may rule for or against any law. The same *checks and balances* which work on the federal level, work in the state. There are a couple of important differences, however, between the two courts. First, a state supreme court has only five members, instead of nine. Second, a state court is considered a *lower court*. This means that the decision of a state court can be reversed by the federal Supreme Court. State government can be strong when the members of the executive branch can work together and the three branches of state government are in harmony.

Questions You Might Ask A Legislator

In what part of the legislature are you?
How long have you been a government official?
What was your job before you entered politics?
What is your party?
What does your party stand for?
How do you work towards the goals of your party and your constituency?

Did you have any special training for your present job?
On what committees do you serve?
Why did you go into politics?
Have you been able to do what you set out to do? How?
Do you enjoy your work? Why?
What bills have you helped pass?

Activities

• Research a member of the state legislature and make a record of what he or she has done.
• Write a report on the duties of some member of the executive branch of the government.
• Make a chart of decisions made by your state supreme court.
• Visit your state capitol and watch the legislature in action.
• Investigate the procedure to become a page in your state legislature and do so, if possible.

Vocabulary

❑ Ratify
❑ Executive
❑ Bicameral
❑ Governor
❑ National Guard
❑ Parole
❑ Treasurer
❑ Comptroller
❑ Checks and Balances

❑ Constitution
❑ Legislative
❑ Senate
❑ Chief Executive
❑ Budget
❑ Lieutenant Governor
❑ Treasury
❑ Auditor General
❑ Political Party
❑ Special Interest Group
❑ Pigeon-Hole
❑ Table
❑ Law
❑ Lower Court
❑ Superintendent of Public Instruction

❑ Constitutional Convention
❑ Judicial
❑ House of Representatives
❑ Enforce
❑ Reprieve
❑ Secretary of State
❑ Auditor
❑ Attorney General
❑ Bill Calendar
❑ Floor
❑ Debate
❑ Pass
❑ Supreme Court
❑ Lobbyist

Tips From Barnabas

Government has been ordained by God. Some governments may be good and others bad, but God is still in control. As Job says in Job 42:2, no plan of God's can be thwarted. Read Romans 13:1-7 and make a list of the things that Paul says about government. Break them down into two groups: the authority of the state and the duties of citizenship.

STOCKS

NAME OF PLACE TO VISIT _____

NAME OF CONTACT PERSON _____

PHONE # _____

ADDRESS _____

_____

BEST TIME TO VISIT _____

Background

*S*tocks are a product of a *free enterprise* economy. They are a way of letting the public share in the profits of companies. A stock represents a particular fraction of ownership of a company. Private citizens buy stocks for a price which equals the specific fraction of the worth of the company. This is an important way for companies to gain *assets* with which to expand. In return, the owner of the stock is paid a *dividend*. The dividend represents the increased value of the company. Dividends are usually paid every quarter—every three months.

There is some risk to the buying of stock. The company does not necessarily make money. The company may lose money. In this case, the value of the stock will decline. This means that the owner of the stock will not receive a dividend. Instead, money will be lost because the stock will not be able to be sold for as much as it cost to buy.

Stocks are not only sold by companies. They are also bought, sold, or traded by owners of stock. This is done at a *stock exchange*. There are stock exchanges in most major countries. There are professionals whose job it is to advise people what stocks to buy or sell and when. These people also do the actual buying and selling. They are called stock brokers. It is their job to look after the *accounts* or *portfolios* of stocks owned by their *clients* and work to increase their worth.

Questions You Might Ask A Stock Broker

Are you a member of the stock exchange?

What are the requirements for membership?

Are you in regular contact with the stock exchange?

On what facts do you base your decisions on whether to buy or sell?

What is the major problem you face in your job?

Why did you choose to be a stock broker?

What are most of your clients like?

What is a blue chip stock?

What causes stocks to change their value?

What causes a stock market crash?

What does it mean "to go public" with a stock?

Activities

- Visit a local brokerage house in your city and ask the above questions.
- Follow a few stocks for a month. Record total gains and losses.
- Research and write a report on the stock market crash of October 24, 1929.
- Write a report on the history of the stock exchange in America or Europe.

Vocabulary

❑ Stock   ❑ Free Enterprise   ❑ Asset
❑ Dividend   ❑ Stock Exchange   ❑ Accounts
❑ Portfolio   ❑ Client

Tips From Barnabas

Stocks are investments. You are buying a small portion of a company which has many owners. In order to buy stock, you must have more money than just what you need to meet your daily expenses. The more you have, the more wisdom it takes to manage it. When you have little, you need wisdom to know how to "stretch" it.

First read the Parable of the Talents in Matthew 25:14-30. This presents the idea that God demands that we responsibly use what He has given us. Now discuss with your parents whether it is wise to invest in stocks, or if there are better uses for "extra" money, such as investing in your own business or helping the poor. There is no "right" answer, but there are "right" principles for using money. If you did decide to invest, how would you decide, in terms of Christian responsibility which company you should invest in. Would you invest in a company that made weapons or chemicals used in abortions? Have your parents help you decide how to make the best choices.

TAXICAB DRIVER/ TRANSIT WORKER

Background

NAME OF PLACE TO VISIT _____

NAME OF CONTACT PERSON _____

PHONE # _____

ADDRESS _____

_____

BEST TIME TO VISIT _____

Unless someone is very rich, he or she probably has to work. This is a fact of life. It is also a fact that the majority of people are not able to work at home. Our world would stop dead if people were not able to get to their offices or the places where they work. That is why inner-city transport is so important. Most cities of any size have some system of *mass transit*. There are several different kinds of transit systems, each one meeting specific needs. It is not uncommon for larger cities to have more than one system. These systems include taxicabs, buses, trains, trolleys, and subways.

Taxis are one of the most common ways of moving people around the city. Taxis differ from most of the other systems in an important way. Taxicab companies are often privately owned, and there may be more than one company in any city in competition with the others. Because cab companies are privately owned, they are able to set their own *rates*. Most other systems, however, are run by publicly-owned companies. One of the results of this is that publicly-owned mass-transit companies cannot set their own rates. Any rate change must be agreed to by public vote. It takes a lot of experience to make a good cab driver. Not only must he or she be a good driver, he or she must know the city well enough to get from one place to another in the most efficient way. Since a cab ride is billed by the mile, a passenger will not ride with a cabby that goes in a round-about way.

All of the other forms of mass transit are usually publicly owned. This means that the company is run by officials usually appointed by the mayor or the governor, and the profits of the company go into the local or state treasury. Probably the most common form of city transport is a system of buses. Some bus systems attempt to be very complete and employ so many buses that most people live within a few blocks of a bus stop. Other cities use buses only to move large groups of workers from the outskirts of town to the downtown area. This second kind of system uses relatively few buses. With this system, people park their cars in large lots out of downtown and ride buses into town. This is to cut down on inner-city traffic. These city bus systems should not be confused with large, national bus companies whose emphasis is inter-city travel. One of the oldest forms of mass transit is the train, including subways and trolleys. These are only found in the largest or oldest American cities. Some cities use trains, usually subways, as a very comprehensive means of *commuter* transit. Others use it as a way of bringing in people from out-lying areas, sometimes even different states. Finally, we must consider ferries as a form of mass transit. In coastal areas, ferries are often used to transport large numbers of people to and from areas that are not connected by bridges.

Questions You Might Ask A Transit Worker

What kind of mass transit system do you work for?
How comprehensive is that system in this city?
Why did you choose to work in mass transit?
Are there any major problems in your job?
How long have you done what you are doing?
What special training did you receive?
What important ability is required to do well in your job?
How are you treated by the public?
How much does it cost to travel by your form of transit?
Do you have regular customers?

Activities

• Make a chart of the types of mass transit in your area with information about how complete their
   service is.
• Take a ride on each form of mass transit that is available in your city and then write a report comparing them.
• Figure out how to use mass transit in your city (any form other than taxi-cab) to get to at least ten
   different areas of interest from your house.

Vocabulary

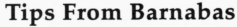

❑ Mass Transit   ❑ Commuter   ❑ Taxi
❑ Rates   ❑ Subway   ❑ Transportation

Tips From Barnabas

Promptness and attention to detail are important, no matter where you look in the mass transit field. Can you imagine what it would be like if each train conductor or bus driver decided they would make up their own schedule? Sometimes we don't realize how even our smallest actions affect other people. Every one that works in the transit field knows how important it is to keep to the schedule! The details of the trips are important too. What if your bus driver decided to stop at the next corner down, rather than the corner where the bus stop sign is? It doesn't seem very important in itself unless you are wanting to catch that particular bus, but if everyone went their own way and arrived only when they "felt like it," they could shut an entire city or country down overnight.

Write a small paper or prepare a talk showing how important promptness and attention to detail is in your own life. Remember to consider the affect your actions would have on others.

TAXIDERMY

Background

NAME OF PLACE TO VISIT _____

NAME OF CONTACT PERSON _____

PHONE # _____

ADDRESS _____

_____

BEST TIME TO VISIT _____

Taxidermy is the preservation of animals for display. Forms of taxidermy have existed for thousands of years. It originated in the practice of keeping *trophies* from the hunt. The most common of these early trophies was the skull or horns of the animal, though sometimes the hide would also be considered a trophy. Besides being distinctive to the animal, these parts were chosen because they are the easiest to preserve or the longest lasting. It takes bone a long time to deteriorate. The ancients were unable to preserve most skin, fur, feathers, or other tender parts of the animals.

The practice of preserving trophies of the hunt has survived up through modern times. Hunters today, however, are no longer limited by primitive technology to keeping only the skull or horns. Through modern methods, skin, fur, and feathers can be preserved intact for long periods of time. Interest in taxidermy blossomed in Europe during the Enlightenment, paralleling the increased interest in the study of animals and the natural world. It wasn't until the early Eighteenth Century, however, that chemicals were developed which could truly preserve skin, fur, and feathers from insects and decay. With this development came the widely increased use of taxidermy in museums. Now, animals could be shown in active, life-like poses illustrating the way in which they actually lived, and the way they would be found in the wild.

Taxidermists now usually use only the skin and skull of the animal. After it is treated, it is sewn onto a frame of wire and straw, in order to make it appear the right shape. Because the framework is held rigid by malleable wire, the figure can be positioned in almost any way. There are a wide variety of plastic and glass eyes. The taxidermist will match the kind of eye natural to the species with the type of glass eye. The animal can then be mounted on a *plaque* or base. Fish are also popular subjects for taxidermy. Modern taxidermy can help us to understand the lives of animals in the wild.

Questions You Might Ask A Taxidermist

With what do you stuff the animals?

How long does it take to complete an animal?

What is the most common animal that you do?

What has been the most unusual animal that you've done?

What determines the price you charge for an animal?

Are there different methods of taxidermy for different species, e.g., mammals, fish, reptiles, and birds?

What chemicals are used?

How long will a stuffed animal last?

What got you interested in taxidermy?

What animals are the most difficult to stuff?

Is any of your work on display somewhere?

Activities

- Visit a local *natural history* museum. Be careful to notice the ways that the animals are positioned and arranged.
- Visit a local taxidermist's shop.
- Write a report on taxidermy.
- Research an animal in your area and design a taxidermic display for a natural history museum, showing the animal in its natural environment.

Vocabulary

❒ Taxidermy   ❒ Natural History   ❒ Embalming
❒ Trophy   ❒ Plaque

Tips From Barnabas

While taxidermy is for animals, the ancient Egyptians had a method of preserving human bodies called *embalming*. We are told in Genesis 50 that Joseph was embalmed.

Even today, in some museums, we can see mummies that were embalmed thousands of years ago. Do some research to find out how much we know today of the methods used back in early Egypt.

TELEPHONE

Background

NAME OF PLACE TO VISIT _____

NAME OF CONTACT PERSON _____

PHONE # _____

ADDRESS _____

_____

BEST TIME TO VISIT _____

The change brought about by the invention of the telephone (from two Greek words: "tele," meaning far, and "phone," meaning sound) is immeasurable. It has affected the entire world, even those people who do not have a telephone. It used to take days, weeks, or even months to pass along the simplest piece of information. Now, information can be passed along instantly. The last half of this century has been called the Information Age. With inventions like the telephone, the television, and the radio, data is instantly available all over the world. With this increased speed of communication comes increased contact in general and that, in turn, creates an increased rate of invention, thought, and change. We owe the increasing pace of our modern lives to the growing ease and speed of communication.

Most of us know Alexander Graham Bell as the inventor of the telephone. Many people do not know, however, that Bell was not the only person working on developing the telephone. The basic principles of phone operation had been known for years. It was basically a race to see who could develop a practical working model first. Alexander Bell was granted a *patent* for the telephone in 1876. Mr. Bell had been working with deaf people, trying to help them hear when he came up with his design. The phones we use today are very similar to Bell's model.

The basic principle of the telephone is to transfer *sound waves* into electric current which can travel through a wire. This change occurs in the mouthpiece. There is a *diaphragm* of thin metal in the mouthpiece of a telephone. It rests against a *variable resistor*. When someone speaks into the mouthpiece, his or her breath makes the diaphragm move in and out. The fluctuations of pressure of the diaphragm on the resistor makes corresponding fluctuations of electrical current. The current fluctuates in the same pattern as the sound of the voice. This current then travels through the wire to the other end of the call. If the call is going a long distance, then the signal will have to be *amplified*. For this purpose there are *repeaters* along the line. Repeaters receive the signals on the line and send them out again with stronger signals. Sound must be recreated at the other end of the line when the signal reaches the *receiver*. The receiver is the part through which you hear the sound. When the signal reaches the receiver, it encounters an *electro-magnet*. The magnetic force of an electro-magnet depends on the amount of electricity. Remember that the variable resistor in the mouthpiece caused a variable, fluctuating amount of current. When this current reaches the electro-magnet, it causes the magnetism to fluctuate in the same way. There is a second metal diaphragm in the receiver. When the magnetism of the electro-magnet fluctuates, it makes this second diaphragm flutter and vibrate in the same way. The vibration of the diaphragm makes sound waves in the air. The two diaphragms vibrate in the same way, so the sound is the same at both ends of the call.

Running a telephone company is a very large and complex job. First, there must be telephone lines running to almost every house, and they must all be kept in good working condition. This is the job of telephone repairmen and *linemen*. Second, there are only so many calls that can go through any wire at a time. The patterns of usage—who is actually on the phone—is changing constantly. All calls, then, have to be switched through the most direct lines that aren't full. This is quite a lot like trying to juggle a million balls at a time. This job is left primarily to computers now. Finally, sometimes people have problems concerning their telephone call; for instance, they need to find out someone's telephone number, or they have special directions about how a call is to be paid for. It is *operators* who must deal with these kinds of problems. You can see that telephone companies must be very large and employ many people to be able to supply everyone who has a phone with all the services that they require.

Questions You Might Ask A Telephone Worker

How many types of jobs are there in the phone company?
What is your job?
What special training did you receive?
How long have you worked for the phone company?
Why did you choose to work for the phone company?
Do you enjoy your job?
How has your job changed in the last ten years?
What do you like best about your job?
How has the divestment of the phone company affected service?
What types of calls are sent through cables and what type through satellites?

Activities

• Schedule a tour of the phone company.
• Write a report on Alexander Graham Bell or any other early researcher in phone technology.
• Write a report on how a phone works.

Vocabulary

❏ Patent
❏ Variable Resistor
❏ Receiver
❏ Operator

❏ Sound Waves
❏ Amplify
❏ Electro-Magnet

❏ Diaphragm
❏ Repeater
❏ Lineman

Tips From Barnabas

Do you think Alexander Graham Bell knew how he would change the world when he invented the telephone? Communication has multiplied, due to his invention. While the telephone is a fairly recent invention, the art of communicating has not changed. The most important part of communication is the content. How it is communicated (e.g., letter, phone, or radio) is not nearly as important.

First, read James 3:1-12 and keep notes about what he says about the tongue. What you say on the phone or in person is very important.

Next, read the following Scriptures and make a list of things or ways we should **not** communicate (put them in your own words):

Proverbs 10:19, 11:13, 17:9, 18:8, 20:19-20; 2 Thessalonians 3:11; 1 Timothy 5:13; and 1 Peter 4:15.

Now read these Scriptures and make a list of things that we should communicate (again, putting them in your own words):

Romans 12:8; 1 Thessalonians 2:12, 4:18, 5:11; and Hebrews 3:13, 10:25.

This should give you some guidelines to think about, the next time you talk on the telephone.

NAME OF PLACE TO VISIT _____

NAME OF CONTACT PERSON_____

PHONE #_____

ADDRESS _____

_____

BEST TIME TO VISIT _____

TELEVISION

Background

Few inventions of the twentieth century have had as much impact on us as the television. Television is from two Greek words: "tele" for far, and "vision" for sight. It affects not only our way of life, but also the way we see the world. In the past, people depended on others to bring them news. Because of the fallibility of us all, these accounts were not always accurate. In ancient times, the tales of fantastic or mythical beasts were a product of miscommunication or of increased distortion caused by a story being passed from one person to another many times. Television, however, leaves little room for doubt. Whatever is being shown, can be seen with our own eyes. We can now decide more for ourselves. And television is not only used to inform but, also, to entertain. Unfortunately, it is often overused in this capacity. Television is passive entertainment and can lead to mental, as well as physical, laziness. The television is a very important invention and has a great capacity to do good things, but we must be careful not to overuse it.

Almost everyone now has a television, but few of us know how it works. We will trace a television show from its origin. A television program usually begins in a studio, but this is not necessary. All that is really necessary is the television *camera*. Inside the camera there are three special *tubes*, called *receptors*. Each of these receptors is sensitive to a particular color of light: one for blue, one for red, and one for green. The entire picture can be broken up into one of these three colors and combinations of them. The *signal* is then sent from the camera through an antenna and outward. The signal weakens after a certain distance, so it is necessary to have *repeaters*. The repeaters receive the television signal, *amplify* it, and send it out again. This way a signal can reach much farther. An alternative to sending signals through the air is the use of *cables*. In this way, the same signal is sent directly, through a wire, to every house that has a cable outlet. This is a more efficient system and makes for more accurate reception of the signal. Each television station has a separate frequency. This is so the *tuner*, or *channel changer*, on the television can tell them apart. The television signal is actually made up of two radio waves called *carrier signals*. One is for the sound, and the other is for *luminance* and *chrominance* (light and color), which are elements of the picture.

When the television signal reaches the television, either through a cable or an antenna, it excites the *cathode ray tube*. You are probably very familiar with the front of a cathode ray tube. It is the television screen. The back of a cathode ray tube is shaped like a funnel. At the small end of the tube is an *electron gun* with three special tubes, each in charge of a particular color: red, blue, or green. The electron gun fires as much of each color, and in the places, that the television signal tells it to. These three colors are recombined on the screen to make all the colors we see. You may have mixed colors before, maybe paints or egg dyes at Easter. If you have, you probably know that if you mix all the colors together, you get black. This is not true when mixing colored light. When all the colors of light are combined, they make white. To help clarify the television picture, there is a screen called a *mask* just behind the television screen. The mask is simply a solid piece of material with rows of tiny slots in it which the electrons from the electron gun pass through on their way to the television screen. These slots help to pinpoint the right color for the right area of the picture and make the picture sharper. The more rows of slots there are, the sharper the picture will be. Televisions in the United States are made with 525 lines of slots per inch. European televisions have 625 lines per inch. The electron gun shoots the picture at the screen fifty times a second. Each of the shots is actually two shots: first the gun will skip every other line, and then it will shoot the whole picture. This also helps clarity. Despite all of the ways it can be misused, television is still a powerful tool for communication and learning.

Questions You Might Ask A Television Show Producer

How many people does it take to put on a television show?
What are their specialties?
What is your job?
What special training have you received?
How long have you been working in television?
Why did you choose to work in television?
Do you like your job?
How is what you do important?
Are there certain methods or "tricks" in television broadcasting to keep the audience's attention?
What are the rules and regulations that you must follow?

Activities

• Visit a television studio set while a show is being taped.
• Write a report on how television affects our lives.
• Write a television script for a drama or a comedy.

Vocabulary

❏ Studio	❏ Camera	❏ Tubes
❏ Receptor	❏ Signal	❏ Repeater
❏ Cable	❏ Television	❏ Carrier Signal
❏ Luminance	❏ Chrominance	❏ Cathode Ray Tube
❏ Electron Gun	❏ Mask	❏ Amplify
❏ Frequency	❏ Tuner	❏ Channel Changer

Tips From Barnabas

Television has given us a much smaller world. You can see what is happening in China, the same day it happens. Not many years ago, it would have taken weeks or months for the news to have spread so rapidly. Television in itself is not evil. It is a tool. It can be used wisely or foolishly. It can be used for good or for evil. Watching television is a very passive activity. You can never "do" good by watching television. But what you watch may provoke you do to good (e.g. giving to the poor), or it may provoke you to do bad (e.g. lying).

Discuss with your parents what their attitude is towards television. If you have a television, decide why you do, and what guidelines are used for watching it. If you do not have one, discuss why you don't.

A WALK THROUGH THE CITY

Background

NAME OF PLACE TO VISIT _____

NAME OF CONTACT PERSON _____

PHONE # _____

ADDRESS _____

_____

BEST TIME TO VISIT _____

If you live in a city, you might think that you could learn nothing by just taking a walk through it. But most people really miss a lot of things because they are around them all the time and get used to them. If you don't live in a city, see if your parents will take you with them for a day in the nearest city or large town.

First of all, notice the people. Notice the various ways that other people are different from you and your parents. Imagine what different people that you see are doing today. They could be going to work, coming home from work, on their way to lunch, going to school, going shopping, or sight-seeing? There are many different things people do in the city. See if you can guess what they're doing, judging by their clothes, their manner, the time of day, and any other clues that you notice.

Go into almost any large office building and look at the directory on the main floor. You'll notice that several different kinds of businesses work in the same building. In a large office building, you might find different types of doctors, lawyers, real estate people, restaurants, government departments, insurance agencies, small shops, employment agencies, banks, engineers, and ad agencies. In office buildings individual offices are rented just like apartments are, only they cost considerably more.

There are different parts to any city. The busiest, and possibly most interesting section, is downtown. Downtown you'll find a lot of department stores and smaller stores, restaurants, business offices, banks, the city's main library, and probably most of the museums that the city has. You will also find a lot of other things, such as apartment buildings and churches, but usually the emphases of the downtown area of any city are business, commercial, and cultural.

The other part of a city that you will want to walk through is the residential district. Usually there is more than one residential district in each city. Some are nicer than others.

As you walk through, notice the differences from downtown. There will be some stores, especially grocery stores, but it won't be nearly as business oriented as downtown was. Think about the advantages and disadvantages to living both in the heart of a city and in the outskirts.

Look at the people that are in the residential area. Try to guess what they might be doing right now. Do you think that they're doing different things than the people downtown?

A lot of people live in the outskirts of a town but need to work or shop downtown. Although a lot of people drive, parking can sometimes be very difficult, especially in a large city. There are usually several mass transit forms in a city. Because a city has so many diverse aspects, there are many things that you can learn from it.

Questions You Might Ask Concerning The City

What is the population of the city?

How did it get its name?

What is/are the city's major newspaper(s)? Buy a copy of one.

What catastrophes (hurricane, fire, tornado, earthquake, blackout) has the city suffered?

What factors have contributed to making the city so large? That is, what things brought a great many people to this one area?

What forms of mass transit are there in the city? Which is the most popular?

Which is the most convenient? Which is the cheapest?

Who is the mayor of the city?

How old is the city?

Is the city the capital of the state?

What museums are in the city?

How does the city's population rank in the state?

Activities

• Get a map of the city. (They are easily purchased at most service stations or bookstores.) Find the parts that you walked through. Notice the names of the streets. What sort of things/people are they named after? Some of the most common ways to name streets are by their geographic location (i.e., next to a certain body of water), by numbers, by letters, or after Presidents, trees, or states. Find streets that fit into each of these categories, if they exist in your city. Find streets that fit none of these categories and see if you can explain how they were named. See if you can find any pattern to the streets. Some cities have streets and avenues running perpendicular to each other. Others have them parallel and alternating (i.e., 21st Street, 21st Avenue, 22nd Street, etc.) Some cities group like streets in one area, such as having all the President streets in the northeast.

• Ride one of the forms of mass transportation with your parents.

• Write a paper on the history of the city.

Vocabulary

❏ Shopping   ❏ Perpendicular   ❏ Apartment
❏ Residential   ❏ Commercial   ❏ Cultural
❏ Mayor   ❏ Avenue

Tips From Barnabas

We find cities mentioned in the Bible from Genesis to Revelation. While times and cultures change, people still congregate in one place in order to transact business and carry on day-to-day activities.

Find a book, such as *The Life and Times of Jesus the Messiah* by Alfred Edersheim, and research what a city like Capernaum was like while Jesus was on earth.

Try to imagine what it would be like if you had lived in Capernaum. Write a story about what profession you would have, where you would attend church, what type of government there would be, where your food would come from, how often you would use money, what forms of transportation you would have, and how you would dress.

If you can, act out a skit based on your story with some of your friends or family.

NAME OF PLACE TO VISIT _____

NAME OF CONTACT PERSON _____

PHONE # _____

ADDRESS _____

_____

BEST TIME TO VISIT _____

A WALK THROUGH A FOREST

Background

There are two types of forest, *coniferous* and *temperate*. Coniferous forests grow where there are long, cold winters and short, hot summers. Large areas of coniferous forest can be found in Canada, Scandinavia, and Russia. Temperate forests grow in areas where summer and winter are less extreme. Temperate forests can be found in the Northeast, Southeast, deep South, Midwest, and Pacific Northwest of the United States, most of Europe, part of Russia, part of China, and some small patches south of the Equator. It is most likely that your walk will be through a temperate forest.

Choose a nice sunny day, but one that is not too hot. Wear comfortable clothes, especially be sure that you have good walking shoes. You might also want to bring binoculars and/or a camera. I also recommend taking a bird, mammal, insect, or plant field guide, or more than one, depending on which of these things you are most interested in. (Field guides should be easily obtainable at your library if you don't want to buy one.)

As you walk through the forest, keep your eyes open. Investigate in bushes, under rocks, inside logs, or in any other crevices you can find. It is very important to leave the forest the same as you found it. Don't leave garbage in it, and don't take anything other than rocks or fallen leaves out of it. See if you can find small mammals and insects in their hiding places, but always be careful so as not to disturb any animal's home.

Look at the trees. They have distinguishing characteristics, just like animals do. See if you can identify some trees by their bark or leaves. If you find a stump, see if you can count the rings in it. There will be as many rings as the number of years the tree lived before being cut down.

If you brought both binoculars and a bird field guide, find a nice place where you can sit comfortably. Now, train your binoculars on the surrounding trees. If you're patient and quiet, you will probably be able to see quite a few birds. (The best times for viewing birds are early morning and late afternoon.) When you spot a bird, note as much as you can about its appearance, and then check for it in the field guide. (This should also be done with trees, mammals, and insects if you've brought any of those guides with you. But you usually won't need binoculars for these things.) Keep a record of everything that you see. If you continue to go to the woods regularly, and keep watching birds or insects or studying trees, you'll soon be able to identify many species very quickly and point them out to your friends or parents wherever you see them.

Questions You Might Ask Concerning The Forest

Which trees can be found in the forest in your area?

Which birds and insects inhabit your forest?

Which mammals live in your forest?

Visit the forest at different times of day. Are there differences in what you see?

Visit the forest in each of the seasons. What are the differences in what you see?

Is your forest temperate or coniferous? Why?

What are the differences in wildlife and plants between temperate and coniferous forests?

What trees seem most attractive to birds?

What are the differences between the homes of various forest mammals?

How many different types of trees can you identify?

Activities

- Put together a leaf collection. Find one good leaf from each kind of tree that grows in your area and label the leaves.
- Do a photo-essay of a particular area of the forest using photographs taken during each season and at various times of the day.
- Keep a log of all the birds, insects, and mammals that you identify.

Vocabulary

❏ Coniferous   ❏ Temperate   ❏ Wild Life

❏ Binoculars   ❏ Field Guides

Tips From Barnabas

After you've taken your walk in the woods, read Psalm 1 and memorize at least verse 3:

"He is like a tree planted by streams of water, which yields its fruit in season and whose leaf does not wither. Whatever he does prospers."

Now try to write your own psalm comparing the righteous man to what you've seen in the forest.

NAME OF PLACE TO VISIT _____

NAME OF CONTACT PERSON _____

PHONE # _____

ADDRESS _____

_____

BEST TIME TO VISIT _____

A WALK
BY THE WATER

Background

Unless you live in a desert region, you probably are close to some type of body of water. Whether it's an ocean, a lake, a pond, or a river, there is a lot you can learn from it. Regardless of what body of water you go to, be sure not to litter and not to disturb any of the animals living there.

Seashore: The best time to study the seashore is during *spring tides*. Spring tides have nothing to do with spring. They are the very high and low tides that occur each month just after the new and full moon. It is best to visit the seashore during this time because the lower beach will be fully exposed then.

After determining on what day to go, next determine when low tide will be on that day. You can find a tide chart at a local fishing or bait shop. If you get to the beach just after high tide, then you can find freshly uncovered sea life as the tide drops.

The oceans are made up of salt water, rather than fresh water. Although humans cannot drink salt water, the sea is full of animals that couldn't survive on land or in fresh water.

There are different zones of seashore, due to the tides. The *upper beach* is usually dry but is covered by the highest tides. *Middle beach* is covered and uncovered every day. *Lower beach* is uncovered only at the lowest tides.

Because of the different amounts of water in each zone, different types of plants and animals grow in each one. The easiest way to distinguish between zones is by the type of seaweed in each. Those in the upper zone are green, the ones found in the middle zone are usually brown, and those in the lower zone are red.

Although there are many types of fish that live in the sea, most of them do not swim close to shore. There are, however, many types of sea birds that should be easy to spot. Sea gulls are the most common, but you may also see puffins, guillemots, kittiwakes, razorbills, or oystercatchers.

One of the most interesting things to do on a seashore is beachcombing. Just walk along the water's edge and see what shells you can collect. Some are very fragile, so you should bring something to put them in. When you get them home, wash them.

If you dig through the sand a bit you may be able to find some shellfish which are still living. You should not collect these to take them home, however. They will be better able to live if you leave them on the beach. But if you bring a clear jar with you, you can fill it halfway up with sand, then the rest of the way with sea water. Now, drop a clam or other *bivalve* into the jar, and you'll be able to watch it dig its way into the sand. After you're done watching it, be sure to replace it in the ocean.

Inland Waters: Rivers, ponds, and lakes all contain a wide variety of plant and animal life. You'll find fish, mammals, insects, plants, flowers, amphibians, and reptiles. All three consist of fresh water and support life that need fresh water to exist.

Many amphibians and insects breed or lay their eggs in the water. Frogs spend the early part of their lives in ponds and lakes as tadpoles and aren't able to leave until they mature. If you look closely, you should be able to spot some.

Some of the animals feed off plants, while others hunt other animals for food. Alligators and snakes hunt for other animals in the water. Otters and other mammals hunt for fish. Frogs eat insects and, in some cases, birds. Birds eat insects. Insects are plentiful around ponds and lakes because the moisture and heat provide an ideal breeding ground.

Because rivers have constantly flowing water, they are usually cleaner. There are still a lot of things living in them though. Take a rock from the water and examine it. You will probably find several *nymphs*, that is, the young of may flies and stone flies clinging to it. Many kinds of insects find shelter in between or underneath the rocks in a river.

If you go to a river in the spring or summer, you'll probably get to see birds and fish try to eat the adult insects which are now emerging from the river.

You are not as likely to find as many birds and mammals by a river as you would by a lake. Some, like raccoons and deer, do go to rivers for food and drink though, and you may get to see some, or more likely, their tracks. Different bodies of water support widely different forms of life. Try to explore as many different types of bodies of water as possible.

Questions You Might Ask Concerning The Water

What colors are most sea birds? Can you explain why?
Why are spring tides higher?
If you live by a river, where does your river originate and where does it end?
What kinds of birds are common to the body of water?
What kinds of insects do you find near the body of water in your area?
What other animals are common to the body of water near you?
What plants flourish near the body of water in your area?
Is the body of water nearest where you live fresh or salt water?
How does your area utilize that body of water?
For what or whom was the body of water in your area named?

Activities

- Collect some sea water in a dish. After it evaporates, notice how much salt is left. This will give you an idea of how salty sea water is.
- Find a book on seashell identification and try to identify the shells that you collected.
- If you find the tracks of an animal near a river or lake, try to identify the animal and see how far you can track it before losing it.

Vocabulary

- ☐ Spring Tides
- ☐ Lower Beach
- ☐ Amphibian
- ☐ Upper Beach
- ☐ Bivalve
- ☐ Evaporate
- ☐ Middle Beach
- ☐ Nymphs
- ☐ Beachcombing

Tips From Barnabas

Water is a frequent symbol in Scripture. Look up the following references, and make a list of the types of water and what they symbolized:

VERSE	TYPE OF WATER	SYMBOL
Psalm 22:14	_____	_____
Psalm 42:1	_____	_____
Isaiah 12:3	_____	_____
Isaiah 32:2	_____	_____
Zechariah 14:8	_____	_____
Mark 9:41	_____	_____
John 3:5	_____	_____
Ephesians 5:26,	_____	_____
Hebrews 10:22	_____	_____
1 Peter 3:21	_____	_____
2 Peter 2:17	_____	_____
Revelation 21:6	_____	_____

Discuss with your parents why you think God chose baptism as the pledge of a good conscience toward God.

WEATHER FORECASTING

Background

NAME OF PLACE TO VISIT _____

NAME OF CONTACT PERSON _____

PHONE # _____

ADDRESS _____

_____

BEST TIME TO VISIT _____

We are all fairly familiar with the day-to-day weather which is typical for the area in which we live. In fact, we depend on the weather for many of our activities. It is often important to be able to anticipate what the weather will be like in the near future. When we can anticipate the weather, we can make plans. The weather person has the job of anticipating the weather. Modern weather forecasting is a complex job which uses highly technical knowledge and devices, such as *weather satellites*. There have been weather forecasters, however, longer than there have been satellites. Modern mechanics only make weather forecasting a little easier and more accurate. These machines are not really necessary. The basics of weather forecasting are fairly simple and readily observable. We will talk here about the basic forces that make weather.

There are three main factors in the creation of weather: heat, air, and water. Weather is caused by changes in one or more of these things. One of the main reasons for change in these elements is movement, either of air or water. There are large-scale and small-scale movements. Movement of air or water on the largest scale is caused by the *rotation* of the Earth. This rotation causes the major *air current* and *water current* patterns. A good example of the way rotation affects *climate* is the United Kingdom. The British Isles are fairly far north, but their weather is generally mild. This mildness is caused by the *Gulf Stream*. The Gulf Stream is a very large current of warm water which flows north eastward from the Gulf of Mexico to the United Kingdom. The warm water keeps Britain's winters mild. This current is caused by the rotation of the earth.

The earth's rotation is not the only cause of air movement. Winds and breezes are caused by differences in temperature. The air is made up of many *atoms* of oxygen, nitrogen, and a few other *elements*. When a substance is heated up, its atoms become more active. You can easily see that boiling water is much more active than cool water or ice. In fact, boiling water becomes so active that it begins to float away as steam. Steam rises for the same reason a hot air balloon rises; hot air is lighter than cold air. This is why heaters are placed low in a room. The heater heats the cold air that has sunk to the bottom of the room and makes it rise, trading places with the warmer air near the ceiling. In this way, the heater creates *circulation* of warm air. On a larger scale, this circulation would be a breeze. This is most apparent on the coast. Water takes longer to heat up and longer to cool down than land. Therefore, during the day, the air over the land is warmer and more active than the air over water. Since the warmer air is more active, it spreads and creates a breeze toward the water. At night, when the land has cooled down and the water is still warm, the breeze comes back the other way. All wind is caused either by the earth's rotation or the difference in the temperature between two areas.

The movement of air is very important to the movement of water. Much of the inland territory would not survive without rain; rain is water carried on the wind. Water is *evaporated* from the seas and other bodies of water. Evaporation is turning water into fast-moving vapor which rises like steam in the kitchen. This vapor *condenses* around dust particles in the sky and produces clouds. Clouds are carried on the wind inland. Warm air can carry more water than cool air. When a warm air cloud cools or meets a cool mass of air, it can no longer hold all of the water it has been carrying. This release, of course, is rain. The amount of rain depends on the amount of water contained in the clouds or the severity of the difference between the warm air and the cool. Other weather formations are also made from the meeting of different temperatures of air. *Tornadoes*, for instance, are caused by the meeting of cold, dry air and warm, wet air. This is why there are so many in the Midwest, which is where cold air from Canada meets warm air from the Gulf of Mexico.

We have only discussed the basic shapers of weather here. These factors would only affect large scale *weather masses*. To be able to predict your local weather you will need to read further.

Questions You Might Ask A Weather Forecaster

How long have you been a weather forecaster?
What training did you receive?
How accurate is forecasting?
What percentage of the time are you correct?
Do you enjoy being a weather forecaster?
Do you mind the complaints you get?
What are the standard weather map symbols?
What weather forecasting devices do you use?
How has man affected the weather?
What causes changes in atmospheric pressure?

Activities

• Read further in weather forecasting and prepare a speech or write a report.
• Set up a weather station and take daily readings and make a chart: take the temperature, measure rainfall, monitor cloud types, and barometric pressure.
• Make a climate chart of other areas of the United States.
• Make a chart, including pictures, of the different types of clouds.
• Make a chart of the different weather-forecasting devices.
• Make a chart of all the different types of weather and what causes them.

Vocabulary

❑ Weather Satellite
❑ Water Current
❑ Atoms
❑ Evaporate
❑ Weather Mass

❑ Rotation
❑ Climate
❑ Elements
❑ Condense

❑ Air Current
❑ Gulf Stream
❑ Circulation
❑ Tornado

Tips From Barnabas

The weather is part of nature that God set into motion when He created the world. Imagine the wide variety of weather conditions there are: the four seasons, winds, storms, sunny and cloudy, rain and drought, and so on. What an infinite variety God has given us.

God uses storms to accomplish His purposes, "He has His way in the whirl-wind and in the storm…" Read how God has His way in the weather in the following verses:

Nahum 1:3-8

Psalm 107:23-31

Job 36:26-37:24

Jonah 1:4-16

Matthew 8:23-27

The next time you are in an thunder storm think of these verses and realize that God is the One behind the storm.

For now, read Psalm 77 and write a poem expressing your thanks to God for your favorite kinds of weather.

NAME OF PLACE TO VISIT _____

NAME OF CONTACT PERSON _____

PHONE # _____

ADDRESS _____

_____

BEST TIME TO VISIT _____

ZOO

Background

A zoo is not only a place to have fun, but there is also a lot to learn. Before you go, call the zoo to find out what time various animals are fed, when there are any demonstrations (such as snake or bird handling), and when there will be any zookeeper talks.

Although traditional zoos have been around for less than two hundred years, the practice of keeping wild animals is an ancient one. For hundreds and thousands of years, kings, queens, and emperors have kept wild animals as pets and curiosities. Usually these animals were treated exceptionally well by the ruler and the court. The practice of one ruler giving an exotic animal as a gift to another ruler was also a very popular custom.

The first American zoo opened in 1824, in Philadelphia. By that time, there were already several large zoos in Europe. Since that time, over thirty major zoological parks have opened in the U.S. Each zoo has its own specialties and feature attractions.

Although in the past most animals were kept in plain, confining cages, *zoologists* have become increasingly aware of the problems with this system. Now you'll find that most zoos primarily have large enclosures, which are copies of the animal's natural *environments*.

Many different people work together in a zoo. Zookeeper, *curator*, exhibit curator, *veterinarian*, *horticulturist*, general curator, engineer, education director, zoo director, and volunteers are just some of the people employed in a typical zoo.

There are also many different types of exhibits in most zoos. Usually animals are grouped together based on their *species* or their natural habitat. For instance, most zoos have a *primate* house where all or most of the zoo's monkeys, apes, and lemurs are kept. Another common exhibit is a "night" animal exhibit that usually contains bats, various night cats and other *nocturnal* animals. Sometimes zoos have exhibits highlighting animals that live in the arctic or in the African *savannah*.

Another feature of many zoos are small sub-zoos. Nearly every large zoo has a children's zoo where you can pet and possibly also feed several different types of animals. There is also often a reptile zoo which will sometimes feature a snake-handling show. Insect zoos are also common.

Zoos are more than just places for people to go to see *exotic* animals. Zoos are becoming increasingly concerned with *endangered* and *threatened* species. Breeding of these species is becoming more and more common as zoologists learn more about the animals' *physiological* and *psychological* needs for successful mating.

Questions You Might Ask A Zookeeper

What are your primary concerns in deciding whether or not to obtain a new species?

What are the most difficult types of species to obtain for the zoo? Why?

What are the major considerations when developing an environmental enclosure for an animal?

How do you determine what to feed an animal? What do you do if an animal refuses to eat?

Where does your zoo get its funding?

What is the difference between the terms "endangered" and "threatened"?

In what breeding programs is the zoo involved?

From where do you obtain your animals?

What are the specialties of this zoo?

How many species are contained in this zoo?

How many animals?

Activities

• Try to go to the zoo during a time that a keeper gives a talk and ask him some of the above questions.

• Pick three wild animals that interest you, one from the cat family, one from the primate family, and one other of your choice. Find out:

1) Where they live in the wild.

2) What type of environment they live in.

3) What food they eat in the wild.

4) If they are endangered or threatened and, if so, why, and what is being done to protect them.

5) What their *gestation* period is.

6) What animals, if any, they hunt or are hunted by, for food.

7) If they are *carnivores,* how they go about obtaining their food. (Do they hunt in groups or singularly, are they *scavengers,* etc.?)

8) What, if any, fables, stories, and myths are connected with them? Is there any connection between the animal's true nature and the way they are portrayed in the stories? How did these myths originate?

• Write reports about each of the three animals.

• Find out what sort of volunteer positions are available at your zoo. Are there any that you could do?

• Write a report on the zoo near you or another famous zoo.

Vocabulary

❑ Environment
❑ Species
❑ Primate
❑ Gestation
❑ Zoology
❑ Horticulture

❑ Endangered
❑ Physiological
❑ Nocturnal
❑ Carnivores
❑ Curator

❑ Threatened
❑ Psychological
❑ Savannah
❑ Scavengers
❑ Veterinarian

Tips From Barnabas

We could probably think of Noah as the first zookeeper. In Genesis 2:20, Adam got to name all of the animals, but they were all loose in their natural habitat.

Read the account of the flood in Genesis 7 and then use your imagination and write a story of what it would have been like to spend a day in the ark. Describe your interaction with all the different types of animals. What kind of work would Noah and his family have to have done?

CHECK LIST

- ❏ Transportation
- ❏ Meals
- ❏ Clothing
- ❏ Housing
- ❏ Maps
- ❏ _____
- ❏ _____
- ❏ _____

NOTES

_____
_____
_____
_____
_____
_____
_____
_____
_____
_____
_____
_____
_____
_____
_____
_____
_____
_____
_____
_____
_____
_____
_____
_____
_____
_____
_____
_____
_____
_____
_____
_____
_____
_____

Field Trip Planner

FT#_____
Subject Key: _____

Date Planned:
___/___/___

Date Completed:
___/___/___

Subject:_____
Topic:_____
Learning Objective:_____
_____

Destination: _____
Field Trip Description:_____
_____

Cost: $_____ Friends to Include: _____
Travel Date: ___/___/___   Time:_____:_____ to _____:_____
Contact Person:_____ Phone:_____
Address: _____
City:_____ State: _____ Zip:_____

Preliminary Reading:_____
Book Title:_____ Page #_____
Book Title:_____ Page #_____

Discussion Questions:_____
_____
_____
_____

Follow Up Activity:_____
_____
_____
_____

Comments:_____
_____
_____
_____
_____

❏ Quiz Administered ___/___/___

Test Scores:

Name:	Score:	Name:	Score:	Name:	Score:
1._____		2._____		3._____	